Louis Botha

A Man Apart

Richard Steyn

Louis Botha

A Man Apart

Jonathan Ball Publishers

JOHANNESBURG & CAPE TOWN

Published in South Africa in 2018 by
JONATHAN BALL PUBLISHERS
A division of Media24 (Pty) Ltd
PO Box 33977
Jeppestown
2043

ISBN 978-1-86842-922-6
ebook ISBN 978-1-86842-923-3

*Every effort has been made to trace the copyright holders and to obtain their
permission for the use of copyright material. The publishers apologise for any errors
or omissions and would be grateful to be notified of any corrections that should be
incorporatd in future editions of this book.*

Twitter: www.twitter.com/JonathanBallPub
Facebook: www.facebook.com/JonathanBallPublishers
Blog: http://jonathanball.bookslive.co.za/

Cover image: *General Louis Botha, 1863–1919. Soldier and Statesman* (Study for
portrait in Statesmen of the Great War, National Portrait Gallery, London) by
Sir James Guthrie. Courtesy of the National Galleries of Scotland. Given by
WG Gardiner and Sir Frederick C Gardiner 1930.

Cover by publicide
Design and typesetting by Triple M Design
Set in 11/15pt Adobe Garamond Pro

Printed by *paarlmedia*, a division of Novus Holdings

CONTENTS

LIST OF MAPS

*The drama, indeed the tragedy, of history, comes from our understanding the
tension that existed between the conscious wills and intentions of
the participants in the past and the underlying conditions that constrained
their actions and shaped their future.*
— Nathan A Finn

*The biographies of men and women, the kinds of individuals they variously
become, cannot be understood without reference to the historical structures in
which the milieu of their everyday life are organised.*
— C Wright Mills, quoted in Charles van Onselen,
The Small Matter of a Horse

*We have an obligation to place historical figures in the context of their times
and to accord them what they, in some instances, did not accord others:
understanding.*
— Richard Cohen, quoted in Harold Evans,
Do I Make Myself Clear?

PREFACE

The year 2019 marks the centenary of the death of Louis Botha, one of the Homeric figures of South African history. Today, his memory and legacy, like those of his close colleague Jan Smuts, are being traduced by members of a modern generation more intent on apportioning blame for historical injustices than making allowance for the times and circumstances in which Botha lived, fought and led his people.

His life was relatively short, but, as Viscount Bolingbroke observed, the duration of great men's lives should be determined by the length and importance of the parts they act, 'not by the number of years that pass between their coming into the world and their going out of It'.[1] By the time of his premature death, Botha had acted out his own part as prime minister of South Africa for nine years, and before that as premier of the Transvaal for three.

Under-educated as a youngster on a remote country farm, and untrained in the arts of warfare, he rose to become the military leader of his people, a fighting commander of such quality as to command the respect and admiration of every one of his adversaries. Bowing, after brave resistance, to inevitable defeat in the second Anglo-Boer War (1899–1902), his political skills were such as to enable his Afrikaner compatriots to win the ensuing peace, all the while ruing the loss of their republics. He was a founding father of the Union of South Africa, and its first premier. In tandem with Jan Smuts, he took the fateful decision to tie his fledgling country's fortunes to those of the British Empire, not out of subservience – as his critics alleged – but because of the imperative of Afrikaner-English reconciliation, and the insurance against invasion and guarantee of economic upliftment that an attachment to the Empire might bring. In the Great War (1914–1918), in order to keep the pledge he had given to the British, Botha took to the battlefield himself – the only Dominion prime minister to do so. He was a man whose word was his bond, who regarded a promise once given as unbreakable.

Louis Botha suffered grievously for following what he regarded as the path of duty and honour. His upholding of his country's constitutional commitment to Empire resulted in his last years on earth being a time of stress and grief. Acutely sensitive to having his motives wilfully misrepresented or misunderstood, he was the victim of frequent spells of depression, made worse by bouts of ill health. The Afrikaner rebellion of 1914 cut him to the quick and caused him more torment than anything else in his life.

Unlike Smuts, Botha was not one to commit his thoughts to paper and left no memoir or trove of documents for researchers to mine. Any account of his life has to be pieced together from three seminal books, as well as the many memoirs and histories of the second Anglo-Boer War (also known as the South African War). Two men from different backgrounds who became closer to him than most were the editor of Pretoria's influential *De Volksstem* newspaper (*Die Volksstem* from 1907), Dr FV Engelenburg, and Britain's governor-general in South Africa, Sydney (later Earl) Buxton, both of whom wrote sympathetic biographies of Botha after his death.

Engelenburg's is the fullest account of Botha's life and the book is enhanced by an eloquent eulogy, '*in memoriam*', written by Smuts in 1929. 'Together as friends and comrades,' Smuts wrote, 'we passed through the gravest crises of our lives; together we had to take the most fateful decisions. I saw him under the most severe tests that can be applied to a human being – tests which would have revealed and brought out any flaws in his inner composition. And it is the way he stood all these tests and showed real greatness of soul that has made him quite outstanding in my memories of the great men whom I have known and worked with.'[2]

Engelenburg, for his part, marvelled that it had taken Botha less than twenty years to become world famous as a soldier and national leader. But fame had come at a price: 'The fifteen years of unremitting political, diplomatic and military prowess that followed, conferred on him the glory as well as the desecration that are the portion of every statesman standing head and shoulders above his contemporaries,' he noted. Seeking to derive a morsel of comfort from Botha's early death, the author wrote, 'To him was vouchsafed the great privilege of departing this life at the very height of his ambition as a South African.'[3]

Earl Buxton, a British cabinet minister sent out to South Africa as governor-general in 1914, formed an unusually intimate friendship with Botha during the last five years of the latter's life. As a leading British politician, Buxton had met many 'big men' in his time, but regarded Botha as the 'most human and loveable of them all'.[4] 'He was imbued,' Buxton wrote, 'with that indefinable magnetism and charm which is innate to its happy possessor, but which cannot be analysed or described.'[5]

Buxton and his perceptive wife, Mildred, provide us with many shrewd insights into Botha's personality – his natural simplicity and inherited shrewdness, his personal warmth and geniality, and his courtesy and consideration for the feelings of others. Yet, in Buxton's judgement, as prime minister Botha was sometimes too tolerant and tender-hearted for his own good. His sensitivity to personal criticism, particularly from his own people, often left him wounded and depressed, and pondering whether he should soldier on in politics.

So much for the personal qualities of this remarkable Boer-Afrikaner, who impressed so many of the great and good of his time. But what should we make of his legacy, after a century of hindsight has thrown into sharp relief some of the failures and misjudgements of his political career? He cannot avoid responsibility for the passing – while premier and also minister of native affairs – of the Natives Land Act of 1913, the baneful effects of which are still with us today. The consequences of this Act – unforeseen though they may have been – have had far-reaching effects on the lives of Africans across South Africa and underpinned other legislation that led to the entrenched segregation of Africans, coloureds and Indians in the decades that followed Botha's demise.

Yet, as Martin Meredith observes, segregation – both spatial and social – was seen by most whites in Botha's time, and even by many blacks, as the remedy for racial peace and the reduction of centuries of conflict. It was the Milner-appointed Lagden Commission no less, staffed by colonial officials representing 'progressive' opinion, that recommended in 1903 that blacks and whites should be kept apart on a permanent basis if tensions were to be averted and 'civilised' white rule preserved. After Lagden, says Meredith, the practice of segregation was elevated to a political doctrine and employed by virtually every white politician as a respectable slogan from then on.[6]

Botha's personal attitude to Africans was a mixture of respectful paternalism towards any individual with whom he came into contact or who worked for him, and a disbelief that blacks as a group should enjoy the same political rights as whites. According to Buxton, with whom he had many discussions on the subject, Botha always took a broad and sympathetic view on matters affecting the 'natives',[7] among whom he had grown up as a boy and whose languages he spoke fluently. His touching concern for Dinuzulu, the Zulu king, who had been unfairly treated by the Natal authorities, must be contrasted with his belief, quoted disapprovingly by a British journalist, that 'no self-respecting white man would sit next to a coloured man in Parliament'.[8]

Mindful of the contrasting views of the Cape and the other provinces on the franchise issue, Botha's overriding concern, according to Buxton, was that the 'native question' should not in any way divide the Afrikaner and English sections of the population. In speech, action and influence, he did his best to prevent any outcome which 'in his opinion would tend to accentuate racial feeling and be injurious to the welfare of the "natives"'.[9]

On the question of Afrikaner-English relations, arguments over the wisdom of Botha's policy of reconciliation reverberate to this day. As for the schism that grew between him and JBM Hertzog and was to split Afrikanerdom asunder, the wisdom of hindsight suggests there was fault on both sides. Hertzog's claim that Botha was intent on subverting South Africa's interests to those of imperial Britain was given the lie by Hertzog's own abandoning of his republican ideal once he had built on the foundations laid by Botha (and Smuts) at successive Imperial Conferences, and achieved Dominion status for South Africa under the Statute of Westminster (1931).

Where Hertzog was probably right, however, was in believing that, unless Afrikaners stood up for their cultural, educational and language rights after the Anglo-Boer War, they were in danger of being overwhelmed and subsumed by an omnipresent English culture. Without the Hertzogites' insistence on equal treatment for Afrikaans in schools, it's quite possible that the language might not have survived, let alone prospered.

As one who almost always spoke only Dutch (or Afrikaans) in public,

Botha disliked language fanatics as intensely as he did 'jingoes'.[10] Yet he was strangely oblivious, says Engelenburg, to the damage done by officials who frequently ignored the equality clause in the Union constitution and gave undue preference to English. His government – he would argue – could not be held responsible for the behaviour of individual civil servants. And when it became clear that a healthy enthusiasm for Afrikaans was being misused as an instrument for anti-English propaganda, his interest in the language issue diminished even further. It was a miscalculation that was to cost him dearly at the polls.

*

The task of the historian, as AJP Taylor reminds us, is to explain the past, neither to justify nor to condemn it.[11] It is also, according to Gordon S Wood, to place the actions of those who came before us in the context of their times, 'to describe their blindness and folly with sympathy, to recognise the extent to which they were caught up in circumstances over which they had little control, and to realise the degree to which they created results they never intended'.[12]

It is in this spirit that *A Man Apart* has been written. It resists the tempta-tion to assess Louis Botha's life through modern lenses and attempts rather to explain, but not necessarily to defend or justify, political attitudes that were commonplace in colonial Africa and most of the world a century ago. As Henry Kissinger observed in his seminal study of Metternich, *A World Restored*, statesmen generally have a tragic quality about them because they are condemned 'to struggle with factors which are not amenable to will and which cannot be changed in one lifetime … It is for this reason that states-men share the fate of prophets, for they are without honour in their own country. A statesman who too far outruns the experience of his people will fail in his domestic consensus, however wise his policies.'[13] In this respect, South African history offers more than one example.

As hindsight makes apparent, many of the politicians of a century ago were victims of demographic, economic, social and cultural forces they could not fully comprehend, nor indeed were even aware of. Understanding Louis

Botha and his generation in this way, and granting them a humanity they did not always see fit to extend to other races, ought to make white South Africans, especially, wiser and less judgemental about our common past. It might also make us all more conscious of the shortcomings and limitations of our perceptions of the present.

INTRODUCTION

The South Africa into which the young Louis Botha was born and grew to manhood was a patchwork region of settler states in perpetual ferment. Earlier in the 19th century, the Mfecane (or Difaqane), a series of convulsions that shattered the traditional structures of African society, had interacted with the Great Trek of Afrikaner farmers from the Cape of Good Hope in ways that affected land habitation and power relationships across southern Africa. Everywhere, people were on the move, journeying to where there was more food, readily available land, grazing for their animals and, above all, liberation from persecution and oppression – whether from tribal chiefs or overbearing colonial authorities.

Britain had taken possession of the Cape in 1806, during the Napoleonic Wars, for one primary reason: she needed a supply station for ships making the long and arduous sea journey around the foot of Africa to India and the Far East. For the world's leading maritime and trading nation, ruling the waves required a network of bases to guard international sea routes, and the Cape was a strategic asset that could not be allowed to remain in French (or other European) hands. Hoping not to be caught up in the internal affairs of another distant imperial outpost, Britain had been drawn inexorably into a complex, financially unrewarding entanglement in and beyond the borders of the southern African colony it established formally in 1814. As the noted historian of empire Ronald Hyam was to write, 'of all the regions of the world where Britain sought to exert influence, none exhibited such complications, and thus presented such intractable dilemmas, as South Africa', where she 'felt herself to be caught

I

between her liberal concern for the whites and her humanitarian concern for the blacks'.[1]

As the occupying power, the British were responsible – directly or indirectly – for protecting the interests of all the Cape's inhabitants, not merely their own kith and kin. These included the descendants of the nomadic San and Khoikhoi peoples; the Afrikaner progeny of the Dutch, and the first Europeans to settle at the Cape in 1652; a large mixed-race (or 'coloured') population; as well as the various Xhosa tribes living along the eastern frontier.

Within less than two decades, however, rural Afrikaners had had more than enough of British rule. Deeply religious and resistant to temporal authority, these Afrikaner farmers (or Boers) had come to regard themselves as a racially pure elect on a black continent, and as the makers of their own destiny.[2] When Britain abolished slavery throughout the Empire in 1833, thereby threatening the Afrikaners' traditional way of life, some 6000 Boer families loaded up their ox-wagons and took off with retainers and livestock into the interior. By 1845, over 15000 burghers (citizens) and their families, accompanied by 5000 servants, had departed the colony in search of new pastures – and freedom from the interfering British.[3]

As Sarah Gertrude Millin colourfully records, '[these Boers] wandered with their flocks, according to the season, from high-veld to low-veld. They lived in tents or in houses of corrugated iron and mud. They rode, slack in seat, long in stirrup, on shaggy horses. Their literature was the Bible – the Old Testament rather than the new. They saw no newspapers. They heard no news. Europe was breathlessly changing and they were unaware of it. They had the freedom and security, the dignity and strength, the lordliness and hospitality – the narrowness, the evasiveness, the idleness, the ignorance, of solitude.'[4]

Most of these Voortrekkers made their way northwards, across the Orange and Vaal rivers, to the high grassland plateau, but some moved eastwards across the Drakensberg mountains into the fertile region of Natal. The spirited resistance of indigenous tribes to the invasion of their land was only overcome by the regular use of firearms. Although these trekkers had a common purpose, they were far from being united. In the small 'republics' they founded in parts of what in due course became the Transvaal and the Orange Free State, they were often at loggerheads with one another, sometimes to the point of armed conflict.

At first, the Cape colonial administration took a hands-off approach to the departing Boers, calculating that their ramshackle republics would eventually founder upon old-fashioned farming practices and a lack of finance, as well as the aggressive resistance of black tribespeople. In Natal, however, Britain took a more uncompromising stance, refusing to recognise any trekker claims to independence because of the risk of Port Natal (Durban) falling into foreign hands.[5]

Anxious to be rid of financial and security responsibility for parts of southern Africa that were of little economic value, and concerned that further Boer expansion to the north and east would bring inter-racial clashes that might undermine peace and stability across the subcontinent, the British reluctantly negotiated independence agreements with the Transvaal and Orange Free State, in 1852 and 1854, respectively. In exchange for agreeing not to progress further northwards, the two Boer republics were given a free hand over their internal affairs, which included control over the far more numerous 'natives' within their borders.

Both republics remained weak and unstable, however. In the Transvaal, where the Venda, Pedi and Sotho-Tswana peoples lived in close proximity to whites, land issues and labour relations were a constant source of conflict. In the far north, unrest in Vendaland led to the entire Zoutpansberg district's being abandoned by whites. In the Free State, there were three wars between Boer and Basotho within the republic's first 14 years.

Elsewhere, the British colonies were in little better state: the Cape was plagued by drought, locusts, a drop in the wool price and a shortage of finance, while in Natal the tiny white population lived in constant fear of an Nguni uprising or an invasion across the Tugela (uThukela) river from Zululand. Not surprisingly, Britain regarded her two investments in southern Africa as 'among the most troublesome, expensive and unprofitable possessions of the British Empire'.[6]

The imperial interest in South Africa was transformed overnight, however, by the discovery of a diamond at Hopetown, in the Cape Colony, in 1867, and other alluvial deposits on the banks of the Orange River in the Free State in 1869. Two years later, the world's richest diamond finds were made on land of the Griqua tribe, on the frontier between the Cape and the Free State. It was not long before Griqualand West became the third British crown colony in South Africa. In 1886, the richest gold seams in the world were uncovered on the Witwatersrand, a rocky ridge on the Transvaal highveld. Within less than two decades, far-off South Africa had changed from economic basket case to highly sought-after treasure house.

Hordes of fortune-seekers from all over the world, especially the British Isles, poured into the diamond and gold diggings in search of instant riches. Known to the Boers as '*Uitlanders*' (foreigners), they – and the mining companies following in their wake – posed a new and unwelcome threat to the Afrikaner way of life and patriarchal style of government.

*

In Natal, the ancestral home of the Zulu people, the small white population of British soldiers and their families at Fort Victoria on the Port Natal coast, as well as the itinerant Boer farmers inland, had been boosted by the arrival – during 1849–1852 – of a further 5000 British settlers under a sponsored immigration scheme. They were followed in 1860 by indentured labourers from India, brought in to cultivate the sugar-cane fields along the coast. These newcomers gave a shot in the arm to the struggling colonial economy, whose development was impeded by impractical land usage and the lack of an adequate communications network. Until a railway was built in the 1870s, the transportation of goods in Natal was by lumbering ox-wagon.[7]

At the time of Louis Botha's birth, the Zulu kingdom was ruled by Mpande. Twenty-five years earlier, Mpande's predecessor, Dingane, had agreed to cede land between the Tugela and Umzimvubu rivers to Piet Retief and his invading Voortrekkers in return for cattle recaptured by the Boers from a rival chief. At the treaty-signing ceremony at Dingane's headquarters, however, Retief's party of 67 trekkers and 30 servants was overpowered and brutally massacred. Eleven days later, Boer laagers along the Bloukraans and Bushmans rivers were overrun by Zulu impis. Five hundred people (mainly servants) lost their lives and more than 25000 head of cattle, as well as sheep and horses, were seized. Revenge followed swiftly. At the Battle of Blood River near Dundee, on 16 December 1838, 470 Boers led by Andries Pretorius inflicted a crushing defeat on Dingane's army, which numbered some 8000 to 10000 men – an event that became etched deeply into Afrikaner folklore. Botha's own father, Louis, then 11 years old, was present with *his* father at the scene.[8]

After the battle, the victorious trekkers established the Republic of Natalia on the land south of the Tugela, which included the tiny British settlement at Port Natal. The deep split in Zulu ranks following the disaster at Blood River caused Mpande to seek the assistance of the Boers in his efforts to overthrow his half-brother, Dingane, an invitation to which they responded with enthusiasm. A few months later, Natalia's Volksraad (parliament) confirmed Mpande as king of the Zulu and installed him as the leader of a vassal state stretching from the Tugela to the Umfolozi (today Mfolozi).

The Boers' hopes of gaining control of a harbour were not to be realised, however. The colonial government still regarded the trekkers as British subjects, and refused to countenance any demand for independence. In May 1842, there was an armed skirmish for control of Port Natal between British troops and Boers encamped at Congella during which the British lost several men. The colonial administration then reluctantly annexed the entire territory between the Umzimkulu (today Mzimkhulu) and Umfolozi rivers, and bordered by the Drakensberg to the north.

In 1845, Natal was formally declared a separate district of the Cape Colony, which brought an immediate end to the short-lived Republic of Natalia. Unlike the Cape, the borders of Natal were now clearly defined, and the colony remained peaceful for as long as the Mpondo in the south and Mpande's Zulu in the north continued to display few signs of aggression. Those Boers who refused to subject themselves to British rule once again headed north for the Transvaal. But others chose to stay on and make their livelihood in verdant Natal – where they were to multiply and prosper. Prominent among them was the family of a trekker from the Cape, one Philip Botha.

CHAPTER I

Growing Up

Early days

Louis Botha, destined to become South Africa's first prime minister, was born on 27 September 1862 on the farm Onrust, near Greytown, in Natal. He was the seventh in a Boer family of 13 children – seven girls and six boys. Like his later political contemporaries Jan Christiaan Smuts and JBM (Barry) Hertzog, he was a subject of Queen Victoria's at birth.

His Botha forebears were German-French, thought to be descendants of a young soldier, Friedrich Boot, who came to the Cape from the German state of Thuringia in 1678. More than a century and a half later, the Botha clan were among the first Boers to leave the southwestern Cape for pastures north and east in order to escape being ruled by the arrogant British, who did not, they believed, have Afrikaner interests at heart.

Louis's grandfather, Philip, made the arduous trek with ox-wagons and cattle from Swellendam in the southern Cape across the Drakensberg mountains east-wards to an unoccupied area of Natal between Durban and Pietermaritzburg, known to this day as Botha's Hill. His own son, Louis, born in 1829, lived on his father's farm until he was 21, when he moved north to De Rust, near Greytown, a village described by Harold Spender, the British journalist and early biogra-pher of Botha, as 'at that time the remotest civilised spot in this part of South Africa, just on the borders of the wildest part of Zululand'.[1]

Louis's mother, Salomina (Minnie), was of Huguenot extraction, the pretty and popular daughter of Gerrit van Rooyen, a well-to-do businessman from Uitenhage in the Cape and close friend of the Boer leader Andries Pretorius. She and Louis's father met and married in Greytown, where 12 of their chil-dren were born.

Life was tough on the De Rust farm: on several occasions the Botha home-stead was burnt down by sparks from the kitchen fire or by Zulu tribesmen objecting to the white man's incursion onto their land. Home comforts were few, and the family, like all their fellow Boers, had to live by the gun for protection from marauders and wild animals and for food from the abundant game.

As his father had done, Louis Botha (Snr) raised cattle and sheep, trading skins and wool in the days before there were markets or railways. He was fiercely independent of mind and temperamentally restless. When Louis (Jnr) was seven years old financial troubles forced his father to sell up and relocate his large family to land at Vrede, in the northeastern Free State, on the road from Natal to Pretoria. Here, in due course, he became a prosperous farmer.

A sunny temperament

Like all Boer children, the young Louis was brought up in a deeply observant Calvinist family. Taught to ride a horse and shoot a rifle at an early age, he received little formal schooling, learning what he could from itinerant Dutch tutors and as much as his parents could teach him. As a result, he read little. While High Dutch was the formal written language of the Boers, Afrikaans was their spoken tongue. Louis only encountered English when visitors came to his parents' farmhouse, never became fluent in the language, and was always hesitant about it in public, even in later life.

From his earliest days on the farm, he lived and played among black children, becoming familiar with their history and customs and fluent in the Zulu and Sesotho languages – although ever conscious of the master and servant relationship between his family and their farmworkers.

Physically, Louis was a fine specimen of youth – tall and strongly built, with an engaging smile and violet-blue eyes, which were to become protuberant in middle age. He had an easy-going personality, enjoyed playing the concertina, much preferred the company of other people to solitude, and made friends wherever he went. Intellectually, he was instinctive rather than cerebral, a man of action rather than a scholar, but there was no doubting his innate intelligence or good sense in picking 'the right men to lead him, the right men to become his close friends and the right men to advise him'.[2] He was blessed also with a natural authority that even in adolescence often saw his elder brothers and sisters deferring to him.

However, as his perceptive biographer Johannes Meintjes points out, Louis's sunny temperament and amiable disposition could not entirely conceal an inner lack of self-assurance and a sensitivity to disapproval or censure. In later life, though always gracious to women and happily married, he needed the close company of men at all times: 'he needed their talk, their warmth and their affection as much as he needed air'.[3] His core characteristic, which he was to display throughout his life, was an unswerving devotion and loyalty to the causes he believed in. Yet his nature was such that he was easily hurt when others criticised him or opposed his course of action.[4]

At Vrede, the Botha farmstead was home to a large and close-knit family, in which the many children looked after one another and shared duties on the farm. In the days before the second Anglo-Boer War, it was not uncommon for Afrikaners and English to intermarry, and some of Louis's sisters wed Englishmen they had met in Greytown. In the hospitable Botha household, all visitors were made welcome. Though members of his family were, in time, to find themselves on opposite sides of the Boer-Brit divide, Louis had no reason to dislike individual Englishmen, and never did.[5]

Teenage years

Most of Louis's teenage years were spent outdoors in the veld, which bred in him a hardy self-reliance and sense of personal responsibility. On more than one occasion, his father tested his resilience by sending him to accompany the flocks of sheep driven down from the chilly Free State to warmer climes in Zululand for the annual winter grazing. An eager learner, he did not take long to pick up the essentials of successful cattle and sheep farming, which remained a passion throughout his life.

When Louis was 15, Natal's influential secretary for native affairs, Sir Theophilus Shepstone (known as 'Somtseu' to Zulu, and 'Stoffel Slypsteen' to Boers),[6] spent a night at the Botha farm on his way to the Transvaal. The youngster was startled to overhear Shepstone, who was fluent in Afrikaans, discussing plans with his father for the possible annexation of the Transvaal on behalf of the British Crown. Botha (Snr) disapproved vehemently of the plan and warned his visitor that the consequences might be disastrous. Under orders from London, Shepstone could pay no heed to this sound advice and the outcome was the first of two bitter conflicts between Boers and British from which both sides were never fully to recover.

Trouble in the Transvaal

The driving force behind imperial Britain's proposed annexation of the Transvaal was the colonial secretary, Lord Carnarvon, known as 'Twitters' to his political colleagues who regarded him as an unreliable eccentric. Twitters had successfully united three British colonies in Canada in 1867 and, with the conviction that so often masks ignorance, saw no reason why he could not also federate the two British colonies and two Boer republics in South Africa under the imperial flag.[7] The timing seemed propitious. After 25 years of independence from British rule, the first South African Republic – the Zuid-Afrikaansche Republiek (ZAR), or Transvaal – was on its knees. A combination of internecine Boer rivalries, looming bankruptcy, the hostility of neighbouring black tribes and the unpopularity of President Thomas Burgers had brought the trekker republic to the verge of collapse. Carnarvon decided the moment was at hand for Britain to acquire the goldfields of the ZAR, and thereafter the Free State – preferably by persuasion but if necessary by armed force.

In violation of the Sand River Convention (which had granted the ZAR its independence in 1852), let alone international law, Carnarvon appointed Shepstone as a special commissioner of the Crown and sent him, along with a 25-strong detachment of Natal Mounted Police, to Pretoria on an assignment that resulted in the annexation of the republic three months later. On 12 April 1877, encouraged by the English-speaking community but over the protests of the burghers, and after making much capital out of the Zulu threat across the republic's southeastern border, Shepstone proclaimed the ZAR's independence at an end.[8] From now on, the Transvaal would be a British colony, run by himself as administrator.

Boer outrage

Although on friendly terms with the British, the Bothas – like all Boers – were outraged at Carnarvon's presumption. It took a while for Paul Kruger and Petrus (Piet) Joubert, successors to the discredited Burgers, to unify the resistance to the new British administration, in which Shepstone had been succeeded by a new proconsul, the arrogant and dictatorial Sir Garnet Wolseley. It was Wolseley who declared loftily that 'as long as the sun shines, the Transvaal will be British territory'.[9]

On 13 December 1880, at Paardekraal, 5 000 burghers reaffirmed their faith in the Almighty and declared the Transvaal to be free once again from British rule. On 16 December, the opening shots of the Boer rebellion were exchanged at Potchefstroom, where a commando led by Commandant Piet Cronje laid siege to the British garrison outside the town. After British encampments in seven other towns were similarly besieged, Sir George Pomeroy Colley and a force of some 1 200 troops were called up from Natal to help subdue the Boers. In response, 800 burghers on horseback under Commandant-General Piet Joubert hurried across the Transvaal/Natal border to cut off Colley and his men.

Colley's first two attempts to capture Boer positions at Laing's Nek and Schuinshoogte ended in failure, with the loss of 340 of his troops. Determined to prove that his men were superior to the unsophisticated enemy, 500 of Colley's redcoats took up positions on the summit of Majuba, a prominent, conical hill north of Newcastle on the main road to the Transvaal. The British troops on the peak were no match for some 150 well-camouflaged Boer sharpshooters who crawled up the hill to pick off their targets outlined against the skyline. Colley himself and 95 of his men were killed, 117 wounded and 60 taken prisoner, against one man killed and a few wounded on the Boer side.

News of the calamity at Majuba reverberated around the Empire and beyond. Ignoring cries to 'avenge Majuba', Prime Minister William Gladstone resisted demands for more resources to be diverted to Carnarvon's over-ambitious endeavour, and sued for peace with Kruger instead. In August 1881, the independence of the Transvaal was formally restored, under certain conditions laid down in the Pretoria Convention. Bitterly divided a mere four years earlier, the Boers of the Transvaal were now united as never before.

In Vrede, Louis Botha (Snr) had spent the war months gathering ammunition for the neighbouring Transvalers, which he took himself by wagon to Boer headquarters in Heidelberg. Young Louis made his own contribution to the cause by cutting adrift pontoons and rowing boats on the nearby Vaal River used by British messengers.[10]

Into Zululand

Around this time, the young Louis Botha's mettle was severely tested on one of his winter-grazing treks to Zululand. The authority of the Zulu king, Cetshwayo, had been destroyed in the devastating Anglo-Zulu War of 1879, with the monarch banished to Cape Town. After the war, Wolseley had established 13 chiefdoms, the most powerful of which was that of Sibebu (Zibhebhu), whose gangs rampaged through the countryside, making it dangerous for visitors. One of these armed bands was led by a notorious captain, Mapelo, who one day cut the throat of a German missionary not far from where Louis was camped. When Mapelo and his armed men rode up later that day, Louis's herdsman fled, enabling the raiders to seize sheep and anything else they could grab.

As Mapelo, whom he knew from past visits, approached, the young Louis clambered aboard his ox-wagon, rifle in hand and only six cartridges in his pouch, and calmly lit his pipe. When the Zulu captain boldly climbed onto the wagon next to him and demanded food for his men, Louis greeted him in a friendly manner and remained outwardly unconcerned. Speaking in fluent Zulu, he engaged Mapelo in conversation, advancing reasons why he and his flocks should not be molested.

After being offered a few sheep on condition he called off his men – and probably not wanting to provoke a Boer unnecessarily – Mapelo suddenly rose, ordered that everything taken should be restored to the young white man, and rode off with his warriors. It was a narrow escape for the shaken Louis, who described the incident afterwards as one of the most disturbing of his life.[11] Yet it had also been an early demonstration of his coolness under pressure, tact and use of friendly persuasion.

To Natal once more

In July 1892, Louis Botha (Snr) died after a protracted illness, during which he had delegated the management of his farming enterprise to Louis (Jnr). His estate was left in the hands of his widely dispersed children. Hoping to keep the parental property intact, the 20-year-old Louis proposed to his brothers and sisters – half of whom were older than he was – that he should carry on managing the farm on their behalf. They declined his offer, choosing instead to sell the property and divide up their father's assets between them.

As was customary among Boers, if you didn't like a decision you inspanned your wagon and trekked off to greener pastures. A disappointed Louis decided to go back to Natal, accompanied by a younger brother.[12] He would cast in his lot with Lucas Meyer, one of his father's closest friends, the leader of the Boers across the natural barrier of the southern Drakensberg.[13]

CHAPTER 2

Making His Mark

A new father figure

Lucas Meyer, known as the 'Lion of Vryheid' (after the town in northern Natal in which he settled), was a larger-than-life character destined to play a significant role in the history of his people. A huge, powerfully built, fully bearded man whose personality dominated any gathering, he was hugely popular among his fellow Boers.

Unlike most of his kinsmen, Meyer was a cultured man, of refined tastes.[1] Born and educated in the Free State, he had trekked with his parents to Natal before moving north to the Transvaal. Fiercely opposed to Britain's annexation of the ZAR in 1877, he took part in the fighting along the Transvaal/Natal border, sustaining a head wound that left him unconscious for 42 days but from which he eventually recovered.[2]

Louis Botha had first met Meyer on his parents' farm in Vrede and was immediately attracted by the magnetism of a man 16 years his senior. The attraction was mutual: Lucas looked upon the young Louis with a fondness that was to deepen in the years ahead. After Botha (Snr)'s death, it was Meyer who became the younger man's father figure and role model. At the age of 21, Louis 'had found himself a hero and a leader, and a deep and lasting friendship was to result'.[3]

Aiding Dinuzulu

In neighbouring Zululand, Cetshwayo's death at Ulundi in 1884 served to heighten the blood feud between Dinuzulu, his 16-year-old son and nominated successor, and the rival claimant to the Zulu throne, the powerful

Chief Sibebu. With the British unwilling to take Dinuzulu's side in his rivalry with Sibebu, the young man turned to the Boers of the Utrecht area for help, offering part of Zululand abutting the southeastern border of the Transvaal in return for their military assistance. Led by Lucas Meyer – Botha's new mentor – the Boers accepted the offer, and began to make preparations for a mounted expedition into deepest Zululand.

On 21 May 1884, on the Ngwibi mountainside 32 kilometres east of Vryheid, Dinuzulu was crowned king of the Zulu at a ceremony attended by some 350 Boers and an estimated 8 000 of his followers. Among those present was Botha.[4] Following the coronation, word went out to every chieftain in the kingdom – including Sibebu, who regarded himself as the virtual ruler of Zululand – that the Zulu crown had been restored to Dinuzulu. As soon as the ceremony was over, Meyer and a commando of more than a hundred fighters left by ox-wagon and horseback for the heart of Zululand to stamp out resistance to Dinuzulu and restore law and order in the kingdom. Another member of the commando was Botha's good friend from the Free State, young Cheere (Cherry) Emett, later to become his brother-in-law and a fellow general in the second Anglo-Boer War.

Overcoming Sibebu

The Boers did not have long to wait for Sibebu's response to Dinuzulu's provocation. At the battle of Magut on the Pongola (Phongolo) River, his impis were put to flight by the Boers' deadly rifle fire, followed by the hot pursuit of 7 000 of the king's loyal but fearful warriors. Meyer's men were now in command of Zululand. In Harold Spender's vivid description, 'after [the battle] everything was over except the shouting, the negotiating, and the division of the conquered lands'.[5]

On campaign on behalf of Dinuzulu, Botha was once again fortunate to escape with his life. After a long day in the saddle setting up landmarks for the Boers, he holed up for the night in an abandoned hut. Wakened by the sound of chanting, he peered out and saw that he was surrounded by assegai-wielding Zulu, who had 'come to kill the white man'. Yelling to them in Zulu, 'Who are you?', the reply came back, 'We are the warriors of Dinuzulu.' 'But I have been fighting on *your* side,' shouted Botha, at which point the chanting ceased and the warriors lowered their spears. They had wrongly assumed the white man to be an ally of Sibebu. When Botha emerged from the hut into the moonlight, he was recognised and hailed as a fellow warrior and friend. But he had been given 'the fright of his life', as he recounted to a friend later. He could easily have been killed in his sleep and his shelter burnt down.[6]

In promising part of his kingdom to the Boers, however, Dinuzulu had not fully realised what he was letting himself in for, and soon became bitter at losing control over three million acres of land – far more than he had contemplated. One hundred and fifteen Boers had fought for him, but no fewer than 800 now applied for 6 000-acre farms.[7]

The Boers were not to enjoy undisturbed possession of their new land for long. As Spender records, no sooner had the much-feared Sibebu been vanquished than 'fugitive Zulus appeared in multitudes from every rock and cranny of the land, trains of women and children, lank, haggard men – carrying their simple household goods on their shoulders and streaming down from the hills to re-occupy the plains. Kraals sprang up like mushrooms …'[8]

The New Republic

Some form of governance for the Boer-occupied part of Zululand was now a matter of urgency, and thus, on 6 August 1884, 'de Nieuwe Republiek' (the New Republic) came into existence, with Lucas Meyer as president and the young Louis Botha a member of the executive council. The popular Transvaler, General Piet Joubert, had been nominated as the fledgling state's first president but had declined, and the well-regarded Meyer was appointed in his stead. Among Botha's first tasks was to divide up the land on which the capital, Vryheid, was to be laid out, into residential plots.[9]

As one of four land commissioners, Botha was also charged with measuring out the acreage ceded by Dinuzulu into the farms which the Boers who had fought for the Zulu ruler had been promised. The task was difficult – and hazardous – for the boundaries of many prospective properties were in far-flung, desolate places. The task kept Botha and his fellow commissioners out in the veld for more than a year.

When the surveying was almost complete, it became obvious that there was not nearly enough prospective farmland to go round, so the laborious exercise had to be repeated. Eventually, some 250 farms were allocated to individual Boers by the drawing of lots.[10] Botha himself drew a landholding near Babanango, which he subsequently exchanged for Waterval (No 130), a 3500-acre farm 38 kilometres east of Vryheid.

Marriage

Before occupying Waterval, Botha, aged only 24, decided it was time to marry. His bride was Annie, the daughter of John Emett, an Irish auctioneer who had settled at Harrismith in the Free State, and the sister of Cherry Emett, Botha's companion on the expedition to Zululand. Annie was a spirited young lady who had been given a good education in Bloemfontein and returned to share the household duties on the family farm. A talented musician, blessed with a lively sense of humour, she had turned her back on her parents' choice of suitor in favour of the 'little Dutch boy' for whom she seems to have fallen instantly. [11]

Annie knew little Afrikaans at first and Louis not much English, but that was no barrier to a long and happy relationship in which both partners were utterly devoted to one another. He always referred to her as '*my maatjie*' (my little mate) and in later life she was known to her friends as 'Maatjie' rather than Annie. As Louis was never comfortable in English, the couple usually spoke to each other in his home language.[12]

Despite the future Mrs Botha's being an Anglican, she and Louis were wed in the Dutch Reformed Church at Vryheid, on 13 December 1886 – the first ceremony of its kind performed in the New Republic. Here, too, the couple agreed that religion would be no obstacle to their relationship, though Annie was eventually to join her husband's church during the Anglo-Boer War. There were five children of the marriage – three sons and two daughters.

There is a charming account, in Spender's biography, of how the Bothas' wedding actually took place in the Free State, shortly after Louis travelled home to attend his mother Minnie's funeral. After a honeymoon spent in the old Vrede homestead, the young couple embarked on the long trek by ox-wagon across the Drakensberg, past 'the shadow of Majuba', to their new home outside Vryheid. Dr CJ Barnard, who interviewed Botha's daughter,

Helen, in 1964, says that the tale was a figment of Spender's romantic imagi-nation, however.[13]

During their early years of married life, the Bothas lived well within their limited means: their first four-room thatched cottage was built by themselves and their farmworkers. In due course, the little cottage was replaced by a large and comfortable sandstone homestead, with a wide stoep and seven bedrooms. Approached through a long avenue of specially planted trees, Waterval became the most attractive and prosperous farm in the Vryheid district.

According to Spender, at Waterval another incident occurred that nearly cost Botha his life. He and his brother Chris were inspecting cattle in a pad-dock when a young bull, a special favourite of his, rushed up from behind and drove its horn into his side. Chris Botha, a powerful man, grabbed the bull and held onto its horns, shouting to the farmworkers for help. As soon as the bull had been safely secured, he ran to help Louis, who looked as though he was dead. Chris picked up his brother and carried him into the house, before returning to shoot the bull. Louis's strong constitution enabled him to recover from his injuries, but he felt their effects for many years afterwards.[14]

Businessman and speculator

Like his father, Louis Botha had a keen eye for business and was never averse to speculation. According to Engelenburg, by October 1899 he had become the owner of some 4000 sheep (including imported rams), 600 head of cat-tle and more than 100 thoroughbred horses. His wealth had been further enhanced by the purchase of several neighbouring farms on which he grew crops and fruit. In addition, his election as the *veldkornet* (field cornet) for the Vryheid area in 1888, his first official military appointment, gave him a salary of 'a couple of hundred' pounds a year to add to his earnings as a native com-missioner, which involved collecting the 'hut tax' from Zulu tribesmen. He also operated, along with Lucas Meyer, a lucrative land syndicate that offered mortgage facilities to would-be property owners.[15]

Botha was to derive additional income from other interests besides farm-ing. In 1891, he bought land on which there were coal deposits (which he was to sell for a handsome profit), and some time later he and Meyer contracted with the Transvaal government to build a railway line from Vryheid to the Buffalo River, a contract eventually sold profitably to an engineering firm. In 1895, the Transvaal government appointed him as a resident justice and native commissioner to look after its interests in neighbouring Swaziland. Botha spent most of that year in Mbabane before returning to Vryheid.[16]

As neither the ZAR nor Natal was prepared to acknowledge the independence of the New Republic,[17] in October 1886 Lucas Meyer took himself to Pietermaritzburg to make British officialdom aware of the Boers' agreement with Dinuzulu. The governor of Natal did not dispute the legitimacy of the agreement, but flatly refused to accept the Boers' claim to control of Zululand. Not long after the meeting, it was announced formally that the Zulu kingdom lay within the Cape colonial government's sphere of influence.

In 1887, the reason for New Republic's existence fell away when Dinuzulu began negotiations with the colonial authorities, and then fled into exile in the British-controlled part of Zululand. Now, the only sensible course for the Boers was to attach themselves to the Transvaal. In July 1888, the New Republic's brief existence came to an end when it became a district of the ZAR, and was given two seats (later four) in the Volksraad. The short-lived mini-state brought with it a surplus of £6 000, which went into the coffers of the Transvaal treasury.[18]

A Transvaal citizen

Louis Botha's first few years as a Transvaal citizen were spent building up the value of his farms, plantations and other business interests. In less than a decade, according to Engelenburg, the value of his assets grew to around £30 000 (several million rands in today's money). Like most Boers, he found himself caught up in politics, but believed that would-be public servants should be free of financial concerns if they were to stand for election.[19]

Encouraged by Meyer, Botha came out in support of the presidential campaign of General Piet Joubert, who stood for progress and reform against the more conservative President Kruger. In a letter to Joubert in August 1892, the aspiring politician left no doubt where his sympathies lay: 'Our country certainly needs great changes, and in you we have the man who carries in his heart the independence of our beloved country, and a true friend of the

Afrikaners ... I hope that the day will speedily dawn when our children will be able to say – away with Kruger's politics, concessions and Hollanders.'[20]

The Jameson Raid

In late 1895, a seismic event occurred that was to alter the course of South African history. The mining magnate and arch-imperialist premier of the Cape Colony, Cecil John Rhodes, had hatched a secret plan to invade the Transvaal, overthrow the Kruger government and force the gold-rich Transvaal into the clutches of the British Empire. What became known as the Jameson Raid, a hare-brained attempt by a mercenary force led by Rhodes' right-hand man, Dr Leander Starr Jameson, to invade the Transvaal from Bechuanaland (today Botswana) and foment an internal uprising against Kruger, ended in fiasco when an overconfident Jameson and his raiders were captured without difficulty by Boer commandos under General Cronje and handed over for trial.

Part conspiracy[21] and part cock-up, the Jameson Raid caused irreparable damage to relations between Britain and the Transvaal and led within a few years to the second Anglo-Boer War. It also inflamed British public opinion against Germany's Kaiser Wilhelm II, who had hastened to send Kruger a telegram of congratulation for having put down the Raid. The telegram read as follows: 'I tender to you my sincere congratulations that without appealing to the help of friendly powers you and your people have been successful in opposing with your own forces the armed bands that have broken into your country to disturb the peace, in restoring order, and in maintaining the independence of your country against attacks from without.'[22]

When the news broke of the Jameson Raid, the outraged Boers of Vryheid immediately turned to their *veldkornet* for counsel. Botha sent the following message on their behalf to Kruger: 'My burghers and I fully approve Government's action towards Johannesburg revolt. We offer assistance, and are ready to start at any moment. We are indignant at Johannesburg's actions, and hope that all rebels will be punished and made [an] example of. We trust the Government and stand by it, come what may. Burghers were never more unanimous than now, and stand by Government like one man.'[23]

In 1897, Botha's healthy financial circumstances enabled him to put himself forward as a candidate for one of Vryheid's two seats in the Transvaal

Volksraad. There were three other candidates in the election, one of them the sitting member, Lucas Meyer, a strong supporter of General Joubert, and the other two followers of President Kruger.[24]

The popular Botha declined, however, to associate himself with either Joubert's 'Progressives' or Kruger's 'Conservatives'. His independent stance brought a stern warning from the editor of Vryheid's newspaper, *De Nieuwe Republikein*, that unless Botha revealed his true colours, he stood little chance of being elected. But the voters of Vryheid thought otherwise. To general surprise, Botha topped the poll in the election, winning 357 votes to Meyer's 330 and leaving his Krugerite opponents trailing well behind.[25]

Before taking up his seat in the Volksraad, Botha made a preparatory visit to Meyer, who was staying in the Transvaal Hotel in Pretoria. Here he encountered a young Afrikaner lawyer, recently arrived from the Cape, with whom he was to form an attachment even closer than his own and Meyer's. His new acquaintance, who would become Kruger's state attorney within a year, was Jan Christiaan Smuts.[26]

On 3 May 1897, Botha was sworn in as a member of the First Volksraad, representing the district of Vryheid. (The Volksraad had been divided into two chambers in 1890, to enable the Boers to retain political control of the ZAR while granting a limited say in local matters to Uitlanders. The First Volksraad was the highest authority over matters of state, while the Second Volksraad gave non-burghers, many of them temporarily employed in the mining industry, some voice in the Republic's affairs.) Among those taking the oath on that day was another politician who was to become one of Botha's closest and dearest friends – the re-elected member for Lichtenburg and future 'Lion of the West', JH (Koos) de la Rey.[27]

CHAPTER 3

WAR CLOUDS

Kruger and Joubert

At the time of Louis Botha's election to the ZAR Volksraad in 1897, the tiny assembly was presided over by the formidable Paul Kruger. Its 30 members, partly elected and partly appointed, met in Pretoria's Raadzaal, usually during February to October of each year. There were no formal political parties, but a vague division existed between the supporters of Kruger and those of his arch-rival, Piet Joubert, who had stood for the presidency (and nearly won) in 1893.

Since Britain's annexure of the Transvaal 20 years earlier, a steady flow of settlers and immigrants had been attracted to the pretty, tree-lined capital, Pretoria. Though since reclaimed from the British, the town had become home to many Englishmen, Hollanders and other incomers, some of whom had built palatial residences. Cultural life, according to Meintjes, 'had become very English'.[1]

The dominant influence in the capital, however, was that of the stern Boer patriarch, Paul Kruger. Born in the Cape in 1825, as a child Kruger had trekked north with his family and settled on land ceded by the Matabele (Ndebele) to the trekker leader, Hendrik Potgieter, at the foot of the Magaliesberg range. By the age of 14 the young Kruger had already been on commando and shot his first lion. At 15, he became a burgher of the Transvaal and a year later was the owner of two farms, one for sowing and the other for grazing. Married at the age of 17 to Maria du Plessis, he was a widower only four years later. In 1847, he wed Gezina du Plessis, a cousin of his late wife, with whom – during a 54-year marriage – he had no fewer than 16 children and 120 grandchildren.

Kruger's daring as a young man was legendary. His retrieval of the body of Piet Potgieter, son of Hendrik, after the massacre of Boer women and children at the hands of the Ndebele chief, Mokopane (Makapan), and his exploits as a hunter – especially blowing off part of his left thumb and cutting off the rest with his pocket knife in trying to escape from a wounded rhinoceros – was the stuff of Boer fable. Commandant-general of the ZAR at the age of 39, he became president when the republic regained its independence from Britain in 1883, and was re-elected no fewer than four times. A huge, ugly, rough-hewn character of gloomy disposition and uncouth manners, he was – to the world outside – the personification of the Afrikaner people.

As a devout member of the ultra-conservative Dopper church, Kruger would rise for prayers each morning at 4 am. Despite having had little formal education, he also was a lay preacher. An inveterate pipe smoker, he liked holding court, Bible at his side, on the front stoep of his modest, single-storey house in central Pretoria, dispensing advice to any burgher who sought it.

Despite his reputation for intransigence, Kruger was an extremely canny and adroit politician who frequently displayed a flexibility of mind and a willingness to adapt to changing circumstances. On one matter, though, he was unbending: the need to preserve the character of the Boer republic. As CT Gordon aptly puts it: 'Preservation of the independence of the state he regarded as a sacred duty, neglect of which would bring down upon him the curse of God.'[2]

On racial questions, Kruger shared the prejudices of his fellow burghers (and most Uitlanders too): the franchise was the preserve of white males and could never be extended to people of colour. Most Boers viewed the 'natives', with whom they clashed repeatedly over land, with hostility and regarded blacks primarily as a source of cheap labour. Yet Kruger was, in some respects, slightly more liberal than his Progressive critics, advocating civil marriages for 'native' people and the partial exemption of educated blacks from the restrictions of the pass laws – measures opposed by, among others, Louis Botha.[3] At a public meeting in 1890, the president flatly refused to agree with a questioner who argued that blacks should have fewer legal rights than whites.[4]

His rival for the presidency of the republic throughout the 1890s, and the informal leader of the opposition in the Volksraad, was the much-loved General Joubert. If Kruger was the first citizen of the ZAR, Joubert was the second.[5] The popular commandant-general had been a member of the triumvirate that ran the Transvaal during the first Anglo-Boer War. He had also led Boer commandos against the British in several battles along the Natal border – including the rout of Colley and his men at Majuba.

Despite his reputation as a warrior, Joubert was essentially a pacifist and political moderate, more interested in business and farming than in making war. Neither anti-English nor anti-Uitlander, he fervently wished to see all citizens of the Republic living together harmoniously.[6] An insecure political leader, his moderate views were often diametrically opposed to those of Kruger, for whom he developed a deep-seated aversion. Among Joubert's staunchest admirers was Lucas Meyer, and another of his supporters was Meyer's protégé, Louis Botha.

Dictatorial tendencies

President Kruger understood, instinctively, that although gold had rescued his ZAR from financial disaster, the much sought-after mineral represented a threat to the Republic's survival. Before long, the Uitlanders flooding into the Transvaal from all parts of the world would outnumber and – if given the franchise – outvote his Boers. British imperialism, then in a belligerent phase, was of constant concern to him. The way to counter the imperial power, he reckoned, was to build up the ZAR's economic independence. That meant handing out monopolies and concessions to local companies and individuals to make and sell bricks, dynamite, liquor, leather and other essential consumer goods, all of which had to be protected by high tariffs.[7]

As Giliomee observes, this protectionist policy made good sense for a predominantly agrarian society trying to develop its own manufacturing sector but not for a rapidly expanding, deep-level gold industry trying to keep down costs so as to be competitive on the world market. Kruger's insistence on dishing out concessions and jobs to his (often incompetent) family, friends and supporters helped to make an already unhealthy system worse.[8]

Discontent with the president's dictatorial tendencies, resentment over the dynamite monopoly (especially) and other concessions, and anger at official corruption and maladministration had driven many younger, more forward-looking MPs in the direction of Joubert's Progressives, who were never strong enough to threaten Kruger but whose members introduced a new and more broad-minded element into the gloomy and stuffy Volksraad. Among the Progressives' brightest lights were Lucas Meyer, Koos de la Rey and Louis Botha. According to Engelenburg, in Botha's first session as a member of the Volksraad, he spoke no fewer than 50 times – on subjects ranging from the iniquity of the diamond monopoly to 'native' policy, the fencing of farms and the leasing of government land. He also seconded a motion to grant members of the Volksraad an annual salary of £1200.[9]

A matter that gave rise to dissatisfaction among the Boers – especially incoming Cape Afrikaners seeking employment – was Kruger's growing dependence upon officials imported from the Netherlands to run the public service, education and the railways. Without a pool of educated and experienced civil servants to draw on, the President had been forced to look to Europe for the skills required by his rapidly expanding administration. But the presence of these incomers, notable among them the highly efficient state attorney, Dr WJ Leyds, and their appointment ahead of home-grown Afrikaners gave rise to (politically exaggerated) resentment, as well as vociferous opposition in newspapers such as *Land en Volk* to 'Hollander rule'.[10]

Joubert wrote to one of his supporters that 'I shall do what my hand finds to do for our beloved country – not only for independence from England – but also from the foreign unhealthy influence which is undermining our existence as a people, and our national character.'[11] Botha, as we have seen, had already expressed to Joubert his own objection to the appointment of Hollanders instead of Afrikaners some years earlier.

Crossing Kruger

Unlike most of his fellow members of the Volksraad, the genial and sociable MP from Vryheid would often bring his and Annie's family of five children – two girls, Helen and Frances, and three boys, Louis, Jantje and Philip – with him to Pretoria to enjoy the bright lights of the capital. One of the ZAR's youngest public representatives, 'with a small moustache and goatee amid that forest of beards', he took no notice of the disapproval of the black-frocked Calvinist element in the Volksraad, who frowned upon his enjoyment of dancing and accordion-playing. As Engelenburg notes, in Pretoria's staid legislative circles such behaviour was regarded as 'nothing less than offensive'.[12]

But Botha did not care; what really mattered to him was opposing official maladministration, the inadequacies of the education system and rampant corruption.

Though always respectful of the president, Botha was mindful of Kruger's limitations and had the self-confidence to cross the much older man occasionally in debate. He was particularly outspoken in his criticism of the lucrative and unpopular dynamite concession. Kruger had given sole rights to the manufacture of dynamite for the mines to a private company in Modderfontein, whose plant rapidly became the biggest in the world. Botha agreed with the mine owners that the monopoly was highly undesirable and supported the argument that explosives should be freely imported if production costs were to be kept down.[13]

In the anxious days of 1899, with war with the imperial power a possibility, the Volksraad appointed the MP for Vryheid to a commission examining the dynamite concession. Finding that the government had bound itself so closely to the concessionaires that it would be unwise, at such an unpropitious time, to terminate the monopoly, Botha raised eyebrows by abruptly reversing his previous stance. For making this U-turn, he was castigated by some sections of the pro-mine-owner, anti-Kruger press.[14]

Kruger's tactics

In Volksraad debates, the domineering Kruger was used to doing as he pleased. His modus operandi was to declare his intentions in a loud booming voice, and, if there was any opposition, to furiously denounce the dissenting members. He spoke as often as he liked, until a measure was put before the assembly to limit him to one speech per debate. After he made it known that, as president, he would take no notice of the restriction, however, the bill was quietly shelved.[15]

If Kruger could not get his own way, his usual tactic was to threaten resignation. Once, when he did so, a mischievous Botha promptly rose and proposed that his resignation be accepted. A lively debate ensued during which the president was forced to back down. Thereafter, he was much more circumspect about offering his resignation.[16]

The Jameson Raid, aptly described by De Kiewiet as 'inexcusable in its folly and unforgivable in its consequences',[17] had revived the flagging political fortunes of the elderly president, who turned 70 in the year of the Raid. The fallout from Jameson's recklessness carried Kruger to a resounding victory in the presidential election three years later. By then, he had become convinced that to give in to Uitlander demands would be the thin end of the wedge. In the meantime, his calm and measured response to the Raid – and refusal to have its leaders shot, as Botha and other hotheads had demanded – elevated him to a figure of world renown, a hero to those in Europe and elsewhere who detested British imperialism. Knightly honours, which he wore proudly on ceremonial occasions, were bestowed upon him by Portugal, the Netherlands, Belgium and France.

Sensing in his bones that another war with Britain was inevitable, Kruger began – with the help of a decidedly reluctant Joubert – to spend gold revenues freely on rearming the ZAR with the best and most modern weaponry, imported from Germany and France. By 1899, the republic was armed to the teeth. The President had also reformed his administration by bringing in younger, well-educated Afrikaners, among them Jan Smuts as state attorney, and widening his circle of advisers to include Marthinus Steyn, president of the Orange Free State. In 1897, Kruger's ZAR and Steyn's Free State entered into an alliance to come to each other's aid in the event of war.

Milner's intent

Kruger's unease about Britain's intentions was well founded. Joseph Chamberlain, the Conservative government's colonial secretary, was an avowed imperialist who believed that consolidating the Empire was essential to Britain's survival as a great power. In 1897, he sent another ardent empire-builder, Alfred Milner, to the Cape as governor of the Cape Colony and high commissioner in South Africa. Milner's idealistic vision was to bring the whole country under British rule as soon as possible, and to add South Africa to a white, English-speaking federation of Britain, Australia and Canada, run by an imperial parliament in London.

The disastrous fallout from the Jameson Raid had made Chamberlain wary, for a time, of acting upon Uitlander grievances and intervening in the internal affairs of the Transvaal. But the impatient Milner had no such scruples.

After Kruger's re-election by an overwhelming majority in 1898, Milner wrote to Chamberlain to say that he saw 'no way out of the political troubles of South Africa except reform in the Transvaal or war'.[18] Determined to force the pace before an economically flourishing ZAR could extend its republican influence over the whole of South Africa, he encouraged the Uitlanders to send London a petition, bearing more than 21 000 signatures, setting out their grievances with the Kruger government, particularly over the franchise qualifications and the dynamite monopoly.

Kruger had already lowered some of the franchise requirements in response to demands from Progressives in the Volksraad, who argued that Uitlander demands for the vote at the cost of their British citizenship was an elaborate bluff. But the President and his supporters believed otherwise. By their estimate, there were more white foreigners in the ZAR than there were Boers. By agreeing to the Uitlanders' franchise demands, they would be putting their own republic at risk.

In a last-ditch effort to ward off armed conflict, President Steyn invited Kruger and Milner and their advisers to a meeting in Bloemfontein. Kruger offered to reduce the residential qualification for Uitlanders from fourteen to seven years, but Milner was unmoved. According to Hyam, he saw the coming war as a 'great game between the Transvaal and ourselves for the mastery of South Africa, the game of uniting South Africa as a British State'.[19] Accordingly, he demanded that the Transvaal surrender its sovereignty and agree to make its laws subject to British approval. 'It's our country you want,' a tearful Kruger claimed despairingly.[20]

Trying to avert war

Following the Bloemfontein conference, Milner continued to manoeuvre determinedly towards confrontation, while Kruger – persuaded by Smuts – further reduced the residential qualification for Uitlander voters to five years. Botha, De la Rey and other Progressives, along with the Free State's President Steyn, enthusiastically endorsed these efforts to avert war, arguing that the Transvaal was not equipped to take on the might of the British Empire. 'We are not strong enough to fight anybody, unless we have to,' declared De la Rey.[21]

The Progressives' patience was not unlimited, however. When the British dispatched an additional 10 000 troops to strengthen their forces in Natal and the Cape, and it became obvious that Milner was intent on going to war come what may, Joubert and his followers gave their unqualified allegiance to Kruger. And, as Meintjes notes, 'once Botha gave his loyalty, nothing on earth would persuade him to change it'.[22]

On 27 September 1899 the Volksraad was called into urgent session to discuss the looming stand-off with Britain. On the streets of Pretoria there was deep apprehension, and the public gallery of the Raadzaal was packed to overflowing. Earlier that day, burgher commandos had been sent hastily to the Natal border and armed men were everywhere in the capital.

In a debate in which the British were harshly condemned, Botha gave vent to his feelings with an impassioned address during which he had to be calmed down twice by the chairman, Lucas Meyer. He was in favour of a defensive posture, Botha declared, but not war. The ZAR should adopt a defiant attitude, saying thus far and no further. In order to acquire the vote, the British government was trying to force its subjects onto the republic, which had gone far enough, in his opinion, in its efforts to preserve peace. He was particularly infuriated by suggestions that the Boers were frightened of the British. 'Already it is being said that the Boers are afraid; they are conceding things all along the line. We have yielded, yes, and we have gone very far because we want peace, but not on account of any fear. That I must strongly deny ...' he declared.[23]

Botha's pugnacious address went down well with members of the Volksraad, who endorsed his sentiments with acclamation and resolved unanimously to defend the rights and independence of the ZAR.[24] After two days of debate, a motion expressing concern at the build-up of British troops on the Natal border, and repudiating responsibility for any war that might break out, was adopted without dissent.[25]

The Volksraad decides

When further negotiations with the British proved fruitless, Kruger called the Volksraad into a secret conclave to take a decision that had become inevitable. In the debate, several of his over-confident supporters asserted that, with the aid of the Cape Afrikaners, the two republics would be more than a match for the British forces. The Boers should strike now, they insisted, before the British could build up their force numbers in South Africa. The time had come to present Chamberlain and company with an ultimatum: remove your troops from the borders of the Republic, otherwise it's war.

The pacific Koos de la Rey was one who had little time for empty bravado, or for the strategy being proposed by some fellow MPs. He was against any plan for aggressive action, he said, that was tactically unsound and politically unnecessary. His argument brought a furious Kruger to his feet to denounce the speaker and describe those who thought like him as cowards. Eyes flashing, an even angrier De la Rey responded that he would do his duty 'as the Raad decides'. Addressing the president directly, he declared contemptuously (and, as it turned out, presciently): 'You will see me in the field fighting for our independence long after you and your party who make war with your mouths have fled the country.'[26]

Stunned by the acrimonious exchange, members of the Volksraad nonetheless rallied behind Kruger. When the decision whether or not to present an ultimatum to the British was put to the vote, only Joubert, Meyer, De la Rey, Botha and three others were against it. However, like President Steyn, if there was to be a fight, they were ready for it.

War between the Boer republics and Britain was declared at 5 pm on 11 October 1899. By then, Joubert, Meyer and Botha had already departed Pretoria for the Natal border. At Sandspruit, near Volksrust, commandos had been mustering in their hundreds in readiness for an invasion of Natal. Armed with the latest German Mauser rifles, a lighter weapon than the British Lee-Metford, which had been in use since 1888, as well as a plentiful supply of ammunition, the mounted and mobile Boers were ready to fight for their land and their lives. The stage now was set for a battle for control over the richest territory on the African continent. It may not have occurred to the combatants that the land they were about to fight over did not belong – in the end – to either side.

CHAPTER 4

THE WAR BEGINS

Note: This chapter and the next few that follow are an account of Louis Botha's role in the Anglo-Boer War, not a detailed record of the war itself.

The Boer plan

Despite his reservations about going to war with Britain, and the painful implications for those of his sisters who had married Englishmen, Louis Botha threw himself wholeheartedly into preparations for the conflict. Though not involved in the planning of Boer strategy and holding no senior military rank, he was appointed as adviser and number two to his fellow MP, Lucas Meyer, the general in charge of southeastern Transvaal commandos.[1]

A war strategy for the Boers had been drawn up in a memorandum prepared weeks beforehand by Kruger's right-hand man, the Transvaal's young and forward-looking state attorney, Jan Smuts. Although the memorandum never became official policy – Commandant-General Joubert had ideas of his own – the plan had three elements: political, economic and strategic. Underpinning all three was Smuts's view of the British Empire as a 'ramshackle structure' inhabited by largely antagonistic tribes (in India, Egypt and South Africa, for example) and without adequate military means of defending itself against attack, or of keeping the peace. As had happened after Majuba, one more British defeat in the field – Smuts believed – would loosen the Empire's shaky hold on southern Africa. At the same time, it would encourage thousands of Afrikaners in the Cape to rally to the cause of their northern neighbours.[2]

Smuts's proposed plan of attack was for the Boers to sweep without delay through Natal and the Cape so as to reach the coast before British troop strength in South Africa could be significantly enhanced. Unlike Britain, the two republics could not afford standing armies – except for small professional artillery units – and had to fall back on the commando system, honed since the Great Trek. Each of the Transvaal's 22 districts and the Free State's 19 provided one commando to the Boer army, and each commando was led by an elected commandant.[3]

The commando system, unique to the Boers, had many drawbacks. There was no military hierarchy to speak of: the commandant-general, commandants and field cornets were all elected by their fellow burghers. As most of these officers had been chosen before war broke out, they were often voted into office for non-military reasons. And, though every eligible burgher had by law to join a commando, he still had to be persuaded to fight. Decisions by a *krygsraad* (council of war) were taken by democratic vote, but once a decision had been reached, it fell to the officer in charge of a commando to explain it to his members and entreat them to carry it out.[4] No law actually compelled a burgher to fight, and he was free to change his unit for another if he wished. In Bossenbroek's words, 'It was the rule rather than the exception for decisions taken by superiors to be debated and sometimes overturned or ignored. Even in combat, every Boer was first and foremost his own man.'[5]

At the outbreak of war, the number of burghers eligible for call-up in the Transvaal and Free State was about 54 000, supplemented by artillery and reservists, uniformed police and some foreign volunteers. By early October 1899, some 14 000 men had assembled at Sandspruit, on the Transvaal/Natal border, while 6 500 Free Staters, under Marthinus Prinsloo, were ready to cross the Drakensberg and invade Natal. A force of 1 500–2 000 men, under Meyer's command, was to head for the Doringberg mountainside, across the border some 32 kilometres northeast of the coal-mining town of Dundee.[6]

Armed and ready

The Boers were equipped with a formidable array of weaponry, financed by mining revenues and imported after the Jameson Raid. Some 45 000 Martini-Henry rifles and an equivalent number of Mausers were sufficient to arm all mobilised citizens, with some kept in reserve in case the Cape Afrikaners decided to join the fight. The Mausers were particularly well suited to the Boers' style of warfare, being relatively light, easy to load and accurate, while

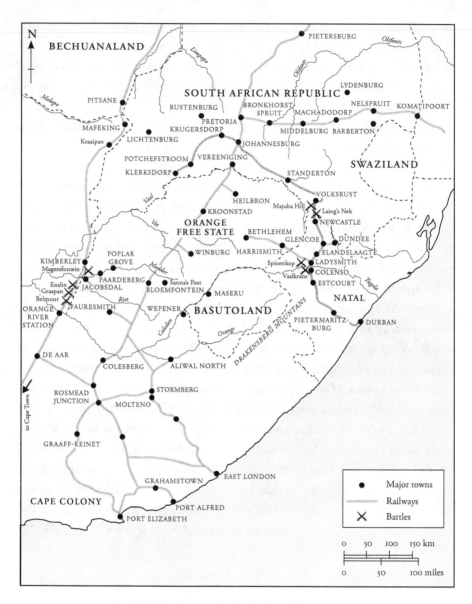

South Africa during the Anglo-Boer War, 1899–1902

their smokeless gunpowder – a recent invention – made them almost impossible for the British to detect.[7]

The Boer artillery was also, to quote Bossenbroek, 'the best that gold could buy'.[8] At their disposal were small Lee-Metford and large Vickers-Maxim machine guns (known as 'pom-poms' because of the sound they made) as well as Krupp field artillery and four heavy French Creusot 155 mm (Long Tom) fortress guns with a range of 10 kilometres – twice the range of the equivalent British guns.

Yet, if the Boers' strategy was to be based upon speed, mobility, the element of surprise and an early superiority in arms, quite the wrong commanders had been chosen to implement it. The elderly commandant-general, Piet Joubert, who hated the thought of losing men in battle, the equally cautious Free Stater Marthinus Prinsloo and other superannuated officers saw their roles as primarily defensive in nature – to protect the republics against invasion rather than to take any bold initiatives against the enemy themselves. Their restraint and lack of aggressive intent were to become a constant frustration to the younger officers around them, including Louis Botha.

The British forces in Natal – bolstered by the recent arrival of 5 600 troops from India – were concentrated at two bases to the north of the winding Tugela River, which flowed through the colony from the Drakensberg to the sea. The largest contingent of men was based at Ladysmith – the junction of the railway lines from the Transvaal and Free State to Durban – where 9 560 troops with 30 guns were garrisoned. Another 4 150 men and 14 guns were positioned further north, in the heart of the Natal coalfields, at Dundee. The officer commanding Ladysmith was another elderly general, Sir George White, while Major General Sir William Penn Symons was in charge at Dundee.[9]

The invasion begins

The Boer invasion of Natal began on 13 October 1899, when three large commandos led by Joubert advanced slowly and deliberately across the border southwards towards the small towns of Newcastle, Glencoe and Dundee. As far as the eye could see, wrote the young Deneys Reitz, 'the plain was alive with horsemen, guns and cattle, all steadily going forward to the frontier.

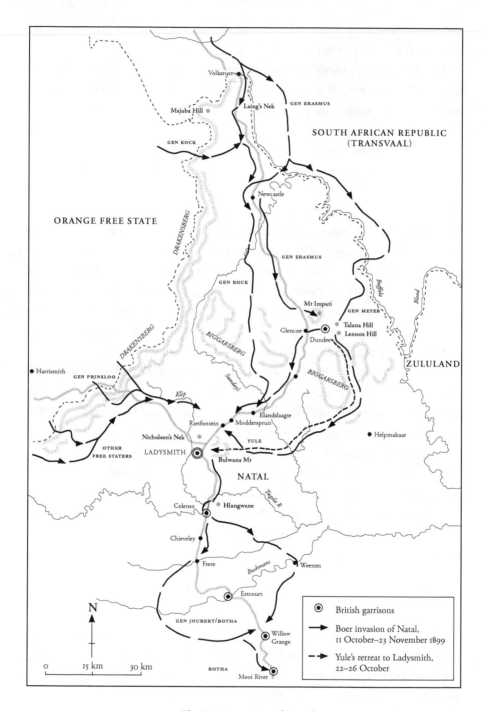

The following labels appear on the map:

Volksrust

GEN ERASMUS

Majuba Hill

Laing's Nek

SOUTH AFRICAN REPUBLIC
(TRANSVAAL)

GEN KOCK

ORANGE FREE STATE

DRAKENSBERG

Newcastle

GEN ERASMUS

Buffalo

Blood

GEN KOCK

Mt Impati

GEN MEYER

DRAKENSBERG

BIGGARSBERG

Glencoe

Dundee

Talana Hill
Lennox Hill

ZULULAND

Harrismith

GEN PRINSLOO

Klip

Sundays

BIGGARSBERG

Helpmakaar

Rietfontein

Elandslaagte

Modderspruit

Nicholson's Nek

YULE

OTHER
FREE STATERS

LADYSMITH

Bulwana Mt

NATAL

Tugela R

Colenso

Hlangwane

Chieveley

Frere

Bushmans

Weenen

N

Estcourt

GEN JOUBERT/BOTHA

Willow
Grange

0   15 km   30 km

BOTHA

Mooi River

⊙ British garrisons

→ Boer invasion of Natal,
11 October–23 November 1899

⇢ Yule's retreat to Ladysmith,
22–26 October

The Boer invasion of Natal

The scene was a stirring one, and I shall never forget riding to war with that great host.'[10]

Fully expecting the war to be over by Christmas and reluctant to damage any infrastructure that might be needed later, the British had left intact the railway line between Natal and the Transvaal, including the key Laing's Nek tunnel, enabling Joubert to bring vital materiel and supplies down by train to undefended Newcastle. From there, his forward wing under General Daniel (Maroela) Erasmus carried on towards Dundee, while another column under Meyer was sent to advance on the town in a pincer movement from the east. A third commando, under General Jan Kock, made directly for Elandslaagte in order to sever the rail link between Dundee and Ladysmith, as the Free State commandos moved simultaneously from the west towards the target of Ladysmith itself. There was little communication between the three columns, however, once they entered Natal.[11]

En route to Dundee, Botha and members of his Vryheid commando were ordered by Meyer to undertake a reconnaissance mission to De Jager's Drift, on the Buffalo River. Here they seized an observation post manned by five men of the Natal Police, who were blissfully unaware of the outbreak of war. Their capture gave Botha the distinction – along with De la Rey, who had unwillingly apprehended an armoured train in the western Transvaal a day earlier – of capturing some of the first British prisoners of the Anglo-Boer War.

Talana

On his arrival in Durban, Sir George White – who had accompanied British reinforcements from India and been put in overall command of imperial forces in Natal – was dismayed to find that Penn Symons, an overconfident officer who had fought in the Anglo-Zulu War of 1879 and was contemptuous of the Boers' fighting capabilities, had already drawn a defensive line across northern Natal. Like the governor, Sir Walter Hely-Hutchinson, Penn Symons believed that to abandon the north might encourage Boer sympathisers to switch their loyalties and perhaps even provoke the Zulu into revolt against Britain's seizure of their territory.

War is in the last resort, to quote Thomas Pakenham, 'a contest of

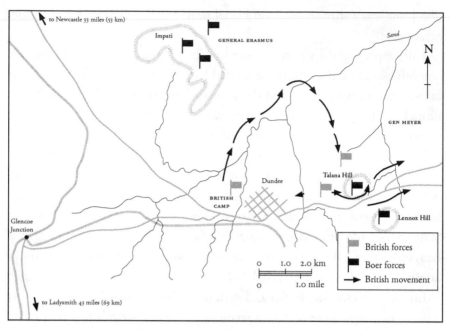

The fighting around Dundee and Talana

blunders',[12] and there were many bungles on both sides in the second Anglo-Boer War. The first great blunder belonged to White, who chose to make his headquarters at Ladysmith, leaving Penn Symons to defend the army's exposed forward position at Dundee against the advancing Boers. The British commander would have been better advised to withdraw his forces south of the Tugela, and wait there until more support could arrive from Britain. On the Boer side, Joubert was responsible for an even greater strategic error – splitting up his forces rather than consolidating them and driving expeditiously through the defences of the dispersed and under-strength enemy.

Early in the morning of 20 October, the first battle of the war broke out when the Boers launched a concerted pronged attack on Penn Symons' encampment at Dundee. From the northwest, General Erasmus and 2 000 men had moved in overnight to occupy a strategic, flat-topped hill, Impati, which rose prominently above the town. From the northeast, Meyer's 1 500-strong commando had also advanced by night on Talana and Lennox, two more hills overlooking the British camp on the eastern side of town.[13]

From his spies, Penn Symons had received ample warning of the Boers' movements, but disdained to take the necessary countermeasures, believing that the inexperienced and untrained Boers would not have the nerve to attack an entire brigade of the British Army.[14] Great was his surprise, therefore, when at daybreak two Boer heavy guns – a Krupp and a Creusot, hauled up Talana Hill in the rain during the night – opened fire on his garrison.

Retaliating quickly, Penn Symons brought up his artillery to bombard Talana and ordered the infantry to make a direct assault on the hill, not realising that frontal attacks were foolhardy against the Boers' accurate rifle fire. He paid dearly for his recklessness by taking a bullet in the stomach himself, from which he was to die a few days later. Despite the loss of many men, the British managed – after several hours of fighting – to force the Boers off the hill, but only after Meyer had realised that his surprise attack on Talana had not succeeded, and had withdrawn his men to safer ground.[15]

Although the first direct engagement of the war had ended, tactically, in a British victory, the cost at Talana had been high: 41 killed, 203 wounded and 231 taken prisoner. The numbers would have been even higher had the colour of British uniforms not changed, since Majuba, from bright red to a utilitarian khaki. On the Boer side, Meyer had lost around 150 men – including 35 dead and 91 wounded.[16] (Casualty numbers in the Anglo-Boer War vary from source to source and are often not reliable.) On the northern side of Dundee, under cover of a thick, swirling mist, Erasmus's men had dragged a Long Tom and other guns up the hillside at Impati, but had been unable to shell the enemy because of the mist. They began bombarding the British camp at dawn the next day, forcing General James Yule, who had taken over command from Penn Symons, to conclude that the Boers' occupation of Impati, and control of the water supply, had made the town indefensible. That night, abandoning valuable equipment, ammunition and three months' provisions, Yule led his men under cover of darkness on a daunting 96-kilometre trek in dreadful weather to the British redoubt in Ladysmith.[17] The British army's ill-considered attempt to hold the line in northern Natal had ended in failure.

Yet the battle of Talana Hill had also given a severe shock to the conscripted burghers, many of whom were farmers encountering the harsh reality of war for the first time. As the British troops retaliated with fixed bayonets, Boer discipline had almost fallen apart. About 1 000 men fled the battle scene, with one frightened Boer racing away on his pony for 80 kilometres without stopping. Although some Boers ran away, many more stayed to fight – picking off the 'khakis' with their Mausers until ordered to retreat to safer ground.

An unwell General Meyer, in overall command of the Boers at Dundee, had been unable to make full use of the opportunity that had presented itself – failing to press home the early advantage gained on Talana by attacking the British infantry from nearby Lennox Hill and cutting off their escape route to Ladysmith, and then pulling his men back too quickly to the safety of the Transvaal side of the Doringberg, 32 kilometres away on the border. On the way there, his own and Botha's roles in the war almost came to a premature end when, during a visit to a farmhouse, they were surprised by an armed British patrol. By slipping out a back door, the two Boer officers were able to steal away to safety. From the Doringberg, a disconsolate Meyer left it to Botha to telegraph an account of the battle to Boer headquarters in Pretoria.[18]

Elandslaagte

On 21 October 1899, the day after Talana, the British won a second Pyrrhic victory when a coordinated attack by cavalry under General John French and infantry under Colonel Ian Hamilton dislodged an 800-strong Boer column under General Kock from the small coal-mining and railway settlement at Elandslaagte, 27 kilometres north of Ladysmith. Kock's men had borne down on the little village from the Biggarsberg mountains, in order to capture the railway station and cut the link between Ladysmith and Dundee. Arriving at the same time as a train from Ladysmith bearing supplies, including a consignment of whisky, the Boers took the station manager and several civilians prisoner. That night there was a boisterous, whisky-fuelled party at the local hotel, during which a British prisoner played the piano and the Transvaal 'Volkslied' and 'God Save the Queen' rang out from the rafters.[19]

But Kock, who always wore a top hat in the field, and his burghers had made the error of advancing too far, too early. The next day, they found themselves hopelessly outnumbered and outgunned by British forces sent up by White from Ladysmith. After heavy fighting, and hundreds of casualties on either side, the Boers had to abandon their defensive position on the ridges of several small hills fringing the railway siding, and were mercilessly cut down as they fled and slashed to pieces by the lances of the charging cavalry. When nightfall came, the battlefield was littered with dead bodies, with many wounded survivors succumbing during the night from exposure to the bitter cold. Kock himself was taken prisoner and died from wounds sustained in the fighting.[20]

The virtual annihilation of the escaping burghers left the Boers with an undying hatred of British cavalry. The partisan Irish MP and journalist, Michael Davitt, wrote after the battle that the spearing of wounded Boers by lancers and others excited a widespread feeling of indignation throughout the civilised world: 'The American and continental press were especially outspoken in condemnation of the brutality which disgraced the British soldiers in their treatment of beaten and wounded foes, after the fortunes of the fight had fallen to the side of the stronger combatant.'[21] Newspapers in Pretoria and Bloemfontein also reacted with revulsion and outrage at what they considered an atrocity on a par with the earlier spearing of 'Christian' trekkers by 'barbarous Zulus'.[22]

The British cavalry's use of 'cold steel' at Elandslaagte had traumatised some in the Boer ranks, who pleaded with their commandant, Ben Viljoen, to be allowed to leave the war and go home. Hoping to be rid of these men, Viljoen gave them passes reading 'Permit – to go to Johannesburg on account of cowardice, at Government's expense'. The fearful burghers grabbed the passes without reading them, giving Viljoen, who managed to escape himself to fight another day, some wry amusement at the thought of the reception they would receive back at Boer headquarters.[23]

Fearing an imminent attack by Free State commandos, White recalled his forces to Ladysmith on the evening of the battle of Elandslaagte, enabling the Boers to reoccupy the station a few days later. The battle for control of the rail link, as well as Joubert's lack of urgency in waiting four days before sending Meyer and Erasmus after the retreating Yule, had enabled Yule's bedraggled, six-kilometre-long column to make its way through thick mud and pouring rain to safety at Ladysmith. There, the entire Natal Field Force of more than 12 000 men and seven artillery batteries had gathered. On 29 October, Lucas Meyer and Louis Botha arrived on the outskirts of the town, where they were joined by Joubert and the Free Staters. The total Boer force outside

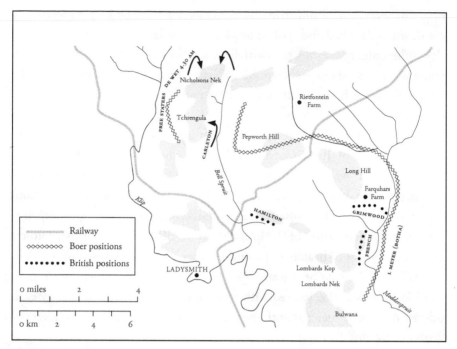

The Battle of Ladysmith (Modderspruit and Nicholson's Nek)

Ladysmith numbered around 10 000, and the battle lines were drawn for a showdown between the two armies.

Ladysmith

Ladysmith was not the sort of place in which any sensible military commander would wish to be holed up. Situated on the banks of a river on the northwestern edge of a broad valley, Natal's third-largest town was 'hot, dusty, disease-ridden and claustrophobic, walled in on every side by a circle of ridges and hills'.[24] So why did White run the risk of being surrounded and cut off by the Boers there? The short answer is that, like Penn Symons, he completely underestimated his foe. Having driven the Boers off Talana and out of Elandslaagte, his army, he believed, was more than a match for the enemy.

The Boer commandos, for their part, bore down on Ladysmith in an equally confident mood,[25] with Joubert setting up his headquarters behind

Botha's tactical acumen during the Natal campaign cemented his reputation as one of the leading Boer commanders. This image, from a postcard, was widely circulated at the time.

Pepworth Hill, the highest of the surrounding hills, a few miles north of the town. He positioned his guns on nearby Long Hill, across the railway track, and on several hills to the east of the town. The Boer line was thus a long semicircle from Erasmus's encampment on Pepworth to Meyer's bivouac (where Botha found himself) near Lombard's Kop, alongside the Modderspruit. Eleven kilometres away to the west, the Free Staters had reached Trenchgula, a flat-topped hill through which the main road to Ladysmith ran, via a pass at Nicholson's Nek. All these movements of men could be clearly seen from an observation balloon hoisted by the British above the town, making White realise that, unless he took offensive action sooner rather than later, his base might become encircled by the Boer army.

On Sunday 29 October, the Boers cut the water supply to Ladysmith. Wary of alienating the enemy by striking back on the Sabbath, White waited until early the following morning before sending out almost his entire force to break through Boer lines. Two infantry brigades, one commanded by Colonel Grimwood and the other by Colonel Hamilton, supported by artillery and cavalry, were sent out in the early hours of Monday morning to capture Long and Pepworth hills, respectively. Earlier, a third force of 1100 men under Lieutenant Colonel Carleton had left on a night march to Nicholson's Nek, where they were to close the pass to fleeing Boers and prevent Free State commandos from joining the Transvalers around Pepworth. White's tactics were a repeat of those used successfully at Elandslaagte: once the Boers had been softened up by artillery fire, first the infantry and then the cavalry would be sent in.[26]

Grimwood and Hamilton's circuitous eastward advance on the Boers' long-range gun emplacements under cover of darkness turned out to be disastrous. As dawn broke, Grimwood discovered that Long Hill had been abandoned during the night, and before long his men were being raked by fire from Meyer's commando, stationed between Gun Hill and Lombard's Kop on the town side of the Modderspruit.

Once again, Meyer's nerves gave way under the strain of battle, leaving his confidant, Louis Botha, in informal control of the 2000-strong commando. For the first time, the 37-year-old Botha was able to display his tactical awareness and uncanny gift for ascertaining what was happening 'on the other side of the hill'.[27] Cleverly moving his men into positions from which they could concentrate their artillery and rifle fire on the British, Botha maintained the initiative throughout what became known as the Battle of Modderspruit, forcing White to recall his forces before noon and beat an undignified retreat back into town.[28]

As the British troops streamed across the open veld towards the safety of Ladysmith, they were at the Boers' mercy, but to Botha's frustration were saved by Joubert's inexplicable refusal to sanction any hot pursuit. It was one of the turning points of the war. As one Boer officer ruefully recorded later, 'if we had chased after the fleeing enemy that day, we could have taken Ladysmith and every khaki in it'.[29]

Sealing the pass

Near Trenchgula, Colonel Carleton's column had run into determined opposition from a Boer commando led not by the elderly Marthinus Prinsloo, but by a fierce-eyed burgher who would soon become world famous – acting commandant Christiaan de Wet. After another intense battle in blazing heat, during which the British sustained heavy casualties, Carleton ordered a cease-fire and surrendered to the Boers, who took 800 prisoners. Deneys Reitz, who was on the scene, wrote afterwards: 'Dead and wounded lay all around, and the cries and groans of agony and the dreadful sights haunted me for many a day, for though I had seen death by violence of late, there had been nothing to approach the horrors accumulated here.'[30]

'Mournful Monday', as 30 October became known in British newspapers, was a humiliation for White, who lost 1200 men, a tenth of his troops in Ladysmith. Had Joubert been more aggressive after the British commander decided to cut his losses and call his troops back to base, the Boers could have turned the British retreat into a rout. But the war-hating general had done enough fighting for one day and refused to heed the urgings of Botha and other younger officers: 'When God holds out a finger, don't take the whole hand' was his response. Thanks to this 'theological view of military tactics',[31] White was able to recall most of his men to the safety of their garrison. Two days later, the Boers cut the railway and telegraph lines outside the town and the siege of Ladysmith began.

CHAPTER 5

TAKING CHARGE

Buller arrives

On 31 October 1899, the day after 'Mournful Monday', Britain's new commanding officer in South Africa, General Sir Redvers Buller, and members of his Army Corps arrived in Cape Town aboard the liner *Dunottar Castle*. They were greeted by the news of the British defeats at Modderspruit and Nicholson's Nek and the lockdown of White's forces in Ladysmith. Buller learnt too that the towns of Kimberley and Mafeking were under siege by the Boers.

The latter news would not have disturbed him unduly, for the numerically stronger Boers were playing directly into his hands. Instead of making a dash for the coast before they became hopelessly outnumbered by reinforcements arriving from Britain – as Smuts had proposed – the Boer generals had unwisely chosen to enforce three comparatively pointless sieges. Buller was given three weeks of precious breathing space while he awaited ships carrying another 50 000 soldiers to arrive in Table Bay.

Having decided that Kimberley and Ladysmith should first be relieved before any attempt could be made to advance on Kruger's capital, Pretoria, Buller assigned the freeing of Kimberley to General Lord Methuen and took the second and more urgent responsibility upon himself. A third force under General Gatacre was to hold the front in the eastern Cape, to prevent the Boers from overrunning the Cape Colony from across the Orange River. Splitting his army to relieve the three sieges instead of driving his entire force up through the Cape to the Transvaal was the first of Buller's several strategic blunders. A second was his belief that he could coordinate the movements of his army in South Africa from a defensive position in the midlands of Natal.

In Buller's mind, keeping the port at Durban in British hands was the immediate priority. If the Boers were to capture the harbour, they would be able to bring in foreign volunteers from countries hostile to the Empire, most notably the Kaiser's Germany. Moreover, nearly all of Buller's cavalry in South Africa were locked up in White's garrison at Ladysmith, putting his forces in the field at a marked disadvantage to the highly mobile Boers.

Buller was no stranger to South Africa. Two decades earlier, as a major in the Frontier Horse, he had taken part in the Ninth Frontier War against the Xhosa. Promoted to lieutenant colonel, he moved on to Natal where he won the Victoria Cross for bravery in helping his men escape from a 20 000-strong Zulu impi on Mount Hlobane. In 1880, shortly after returning home, he was sent back to South Africa for the duration of the first Anglo-Boer War, in which he served as military secretary to the commander-in-chief of the Cape Colony.

Ponderous and blimpish in appearance, Buller possessed 'great girth, multiple chins, a flushed complexion and a walrus moustache'.[1] A taciturn man who avoided the limelight, he was a 'soldier's general', respected for his fighting as well as his administrative abilities, and revered for his obvious concern for the rank and file. A 17-year-old soldier said of him: 'Tough and brusque he was, but his troopers discovered that he was both accessible and sympathetic. If we were lying in the rain, so was Buller. If we were hungry, so was he. All the hardships he shared equally with his men. Never did Buller, as commander, have a patrol tent to sleep under whilst his men were in the open. He was the idol of us all.'[2] In the past, he had got on well with the Boers, whose fighting skills and mobility he respected.[3] He was not really looking forward to fighting them again.

Admiration for Buller's military abilities was not universal, however. On the long voyage to Cape Town, he had been accompanied by the military correspondents of several British newspapers, among them the precocious young Winston Churchill, as ever in search of fame. Having seen action in the army himself, Churchill regarded most generals of Buller's age (nearly 60) as being well past their prime. His memorable description of the commander-in-chief – whom he quite liked personally – was that Buller was 'a man of considerable scale. He plodded on from blunder to blunder and one disaster to another without losing either the regard of his country or the trust of his troops, to whose feeding as well as his own he paid serious attention.'[4]

General Sir Redvers Buller (drawing by S Begg, 1900) commanded British forces at the start of the Anglo-Boer War.

Towards Estcourt

Having failed to heed Buller's earlier warnings – issued repeatedly via the War Office in July and August – not to cross the Tugela, White had had enough sense not to confine all his troops to Ladysmith. Before the siege, he sent about 2 300 men across the river to Colenso, 40 kilometres north of Estcourt, in order to bar the way to any Boer forces who might bypass Ladysmith on their way south. Only this small British contingent stood between the Boers and the capital of the colony, Pietermaritzburg.

On the Boer side, Piet Joubert was as uncertain as ever whether his strategy should be offensive or defensive. Alarmed at the number of men who had simply melted away from Ladysmith without his permission, or gone on unofficial 'leave', he cabled despairingly to Pretoria: 'Unless the government publishes an order to send back the absent burghers, I shall shortly have no commandos at all.'[5]

It took a full week after Ladysmith had been besieged for Joubert to mount a half-hearted and uncoordinated attempt to overrun the town, which the British defenders managed to ward off easily. On 9 November, the commandant-general called a council of war outside his tent. By now, Meyer had departed for medical treatment in Pretoria, and Louis Botha had been officially designated as an assistant general. With the British now encircled in Ladysmith, at Botha's urging it was decided that a mounted force of 1 500 Transvalers, drawn from three commandos and supplemented by 500 Free Staters, would drive onwards into southern Natal.

Botha was to be in charge of the commando, but to his dismay Joubert insisted on accompanying him, to ensure – the cynics said – that his inexperienced new commander did not overreach himself. Botha understood full well that the Boers were now in a race against time. Buller was in South Africa, and before long 20 000 British reinforcements would land in Durban and begin making their way inland towards the Tugela front. Leaving Ladysmith to be guarded by several thousand burghers, he and Joubert pressed southwards across the river towards Estcourt. They hoped to reach Pietermaritzburg and Durban before the khakis could arrive in numbers.

Hugging the railway

By 14 November, Botha's commando had bypassed Colenso and reached Chieveley, 32 kilometres north of Estcourt, on the rail line to Ladysmith from Durban. The railway was a lifeline for the British, who depended on armoured trains (of which they had 13 initially) for moving large numbers of men, materiel and supplies around the country, and for reconnaissance purposes. After the loss of Ladysmith, the small British force sent to guard the strategic rail bridge over the Tugela at Colenso had scuttled back to the safety of Estcourt. They used an armoured train to patrol the Estcourt-Ladysmith railway line regularly.

Every day, like clockwork, the train – consisting of an engine sandwiched between two or three armoured trucks, and a seven-pounder naval gun – would chug its way from Estcourt to Colenso. After its occupants had checked the line and tried to ascertain what the Boers were up to, it would turn around and slowly return home. 'Nothing looks more formidable and impressive than an armoured train,' wrote Churchill, 'but nothing is in fact more vulnerable and helpless.'[6] A more tempting target for Botha and his men would have been hard to find.

Churchill captured

Soon after dawn on 15 November, a Boer patrol spotted the train steaming along the line towards Chieveley. On board, under the command of Captain Aylmer Haldane, were 164 troops, railway workers and ratings manning the naval gun, as well as the correspondent of the London *Morning Post*, the adventurous young Churchill. From a nearby hill, Botha and 500 men of the Wakkerstroom and Krugersdorp commandos watched as the train went by. While they waited for its reappearance, they scattered rocks across the track around a corner and down a steep incline near the Blaauwkranz River.

As the returning locomotive neared the obstruction, the Boers let fly with cannon fire, causing the startled engine driver to pick up speed and crash with even greater force into the obstruction across the track. Two trucks in front of the locomotive were wrecked and a partially derailed third barred the way forward. Bullets and shrapnel rained down upon Haldane's men, who made a spirited reply with their own cannon and rifle fire.

While the fighting raged around him, Churchill took it upon himself to organise the removal of the rocks obstructing the locomotive and its tender. Displaying conspicuous bravery under fire, he managed after an hour to clear the track and send the engine, with more than 40 wounded men clinging to its cabin, on its way back to Estcourt. Riding for a few hundred yards himself before jumping off to help Haldane and his troops, Churchill had not gone far before he was accosted by an armed Boer and – on finding that he had lost his Mauser pistol while clearing the line – was forced reluctantly to raise his arms in surrender. Along with Haldane, he and 53 others were taken into captivity, to be sent up to Pretoria via the Boer headquarters on the outskirts of Ladysmith, as prisoners of war.

A household name

Newspaper reports of Churchill's subsequent escape from Pretoria and dramatic return to the British front line in Natal via Lourenço Marques (today Maputo) and Durban made the *Morning Post*'s daredevil correspondent a household name throughout the Empire. It also helped propel him into a career in politics. As he later reflected in print, if he had not climbed aboard the armoured train, he'd not have been captured, and if he'd not been taken prisoner, he could not have escaped, and if he'd not escaped, he would not have had enough material to write a best-selling book or give the lectures that assured his financial independence and enabled him to buy his way into a parliamentary seat in 1900.[7]

Years after the war, the legend grew that it was Louis Botha himself who had captured Churchill near Chieveley. It was the result – one must surmise – of a 'misunderstanding'. At a lunch in London after the war, at which Botha was present, Churchill was describing his capture when the Boer general – with a twinkle in his eye, no doubt – claimed that he had been the one who had taken Churchill prisoner. That was enough reason for the journalist Churchill to write later, in *My Early Life*, of his capture at the hands of one of the Boers' most eminent leaders. It was, to use one of Churchill's most famous expressions, a 'terminological inexactitude'. His actual captor was the 'Red Bull of Krugersdorp', one Sarel Oosthuizen.[8]

Buller's Army Corps arrives

Three days before the armoured train incident, almost 10 000 troops of Buller's Army Corps landed in Durban from Cape Town and began to make their way northwards to the Tugela. A day after the skirmish, the vanguard reached Estcourt. By now, the ever-apprehensive Joubert had split his commando in two: one column of 1500 burghers under himself and Botha, and another of 600 men under David Joubert (no relation). The two columns were to swing round the British forward position at Estcourt and converge lower down the line at Willow Grange, a small village on the railway line near Mooi River. There was a fear that the two advancing British brigades, only 32 kilometres apart, might join forces and overpower the Boers, but Botha reckoned that to be unlikely as long as the Boers remained in control of the railway.[9]

On the night of 22 November, newly arrived British troops under Colonel Walter Kitchener, brother of Lord Kitchener, attacked the Boer positions in the hills to the south of Willow Grange. As the battle began, a ferocious thunderstorm killed one Free Stater and six horses, causing slightly less damage than Kitchener's men, who killed two Boers and wounded two others, but lost 11 men and sustained more than 86 wounded themselves.[10]

Three days later, Buller himself disembarked in Durban and left immediately for Pietermaritzburg, where he spent the next few days attending to administrative matters and overseeing hospital arrangements for his sick and wounded.[11] Only then did he set off for Frere to inspect his forward positions and weigh up his chances of crossing the Tugela and relieving White in Ladysmith.

Fate intervenes

Having won a tactical victory at Willow Grange, Botha had little time to decide what to do next. At that moment, fate intervened: Joubert was thrown from his horse, suffering severe internal injuries from which he was never to recover. By now, the elderly commandant-general was a man broken in body and spirit. Desperate not to lose more burghers in what he believed was an unnecessary war, he refused to allow Botha's men to press on towards Durban. In a telegram to Kruger, he proposed an immediate retreat in the face of overwhelming British numbers and suggested peace talks with the enemy. The president would not hear of it, and ordered the commando to stick to its task, 'dead or alive' (*'dood of leven'*). There was no chance of the British accepting a peace proposal from the Boers, Kruger declared.[12]

Joubert's injuries brought a halt to the commando's further progress towards the coast. At a council of war on 25 November, it was decided that the commandant-general would be escorted back to Volksrust, and that the commando itself would withdraw to a defensive position above the Tugela, where heavy rains were threatening to cut off access to the north. Taking with them hundreds of horses and cattle, as well as provisions captured in southern Natal, the Boers and their wagons made their way unhindered, via Weenen, back across the Tugela. On 28 November, their engineers blew up the key railway bridge across the river at Colenso, leaving the wagon bridge as the only route through the little town.

With Joubert on his way to Volksrust, Botha was now in sole charge of the commando. In Pakenham's words, the Boers had now 'entrusted their most critical operations to the youngest and most energetic of all their generals, who had shown himself, by his raid on south Natal, to be the most brilliant tactician in the war'.[13] But Botha, always respectful of seniority, chose to tread warily. His old mentor and friend, Lucas Meyer, had returned to Colenso, and the vice president of the ZAR, Schalk Burger, was among other Boer generals on the outskirts of Ladysmith. Requested by Kruger himself to take command in Natal, the deferential Botha agreed only to help with the defence of the Tugela and not to accept any formal or permanent appointment.[14]

This loose chain of command failed to satisfy Joubert, recuperating at his base in Volksrust. He was still commandant-general and the recipient of repeated requests for help and direction from senior Boer officers. Putting Botha in full command of operations along the Tugela, Joubert made it clear that Meyer and Burger were now the much younger man's subordinates. For most Boers in Natal, this was a highly popular decision. As a member of the Soutpansberg commando was to record later, 'The influence that Louis Botha had among the burghers at that time was simply marvellous. The mere mention of the fact that Louis Botha was in command and on the spot was sufficient to inspire the burghers with courage and confidence, no matter how despondent they may have been before.'[15]

Yet not everyone was in thrall to the new commander. Many old-guard

On the Natal front, 1900: Louis Botha stands in the centre, flanked by his old mentor
Lucas Meyer (left) and General Daniel Erasmus (right) of the Pretoria commando.

SÜDDEUTSCHE ZEITUNG PHOTO/ALAMY STOCK PHOTO

burghers resented the rapid rise of a dynamic and popular young officer, whose boldness was so far removed from their own. In the words of American journalist Howard Hillegas: 'The Boer mind would not grasp the fact that a man of thirty-five [sic] could be a military leader, and for a long time the Boers treated the young commander with a certain amount of contempt.'[16]

Realising that his orders would not be obeyed unquestioningly, Botha made a point of always consulting his elders about tactics, and of ensuring that the flap of his tent was open to them. He had the rare gift of making individuals feel they were special and that their opinions mattered to him.

Preparing for Colenso

As the new commander in Natal, Botha's immediate task was to fortify the Boers' defensive line north of the Tugela. The unforgiving terrain presented a

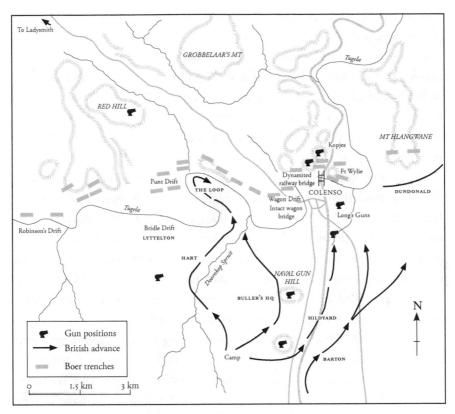

The Battle of Colenso, 15 December 1899

formidable challenge. Above the river at Colenso, an 11-kilometre trench had to be dug from low koppies below Red Hill to the northwest across the railway line to Hlangwane, the mountain that dominated the eastern approach to the town. Botha knew that Buller would have no choice but to fight close to the railway line, along which men and materiel could be brought up to Ladysmith. He accordingly prepared the defences of his 4 500-strong force, which had five guns, using dummy trenches and false gun emplacements so as to deceive the enemy when the fighting began. He was fortunate to be able to draw on a ready supply of black labour to help excavate rifle pits out of the reddish, rock-strewn earth.

Nineteen kilometres to the south, Buller had chosen to concentrate his troops at Frere and Chieveley, on the railway line between Estcourt and

Colenso. Here, he assembled an army of 20 000 men in 16 battalions, supported by cavalry and field artillery – the biggest force of men, guns and
animals ever seen in southern Africa.[17] A heliograph enabled him to exchange
messages with White and his men, holed up in Ladysmith. On 12 December,
Buller moved his headquarters up to Naval Gun Hill, beyond Chieveley, and
brought his troops up to a mere six kilometres from where the Boers were
positioned across the Tugela. To Botha, it was obvious that the British attack
would come at Colenso.

Buller was well aware of the inadvisability of a frontal advance along
the main road through the town, which had already been mined by the
Boers. He ordered, therefore, a hazardous flanking attack, which required
an 80-kilometre detour via Potgieter's Drift, 24 kilometres upriver. But that
plan had to be abandoned when the shattering news reached him that in the
Battle of Stormberg, near Molteno, in the eastern Cape, General Gatacre had
lost 26 men killed and 696 captured. The next day came news of General
Methuen's defeat at Magersfontein, outside Kimberley.

Buller decided he could no longer risk losing the only mounted troops
he had available to him in Natal. As he explained afterwards: 'Colenso was
in front of me. I could attack that and control the result. But Potgieter's
... I could not pretend I could control that. I might easily have lost my
whole force.'[18] On Thursday 14 December he heliographed White: 'I have
been forced to change my plans. Am coming through via Colenso and
Onderbroekspruit.'[19] The relief of Ladysmith, which would enable the British
commander to return to and direct the war from the Cape, had become a
matter of the utmost urgency.

CHAPTER 6

BULLER OUTWITTED

Colenso

On the afternoon of 13 December, Buller gave the Boers early confirmation of his intention to attack at Colenso by shelling Boer positions on Hlangwane, the 1102-metre-high, strategically important hill overlooking the town from the British side of the winding Tugela River. At the foot of the hill, the Tugela twists so much that Hlangwane commands the ground on both sides of the river.

Buller was not to know it, but his fusillade provoked utter panic in Boer ranks. During the night, a jittery Soutpansberg commando of some 250 burghers fled away from the hill, and it took two councils of war, much pleading from Botha, a telegram from Kruger and the drawing of lots before 800–1000 Boers from various commandos consented to reoccupy Hlangwane.[1] If Buller had been more astute, he would have made the retaking of the hill a priority, as it would have enabled him to bring his heavy artillery to bear on the Boer lines while his infantrymen went about fording the river.[2]

The British assault on the town of Colenso itself began before daybreak on Friday 15 December, when massed columns of infantry, two miles wide and a mile deep (3.2 kilometres and 1.2 kilometres, respectively) and accompanied by field artillery, began marching across the dusty veld from Chieveley towards the Tugela. Simultaneously, guns on Naval Gun Hill began shelling what the British imagined to be Boer positions across the river.

Buller had split his forces into three columns: the central and largest, under General Hildyard, was to attack via the road bridge at Wagon Drift; an Irish Brigade under General Hart (on the left) would try to cross at Bridle Drift further upriver; while a third force under Lord Dundonald would attempt to dislodge the Boers from Hlangwane. Concealed in their trenches above four potential crossing points north of the river, Botha's men lay in wait and held their fire.

Buller's plan went wrong from the outset.[3] Before Hildyard could launch the main infantry attack across the road bridge, Hart's Irish Brigade had been caught in a loop of the river and raked by Boer rifle fire, while Dundonald, to the right, lacked sufficient manpower to take Hlangwane. But the real disaster occurred in the centre. Instead of supporting Hildyard's advance, the officer in charge of artillery, Colonel Long, had pushed on a mile ahead of the infantry 'as though on parade at Aldershot'[4] and opened fire on the Boers with his 18 guns. His premature action, according to Pakenham, 'adhered to one of the great traditions of the British army – courage matched only by stupidity'.[5] An amazed Botha, who had planned to lure British troops across the Tugela before trapping them with the river at their back, ordered his artillery – positioned on a high ridge above the river – to fire away. Within half an hour, all of Long's field guns had been silenced and his surviving gunners had taken refuge in a donga.

Hildyard's attack on the town depended upon his force being supported on its flanks by Hart and Dundonald, who were now in difficulties of their own and could offer no help. Having lost Long's guns, as well as many men killed or wounded, Buller decided – after several hours of fighting – that it would be reckless to try to cross the river, and ordered Hildyard to extricate the guns with the least number of casualties to his own brigade. In the afternoon, the commander-in-chief sounded a general withdrawal of British forces. Buller had lost 143 men killed and another thousand injured or captured, while the Boers had sustained only 38 casualties, including seven killed.[6]

With their drab clothing, the Boers blended seamlessly into the landscape and were so well concealed above the river as to be virtually invisible. Their use of smokeless gunpowder, invented by Alfred Nobel a dozen years earlier, had made it almost impossible for the British to locate where the opposing sniper fire was coming from. General Lyttelton, commander of the reserve brigade at Bridle Drift, said afterwards he hardly saw a Boer all day. He described the battle of Colenso as 'one of the most unfortunate in which the British army has ever been engaged and in none has there been a more deplorable

LE GÉNÉRAL LOUIS BOTHA
Gravure du Journal l'Illustration

Boer successes on the Natal front increased Botha's reputation as a commander.
Images of him and the white horse he invariably rode while on campaign
circulated widely in Europe at the time.

tactical display. No proper reconnoitring of the ground, no certain information as to any ford by which to cross the river, no proper artillery preparation,
no satisfactory targets for the artillery, no realisation of the importance of
Hlangwane.'[7]

That evening, a victorious Botha sent a dispatch to President Kruger that
read: 'The God of our forefathers has today given us a brilliant victory. We
have repulsed the enemy on all sides, at three different points ... The enemy's
losses must have been terrible. They are lying on one another – I think possibly 2 000 men. We have about 30 killed and wounded. I shall later send you
exact reports. With a thankful heart I can congratulate you and the Afrikaner
people on this brilliant victory ... and I respectfully request the Government
to proclaim a general day of prayer to thank Him who gave us this victory.'[8]

John Buchan, the Scottish aristocrat, historian and novelist, wrote in his account of the war that Kruger believed that God had given his people a final victory at Colenso. 'But the Great Man who commanded the Boers on the Tugela thought differently,' recorded Buchan. 'In the very moment of that triumph, Louis Botha realised that the war was lost – when, as he afterwards said, he saw the British soldier, mishandled, and misled, advancing stolidly to death with unshakeable discipline.'[9]

Black Week

Buller's loss was the third suffered by the British army in South Africa in what became known as 'Black Week'. The Empire was widely disliked in Europe, not only because of Britain's treatment of the Boers, and so there was much jubilation at the Boers' successes. In Britain, the news of the army's three defeats at the hands of farmers and part-time soldiers was met with incredulity. In his history of the war, Arthur Conan Doyle described the week as 'the blackest one known during our generation and the most disastrous for British arms during the century'.[10] Reports from the battlefront that the British commander had withdrawn his forces too early from the battle brought volleys of abuse down upon Buller's head.

The secretary for war, Lord Lansdowne, was thoroughly disillusioned with his commander in South Africa, a sentiment compounded by the despairing tone of Buller's report of the battle, which read in part, 'Colenso is a fortress which … if not taken on a rush, could only be taken by a siege … My view is that I ought to let Ladysmith go, and occupy good positions for the defence of South Natal and let time help us … I consider we were in the face of 20 000 men today. They had the advantage both in arms and in position. The moment I failed to get in on the run I was beat. I now feel that I cannot say I can relieve Ladysmith with my available force and the best thing I can suggest is that I should occupy defensive positions and fight it out in a country better suited to our tactics.'[11]

The next day Buller sent another message to White suggesting that if he could not hold out for another month, he should shoot away his ammunition and negotiate the best terms of surrender he could. But he failed to make clear that Ladysmith should be left to itself for the time being, while the bulk of the British army was sent to advance across the Free State. The British commander's message, says Pakenham, was 'a gift' to his enemies.[12]

By this time, the siege of Ladysmith had captured the imagination of the British people, who regarded the small Natal town as a symbol of the success or failure of their army in South Africa. Far away in London, Lansdowne could not comprehend why the combined forces of White and Buller, so much greater than the Boers in number, found it impossible to relieve the town. Disliking defeatist language of any kind, the secretary for war decided to make a change in overall command: Buller would remain in charge in Natal, but be superseded as commander-in-chief in South Africa by another holder of the Victoria Cross, 67-year-old Field Marshal Viscount Lord Frederick Roberts, whose son Freddie had been among those killed at Colenso. Assisting Roberts as chief of staff would be the hero of the recent campaign in the Sudan (1898), the much younger Major General Herbert Kitchener.

If the litmus test of generalship is being able to win a victory with fewer resources than your enemy's, the 37-year-old Louis Botha had given the older, more experienced Buller a tactical lesson at Colenso. By means of stealth and clever planning, his much smaller force of 3 000 men and five heavy guns had defeated a British army of 20 000 men and 44 guns. Before long, newspapers in Britain and beyond had made the name of the youthful and charismatic Boer commander, who had suddenly emerged as a potential leader of his people, known to readers around the world. In CJ Barnard's opinion, 'Colenso was … the first important rung on the ladder that was to carry [Botha] only ten years later to the head of his country's affairs.'[13]

Platrand

After Colenso, there was a lull on the Tugela front while Buller regrouped and awaited the arrival of reinforcements from the 5th Division, led by Lieutenant General Sir Charles Warren. His army now numbered 30 000, supported by as many as ten artillery batteries. Buller did not much like the ill-tempered Warren, who had been sent to Natal as his de facto deputy, and the friction between these two generals was to manifest itself during the next stage of the Tugela campaign.[14]

Alarmed at the steady build-up of British forces south of the Tugela, the Boer command outside Ladysmith decided, on 6 January, to make another attempt to capture the besieged town. While Botha kept an eye on Buller across the river, several thousand burghers were pulled back from Colenso and sent to storm two weakly defended hills, Wagon Hill and Caesar's Camp, on the Platrand, a flat-topped ridge on the southern side of Ladysmith. Joubert had correctly surmised that if the Boers could establish themselves on the Platrand, they would be able to make Ladysmith not only impossible to defend but also more difficult for Buller's forces to relieve. White had come to the same conclusion and had given Colonel Hamilton the task of defending the double-humped hill.[15]

After 16 hours of fierce fighting, interrupted by a huge thunderstorm that reduced visibility at one stage to less than 90 metres, the Boers were forced to fall back and break off their efforts to capture the Platrand. Against more than 400 British casualties, including 183 killed (more than at Colenso), the Boers lost more than 230 men killed and wounded – more than enough to persuade Joubert to abandon any further thoughts of overrunning Ladysmith.[16]

Potgieter's Drift

On 10 January 1900, the day on which Roberts and Kitchener arrived in Cape Town, Buller began his second attempt to ford the Tugela by way of pontoons at Potgieter's Drift. The addition of Warren's troops created a combined force of some 23 000 men, whose supplies were carried on 650 wagons drawn by horses, mules and oxen. Twenty-seven kilometres in length, this immense supply train slowly ploughed its way through a quagmire created by torrential rain. On the hills north of the river, Botha's burghers looked on in amazement at 'the unprecedented spectacle in South Africa of thirty thousand white men on the move'.[17]

War correspondents with the British forces were scornful of Buller's huge, slow-moving caravan, which contrasted so strongly with the mobility of the Boers. A disapproving Churchill, now back from his exploits as a prisoner of war, criticised the string of wagons carrying one tent for every soldier. 'The consequence is that the roads are crowded, drifts are blocked, marching troops are delayed and rapidity of movement is out of the question. Meanwhile the enemy completes the fortification of his positions and the cost of capturing them rises. It is poor economy to let a soldier live well for three days at the price of killing him on the fourth,' he wrote.[18]

On the northern banks of the Tugela, Botha and his men busied themselves by shoring up their defensive lines, despite being shelled periodically by British naval guns. When Buller began his advance on Potgieter's Drift, however, Botha had to call urgently for reinforcements. By the time the British cavalcade had reached the river crossing, 4 000 Boers in four commandos, and their guns, had taken up concealed positions on the crest of hills above the winding river.

Acton Homes

The British advance across the Tugela began on 16 January 1900. Once again, Buller had decided to split his forces, sending 15 000 troops under General Warren to cross the snaking river eight kilometres further upstream at Trichardt's Drift, while a smaller force of 8 000 under General Lyttelton would ford the Tugela (and concentrate the Boers' attention) at Potgieter's Drift. As it was, Lyttelton's crossing was uncontested by the Boers who had moved westward to counter the crossing at Trichardt's Drift. It took Warren 37 hours to move his men, ox-wagons and supplies across the river.

Ahead of Warren, Lord Dundonald and his cavalry were sent on a great leftward arc towards Acton Homes, on the road from the Free State to Ladysmith. Warren's own target was the crucial Tabanyama plateau, 27 kilometres west of Colenso, defended (though he did not know it) by a mere 500 Boers. If British troops could capture Tabanyama, he correctly surmised, the way to Ladysmith across the veld would be wide open.[19]

On 18 January, Dundonald's mounted brigade ran into a Boer patrol about three kilometres south of Acton Homes, and a sharp skirmish ensued in which 35 men lost their lives. Among those involved was Churchill, in his dual role as war reporter and officer in the South African Light Horse. In a dispatch to his newspaper, Churchill wrote sadly of how the Boer dead aroused in him the most painful emotions: 'Here by the rock under which he had fought lay the Field Cornet of Heilbronn, Mr de Mentz – a grey-haired man of over sixty years, with firm aquiline features and a short beard. The stony face was a man who had thought it all out, and was quite certain that his cause was just, and such as a sober citizen might give his life for. Nor was I surprised when the Boer prisoners told me that Mentz had refused all suggestions of surrender, and that when his left leg was smashed by a bullet he had continued to load and fire until he bled to death; and they found him, pale and bloodless, holding his wife's letter in his hand.'[20]

Spioenkop

With Warren's huge force now in action at Tabanyama, it was only Botha's superior tactical positions on the plateau that enabled the Boers to keep the British at bay during three days of artillery bombardment and heavy fighting. On 23 January, urged on by an impatient Buller, Warren unwisely decided to send a column of 1700 men, under Brigadier General Woodgate, to ascend Spioenkop, the highest peak on the ridge of the Tabanyama plateau. At just before 4 am next morning, having put a small picket of Boer sentries to flight, Woodgate occupied the mist-shrouded summit of the hill. Warren had miscalculated badly, however: Spioenkop was not on the flank of the Boer lines, as he had thought, but slap in the middle and the terrain atop the hill was so rocky that Woodgate's men were unable to dig themselves in properly. What is more, they thought they had reached the crest of Spioenkop, but once the mist had cleared, they could see that the crest lay further on. By this time, the Boers had advanced up the side of the hill, unseen.

From his headquarters on an adjacent koppie two kilometres to the north, Botha gave the order at daybreak for Spioenkop to be recaptured from the khakis. As his seven guns pumped deadly fire into British ranks and the mist began to rise, Boer reinforcements, urged on by their commander, crawled up the nearby slopes. The ensuing fight for possession of the Kop on a pitilessly hot day was one of the most savage and bloody engagements of the war. Some 2000 of Warren's men crowded onto the summit, on which there was cover for only 1000. Despite losing Woodgate, and sustaining horrific casualties, the British managed to hold the Kop until nightfall, when their replacement commander, Thorneycroft – unable to communicate with Warren and Buller – decided to abandon the hill. Some hours earlier, Botha had realised he was not likely to regain the Kop that day and also ordered the withdrawal of his

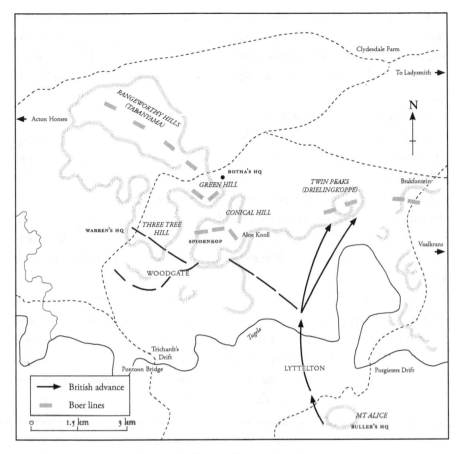

The Battle of Spioenkop, 24 January 1900

men and guns. Such was the confusion that both sides evacuated their side of the summit of Spioenkop at more or less the same time.[21]

Deneys Reitz, the 17-year-old son of the Transvaal state secretary, described how Botha had spurred on his burghers during the height of the battle for control of the peak: 'He addressed the men from the saddle telling them of the shame that would be theirs if they deserted their posts in this hour of danger; and so eloquent was his appeal that in a few minutes the men were filing off into the dark to reoccupy their positions on either side of the Spioenkop gap. I believe he spent the rest of the night riding from commando to commando exhorting and threatening, until he persuaded the men to return to the line, thus averting a great disaster.'[22]

Before dawn on the following morning, an astonished Botha was informed that the British forces had abandoned the Kop and the adjoining Twin Peaks (successfully captured by General Lyttelton's brigade) and withdrawn to the southern bank of the Tugela. The Boers were left in command of the Tugela hills.

On Spioenkop, the British dead lay three deep in their trenches, many horribly mutilated by artillery shells.[23] Churchill described his own journey up the hill late on the previous afternoon: 'We passed through the ambulance village, and leaving our horses climbed up the spur. Streams of wounded met us and obstructed the path. Men were staggering along alone, or supported by comrades, or crawling on hands and knees, or carried on stretchers. Corpses lay here and there. Many of the wounds were of a horrible nature. The splinters and fragments of the shell had torn and mutilated in the most ghastly manner.'[24]

Reitz also wrote of the scene on the summit the day before: 'The English troops lay so near that one could have tossed a biscuit among them, and whilst the losses which they were causing us were only too evident, we on our side did not know that we were inflicting even greater damage upon them. Our casualties lay hideously among us, but theirs were screened from view behind the breastwork, so that the comfort of knowing that we were giving more than we received was denied us.'[25]

On the day after the battle, both sides agreed to an armistice to enable the dead to be buried and the wounded to be carried off. Warren's folly had cost over 1750 men killed, wounded, missing or taken prisoner; Boer casualties were under 400, though these were burghers who could not easily be replaced.

With only a fraction of Buller's manpower at his disposal, Botha had once again outmanoeuvred his British counterpart, whose second attempt at crossing the Tugela had ended in failure. The Boer commander's tactical mastery lay in his clever concealment of guns and troops, as well as the energy and enthusiasm with which he urged on his frightened burghers. Earlier in the day, General Schalk Burger, under fire elsewhere on Tabanyama, had sent him a despairing message to say that further resistance was futile as his fighters could no longer hold their line. 'Let us fight and die together, but, brother, please do not let us yield an inch to the English,' was Botha's reply.[26] In Rayne

Kruger's judgement, though, there were men on both sides who fought with unbelievable courage. What told in the end was the quality of a single man: 'The victory at Spioenkop was Louis Botha's.'[27]

CHAPTER 7

THE TIDE TURNS

Vaalkrans

Buller's withdrawal across the Tugela led to a lull in the fighting that gave an exhausted Botha the opportunity to slip away by train to Pretoria for a few days' home leave, leaving General Schalk Burger in command. Botha travelled incognito and gave no indication en route that he was anyone other than an ordinary burgher. Despite his newfound fame as the victor of Colenso and Spioenkop, not a soul was there to greet him on his arrival in Pretoria. After reporting to Kruger, he spent two days relaxing with his family. Annie presented him with a simple coat without insignia she had made for him to wear on the battlefield.[1]

While Botha was away, Boer intelligence got wind of Buller's plans to cross the Tugela at Potgieter's Drift again and make a third attempt to breach the Boer defences, this time in the vicinity of Vaalkrans. Joubert urgently recalled the commander in whom he now had such faith. Buller, as usual, took his time preparing his forces for the attack, which enabled Botha to return to the front just as battle was rejoined.

Vaalkrans is the highest of a semicircular group of low hills between Spioenkop and Colenso that commanded a clear view of the open plain that led to Ladysmith. Many burghers had followed Botha's lead and taken off for home, leaving the Boer army on the Tugela with a mere 3 600 men equipped with two pom-poms and ten other guns against Buller's massive, well-armed force of over 26 000 troops and 72 guns.[2]

While Botha was away, President Steyn of the Free State had caused fresh confusion in Boer ranks by insisting on the appointment of General Marthinus Prinsloo as overall commander in Natal. An exasperated Botha ignored the provocation and continued to report to Joubert, advising the commandant-general that he planned to hold the line above the Tugela by maintaining heavy artillery fire on all sides of Vaalkrans. The Boer gun batteries were boosted by the arrival, shortly before the British attack began, of the Long Tom dragged across from Ladysmith to the high ground of Doringkop away to the east.

Buller's plan was to cross the river via a pontoon bridge at Potgieter's Drift under cover of an artillery bombardment, and to attack the heights to the west of the Vaalkrans ridge. This was a feint to distract the Boers while a second pontoon bridge was built directly south of Vaalkrans, across which thousands of British troops would pour. The ensuing shelling around Vaalkrans from both sides was the most intensive thus far in the war.[3]

The British crossing began on 5 February, and by afternoon on the first day the Boers had been forced to retreat from Vaalkrans to behind neighbouring Groenkop, leaving Vaalkrans to be occupied by a British force, which dug itself in during the night. Early next morning, the Boers' Long Tom began to bombard the exposed summit of Vaalkrans from Doringkop, causing the irresolute Buller once again to have second thoughts. Afraid of another long casualty list, he decided that General Lyttelton should bring his men down from Vaalkrans to safer ground.

An incredulous Lyttelton ignored the order at first, remaining on the hill all night and for most of the next day.[4] While he (Lyttelton) was there, Buller telegraphed Roberts asking whether he should persist with the attack on Vaalkrans if it meant possibly losing another 2 000 to 3 000 men. When Roberts told him to persevere, Buller relieved Lyttelton's force with a brigade led by General Hildyard, who set about fortifying his defences on the Vaalkrans summit.

Botha's tactical skills, however, had induced Buller to believe the Boer force against him numbered as many as 12 000 to 16 000 men. By the next day, 7 February, after another ferocious artillery duel during which the Boers kept pounding away at Hildyard's men, the British commander had had enough. To the relief of the exhausted burghers, Buller ordered a complete withdrawal of all his forces from their positions on and around Vaalkrans, the removal of the pontoon bridge from the river, and a return to base at Chieveley. The British had lost, to no purpose, 34 officers and men and sustained 350 casualties,[5] while the Boers – who could not easily call up replacements – had suffered losses of 38 men killed and nearly 50 wounded or missing.[6]

Buller's dispirited senior officers were less than impressed with their commander's decision. When Buller observed with satisfaction that the withdrawal from Vaalkrans had been carried out 'uncommonly well', his chief of staff replied grimly, 'Yes sir; we've practised it twice.'[7] Back home, there was disbelief that the British army had at first captured and then abandoned another strategic position to the Boers. Buller was derisively dubbed 'Sir Reverse', and popular newspapers dubbed him the 'Ferryman of the Tugela'.[8]

Numbers tell

The sheer weight of numbers, however, turned the tide, with Boer ranks being thinned out at every battle. In early February, in response to an urgent request from Kruger, 800 badly needed burghers had to be rushed from Natal to the Free State border to help prevent a breakthrough by the British in the vicinity of Colesberg. They were not replaced. Joubert was one of the few Boer leaders who realised that the dogged Buller was never going to give in, and feared that the disparity in forces would be eventually be decisive: 'A blunderer and a cautious man himself, [Joubert] understood that persistence is the one quality to be feared in an enemy.'[9]

On 12 February, Botha and a reconnoitring patrol clashed with a force of Royal Dragoons at Munger's Drift, near Vaalkrans, inflicting a loss of 13 men (four wounded and nine prisoners) on the enemy. It was to be the Boers' last military excursion across the Tugela. On 14 February, the implacable Buller resumed his offensive. By now, he had learnt by trial and error that the route to besieged Ladysmith lay across the river, away from the railway line and through the hills to the east – not the west – of Colenso.

Magersfontein

Elsewhere in South Africa, the war was going badly for the Boers. While Buller was planning his fourth foray across the Tugela, almost 500 kilometres away Lord Roberts had assembled a huge force west of the Free State, hoping to draw Boer commandos away from the sieges of Kimberley, Mafeking and even Ladysmith towards the border between the Free State and the Cape Colony.

Two months earlier, during Black Week, Lord Methuen's advance along the railway line towards Kimberley had been abruptly halted, first at Modder River and then below the Magersfontein ridge. At Magersfontein, General Koos de la Rey's tactic of taking up defensive positions in well-concealed trenches on low-lying ground rather than on the slopes of the hills had proved more than a match for the British, who were mown down as they marched across the open veld, as if on parade. British casualties at Modder River and Magersfontein numbered in the hundreds, and far exceeded those of the Boers. A chastened Methuen had retreated to lick his wounds and await reinforcements.

By early February 1900, Roberts had reached Methuen's camp at Modder River, where his 45 000-man army, which now included three cavalry brigades, prepared for a direct advance on Bloemfontein. These plans had to change, however, when former Cape premier Cecil John Rhodes, holed up in Kimberley and openly contemptuous of the British army for not ending the siege sooner, insisted that the relief of the town could not be postponed any longer. Although hampered by long and cumbersome supply lines, Roberts's troops managed to circumnavigate the Boer defences at Magersfontein and, on 15 February, a massed cavalry charge led by General French split the Boer line asunder. Encountering little resistance outside Kimberley, French's men entered the town at 4 pm. After 124 days, the siege of Kimberley was over.

The relief of Kimberley and Methuen's relentless artillery bombardment of the Boer trenches at Magersfontein were enough to persuade General Piet Cronje, in joint command of the 5 000-strong Boer force entrenched around Magersfontein, to beat a retreat towards Bloemfontein. Hotly pursued by French's cavalry to Paardeberg Drift, further along the Modder River, Cronje's burghers – with wives, children, 400 ox-wagons and horses in tow – dug in along the river bank to take stock of the situation.

Sensing a change in the fortunes of the war, the correspondent for the *New York Tribune* observed: 'The relief of Kimberley and the retreat of Cronje have completely transformed the whole aspect of the war. The fighting is now transferred from British to Boer soil. The advance on Bloemfontein and Pretoria has actually begun and the investment of Ladysmith is likely to be abandoned. The Boers must relinquish their schemes of conquest and fall back in defence of their own territory.'[10]

Paardeberg

On 18 February, Kitchener led a frontal attack on Cronje's laager at Paardeberg, but was unable to break through and sustained heavy casualties in the attempt. Roberts then brought 40 000 men and almost 100 guns to bear on a Boer force now down to around 4 000 and only five guns. General De Wet made a daring attempt to open a corridor of escape for Cronje by taking some hills to the south, but the elderly Cronje was stricken with indecision and refused to move unless he could take his wagons and supplies with him.

On this occasion, Goliath slew David. After enduring nine days of a battle against British forces led by French from the north and Kitchener from the south, which turned into a siege of his encampment, a deeply despairing Cronje was forced to surrender on 27 February, the anniversary of Majuba. He was taken to Roberts, who greeted him with courtesy: 'I am glad to see you. You have made a gallant defence, sir.' Cronje and his men were taken prisoner, with many sent to the island of St Helena. To make matters worse, the carcasses of men and horses polluted the Modder River, leading to a typhoid epidemic that cost many Boer, British and civilian lives.

Cronje's defeat at Paardeberg, in which the Boers lost or surrendered almost a tenth of their army, dealt a devastating psychological blow to republican morale. It meant the end of the Boer western front and opened the way for Roberts to march on Bloemfontein. Many burghers simply gave up the fight, saddled up their horses and rode off home. There, according to Bill Nasson, they encountered animosity for having abandoned their patriotic duty to protect the homeland from invasion.[11]

Ladysmith relieved

With Kimberley liberated and the Boers in retreat towards Bloemfontein, the initiative in the war had passed to the British, now poised to resume the offensive outside Ladysmith. Despite efforts to stop them, many burghers had already drifted away from the besieged town. In despair, Botha telegraphed

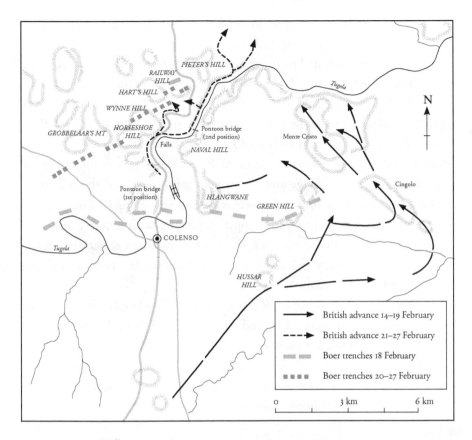

Buller's breakthrough at Ladysmith, 14–27 February 1900

Joubert and Kruger to warn that desertions might mean his abandoning the encampments above the Tugela and retreating to the Biggarsberg. Kruger replied with a long religious exhortation to the burghers to hold the Tugela line at all costs: retreat would have a disastrous effect on Boer morale on the western front, he said.[12]

Thanks partly to the urgings of Kruger, Botha and Meyer, and partly to the slowness of Buller's advance, the disintegration of Boer forces came to a temporary halt. Buller's tardiness enabled the Boers to establish a new nine-kilometre defensive line running northeast from Red Hill above Colenso to Pieter's Hill outside Ladysmith. Botha took command of the sector west of the line, leaving Meyer in charge of the east, where a mere 1500 men were strung out across the crucial Hlangwane-Green Hill section. The ever-respectful

71

Botha had no wish to supersede his old friend, even though he knew Meyer was incapable of commanding on his own.[13]

Buller, by this time, had come up with a better tactical plan for taking on the Boers, whose numbers had risen again to some 5 000 against the enemy's 25 000. Having failed with frontal attacks on Boer lines at Colenso, Spioenkop and Vaalkrans, he now realised the importance of flanking actions across the Tugela and to the south of Ladysmith. On 21–22 February, while Roberts and Kitchener were in action at Paardeberg, Buller's forces crossed the river by pontoon bridge and began taking possession of the hills overlooking Ladysmith, including the weakly defended but crucial Boer redoubt on Hlangwane. Advancing from koppie to koppie, with infantry and artillery now working closely together, the British mounted concerted attacks on Pieter's Hill, Railway Hill and Inniskilling Hill, the last Boer strongholds outside the besieged town.

Towards dusk on 27 February, after a massive artillery bombardment of their crowded trenches on Pieter's Hill and an all-day battle with Buller's infantry, the demoralised, outnumbered and outgunned Boers began slipping away from the three hills. For the British, the road to Ladysmith now lay open. From Meyer's tent later that night, Botha telegraphed Joubert asking for permission to withdraw Boer forces from all positions north of the Tugela, including those outside Ladysmith. The next day, 28 February, Lord Dundonald and his cavalry rode unopposed into Ladysmith to relieve the 118-day siege.

Botha had returned to his camp on the previous, rain-swept night and given orders for an orderly withdrawal via Elandslaagte to the Biggarsberg. The news of Cronje's defeat at Paardeberg meant that the Boer retreat was anything but orderly, however. The next morning, Botha, Meyer and 150 men formed a small rearguard unit to discourage any British pursuit of Boers retreating from the Tugela line.[14]

Deneys Reitz described the scene vividly: 'The rain now stopped and the sun rose warm and bright, but it looked on a dismal scene. In all directions, the plain was covered with a multitude of men, wagons and guns ploughing across the sodden veld in the greatest disorder … Had the British fired a single gun at this surging mob everything on wheels would have fallen into their hands, but by great good luck there was no pursuit and towards afternoon the tangle gradually straightened itself out.'[15]

Fortunately for the Boers, Buller was more intent on celebrating the raising of the siege of Ladysmith with due pomp and ceremony than in risking further casualties by pursuing the fleeing Boers. As Winston Churchill wrote afterwards, 'My personal impression is that Sir Redvers Buller was deeply moved by the heavy losses the troops had suffered and was reluctant to demand further sacrifices from them at this time.'[16]

In his war diary, *London to Ladysmith via Pretoria*, Churchill wrote of the high price paid by the British for victory at Ladysmith: 'In the fortnight's fighting, from February 14 to February 28, two generals, six colonels commanding regiments, a hundred and five other officers, and one thousand five hundred and eleven soldiers had been killed or wounded out of an engaged force of about eighteen thousand men; a proportion of slightly under 10 per cent. In the whole series of operations for the relief of Ladysmith, the losses amounted to three hundred officers and more than five thousand men, out of a total engaged force of about twenty-three thousand, a proportion of rather more than 20 per cent. Nor had this loss been inflicted in a single day's victorious battle, but was spread over twenty-five days of general action in a period of ten weeks; and until the last week no decided success had cheered the troops.'[17]

Protecting the border

On 3 March, the retreating Botha and Meyer reached the Boer supply centre at Modderspruit station, near Elandslaagte, to find that Joubert had already departed for the north. Botha was disgusted to find that the depot had been plundered and set on fire by fleeing burghers supposedly intent on preventing supplies falling into British hands. To stem the tide of absconders, he threatened to shoot the horses of anyone who wanted to leave for home. On reaching Glencoe, north of the Biggarsberg, by train, exhausted after days of fighting and weighed down by his responsibilities, a dispirited Botha wired Annie in Pretoria to say he was 'safe and well but heartsore over the loss of the Colenso fighting line, where he had not lost a single position ... Brave friends of mine, dead, wounded and captured ...'[18] he wrote.

For the Boers in northern Natal, it had become vital to protect the borders of the Orange Free State and Transvaal from the British, who were now

threatening an advance from the south. While the retreating Free State commandos took up positions on the mountain passes through the Drakensberg,
in the nearby Biggarsberg Joubert and Botha set about establishing a new
defensive line stretching over 160 kilometres from the Drakensberg to
Vryheid.[19] By now, the main focus of the war had shifted to the Free State,
however, where Lord Roberts was advancing relentlessly on Bloemfontein.

CHAPTER 8

ON THE BACK FOOT

Drawing the line

For the Boers in northern Natal, there was no time to waste. Joubert and his generals had to decide where exactly to draw their defensive line against the British and then reassemble their by now widely scattered commandos.[1] In the meantime, the Free Staters had taken up positions along the Olivier's Hoek and Van Reenen's passes in the Drakensberg, while the Transvalers were stationed closer to the railway line along the Biggarsberg range above Dundee.

Among the senior Boer officers, there was no unanimity about the Biggarsberg being the right place for a new front. Vice President Schalk Burger was in favour of Laing's Nek, to the north of Newcastle and close to the Transvaal border, and so was Joubert, now in poor health and in such despair that he again telegraphed Kruger to suggest it was time for the Boers to sue for peace. Even the ailing commandant-general realised, however, that negotiations had no hope of success as long as the Boers remained encamped on colonial territory.

On 2 March, Paul Kruger himself came down to Glencoe to instil some fight into Joubert and the disheartened burghers before going on to Kroonstad for an emergency meeting with President Steyn. The upshot of the Kroonstad discussion was a message to the British prime minister, Lord Salisbury, offering an end to the fighting on condition that the sovereign independence of the Boer republics was recognised. Salisbury rejected the offer out of hand, asserting that his government had no intention whatsoever of granting the Boers their independence.[2]

Change in command

On 5 March, Joubert called a *krygsraad* at which he announced to his stunned officers that he felt too weak to continue as supreme commander in the field and wished to appoint Louis Botha as his chief assistant and second in command. Though not elected according to Boer custom, Botha was now the Transvaal's de facto military commander. Another decision, taken by vote this time, was to draw the new defensive line in Natal in the Biggarsberg.

Botha's sudden appointment was well received by the commandos, who were given instructions as to where they should position themselves along the Biggarsberg line. Responding to a pious and presumptuous letter of advice from a member of the Transvaal executive council that he should not let his appointment go to his head, Botha replied – with commendable restraint – that he had never sought the position and would rather not have it, but had felt himself duty-bound to accept. As to the military situation in Natal, he believed there was no cause to be disheartened. The burghers were in position and regaining their confidence, and, with the help of the Lord, would fight to the death.

Dealing with Kruger

On 9 March, Joubert left Glencoe by train for Pretoria for further discussions with Kruger. Botha was never to see him again. The Boers' new commander immediately moved his headquarters to Glencoe, from where he could more closely supervise the deployment of the commandos in the Biggarsberg. A few days later, he received a message from Kruger saying that Bloemfontein had fallen, without opposition, to the advancing British. The great danger now, said the president, was that the enemy would burst through the Free State and drive on towards the Witwatersrand and Pretoria. It did not help to have 10 000 burghers out of action in Natal while the safety of the republics was at risk. Could Botha send 2 000 of his best mounted men, with ammunition and supplies, to the Free State as a matter of urgency?

After consulting Meyer and his other generals, Botha replied to Kruger that he did not have 10 000 men at his disposal, but only 6 000 to defend the 164-kilometre line from the Drakensberg to Vryheid, a distance of 22 hours on horseback. However, he would send 1200 men to the Free State immediately, in two commandos. Because many burghers were still absent without leave, he asked the president to conscript as many able-bodied men into the Boer army as possible. He also ordered district *landdroste* (magistrates) in the Transvaal to send back everyone on home leave.[3]

Kruger's insinuation that the Boer force in Natal was merely marking time bothered Botha, who responded by proposing to the president and Joubert that the commandos in Natal be withdrawn to Laing's Nek, which would shorten the defensive front and bring them closer to the Free State. His proposal was not made lightly, as his own farmhouse and properties in the Vryheid and Utrecht districts would be left unprotected against the advancing enemy. But sacrifices had to be made if the republics were to be saved.

The Transvaal government approved Botha's proposal to withdraw from the Biggarsberg to Laing's Nek on condition that Boer women and children and their possessions were moved to safety under the protection of commandos, and that the railway line, bridges and the coal mines at Dundee were put out of action or blown up. Botha advised Kruger that he would carry out his orders, but was not in favour of damaging the coal mines, or even the mines of Johannesburg, because Christians should not wage war on private property and the shareholders in mining companies came from many countries besides Britain. (As it happened, the fighting in the Free State died down temporarily so the withdrawal to Laing's Nek was never carried out.)

On 17 March, a historic *krygsraad* took place in Kroonstad, attended by presidents Steyn and Kruger and many senior Boer officers, including generals Joubert, De Wet, De la Rey and Botha's brother, Philip, who had distinguished himself in battle in the Free State. It was agreed that after the failure of the peace overture to the British, the republics had no alternative but to carry on fighting. However, having learnt the lesson of Paardeberg, those present took the decision that there would be no more ox-wagon laagers or women and children allowed at the front: greater mobility was now essential against Roberts's more conventional tactics. This important change in strategy heralded the start of the Boer guerrilla campaign, which was to prolong the war by another two years.[4]

Joubert dies

The day after the *krygsraad*, Joubert informed Botha of the new strategy but urged him not to vacate the Biggarsberg in a hurry. On 27 March, the much-loved commandant-general died at his home in Pretoria, after a three-day illness. He had never recovered fully from the injuries sustained from falling from his horse while on commando in Natal.

The news of Joubert's death was greeted with shock and sadness across the war front. Kruger was moved to tears by the loss of someone 'who stood beside me since we were both youths, many years ago. I seem at present the only survivor of the many who in the past fought for land and people …'[5] The Free State's President Steyn wrote to Mrs Joubert saying that in everything his friend the general did, he always revealed a strong loyalty to duty and a deep love for his fatherland.[6]

Among those who also sent sympathies to Kruger by telegram was Lord Roberts: 'I have just received the news of General Joubert's death and I desire at once to offer my sincere condolences to your Honour and the Burghers of the S. African Republic on this sad event. I would ask you to convey to General Joubert's family the expression of my most respectful sympathy in their bereavements and to assure them also from me that all ranks of Her Majesty's forces, now serving in South Africa, share my feeling of deep regret at the sudden and untimely end of so distinguished a general who devoted his life to the service of his country and whose personal gallantry was only surpassed by his humane conduct and chivalrous bearing under all circumstances.'[7] Such were the proprieties observed – even towards one's enemies in war – in the late Victorian era.

Before Joubert's burial on his farm, Rustfontein, in the Volksrust area, a memorial service was held in Church Square in Pretoria. Accompanying the coffin to the station, where it was put on a special train, was President Kruger, who paid a sorrowful tribute to his erstwhile political opponent and announced to the assembled crowd that it was Joubert's desire to be succeeded as commandant-general by Louis Botha. The late general's wish would be respected and the government would put forward no other nominee until the people were able to make their own choice – as laid down by the constitution.[8] It was hardly the ringing endorsement the ZAR's new military leader – who had never been afraid to cross swords with Kruger – might have expected from his president.

Botha only learnt of Kruger's announcement the following day, 30 March, shortly before he left Glencoe himself for the funeral. Occupying the commandant-general's place of honour at the ceremony, he told mourners at the graveside that Joubert had resolutely refused to submit to the yoke of the English and his example should inspire them to offer up everything for the ultimate prize – sovereign independence.

Soon after Joubert's interment, the ever-sensitive Botha asked for a private meeting with Kruger and was angered by the president's response that he (Botha) should not come to Pretoria because matters could go wrong in his absence from Glencoe. He wrote immediately to the president to say that the government should not feel bound by Joubert's choice. His new appointment was not about honour or titles but duty, and he would happily work with whomever the government wished to appoint.

Once again, he was informed, unofficially, that Joubert's wish would be honoured until a proper election could be held. As CJ Barnard records, Botha found this highly unsatisfactory. His mandate confined him to the Transvaal and Natal, yet the focus of the war was now in the Free State. He requested FW Reitz, the ZAR's state secretary, therefore to clarify his exact role and responsibilities as a matter of urgency.

Botha's unease was compounded by a private letter from Smuts informing him that the government had intended to make him *acting* commandant-general for all Boer forces, but was afraid of arousing provincial jealousies and wished to maintain the status quo by leaving him in command in the Transvaal, with De la Rey in de facto charge of the Free State. This arrangement, Smuts believed, was to continue until the war's end because of the difficulty of arranging an election with so many Boers in captivity on St Helena and elsewhere.

The new commander

On 14 April, Botha received a letter notifying him formally of his appointment as commandant-general of the ZAR, retroactive to 28 March. In a letter of congratulation, his brother Philip echoed the feelings of many admirers when he said that Botha had gained the distinction not by favouritism or influence, but entirely by his merits on the battlefield. Still the Boers' youngest general at the age of 37, Botha's rise from ordinary burgher to commander of the ZAR forces within a mere five months had been meteoric.

The rapidity of Botha's advancement through the ranks had few parallels in military history.[9] The war correspondent of *The New York Times*, Thomas F Millard, wrote of him: 'Never have I encountered a more winning personality, a quality which greatly enhanced his influence with the independent spirits who composed the Boer commandos.'[10] After his successes along the Tugela, another American journalist with the Boer forces, Howard Hillegas, wrote that it seemed providential that Botha should step out of the ranks and lead his men with as much discretion and valour as could have been expected from far more experienced generals. The younger Boers, noted the admiring Hillegas, were quicker than the hoary old *takhaars* (backvelders) to discern the worth of their new commander, 'and without exception gave him their united support'.[11] Even diehard political opponents, such as the Nationalist Oswald Pirow, later acknowledged that Botha was the finest military tactician ever produced in South Africa.[12]

The new commandant-general lost no time in breathing new enthusiasm into the Transvaal forces under his command. He tightened discipline, banned women from the war front, reorganised transport and supply lines and replaced underperforming senior officers with younger, more energetic men. As Meintjes notes, among the undisciplined Boers, personality and strong leadership were of the utmost importance. While Botha drew men to him by sheer force of personality, De la Rey kept his burghers together through awe, respect and terror, while De Wet attracted disciples by his fearlessness and daredevilry.[13] In the field, these three leaders formed a formidable triumvirate, whose example and deeds of daring galvanised their fellow burghers into renewed action.

Hit-and-run tactics

Delaying his advance through the Free State for a fortnight while his exhausted troops recovered their strength, Lord Roberts also took advantage of the break in fighting to weed out the less competent officers in his upper ranks. Of the generals defeated during Black Week, Gatacre was dismissed but Methuen and Buller were allowed to keep their commands. By the end of

April, Roberts was ready to lead his huge army out of Bloemfontein. With
170 000 troops now at his disposal in South Africa, he decided that 100 000 of
them would march northwards to the ZAR, while 70 000 would stay behind
to guard crucial supply and communication lines for the main army.[14]

The British commander-in-chief planned to invade the Transvaal by dis-
patching mounted columns from different points across a front extending
from Kimberley to Ladysmith. He would head the main column of almost
40 000 troops and 100 guns himself, while Methuen, on his left flank, would
march along the railway line north with another large contingent. Roberts
hoped that Buller might arrive from Natal to guard his army's eastern flank,
but, after Buller took his time and found every excuse not to get his men
moving, the impatient Roberts left him to find his own way to the Transvaal.

Despite being on home ground and not having to defend any supply lines,
the Free State Boers, now only 5 000 in number, had no hope of holding up
the British juggernaut by conventional means. Instead, they resorted to guer-
rilla-style hit-and-run attacks – aimed principally at disrupting the enemy's
supply lines and communication links – a tactic that would confound and
amaze the watching world.

Christiaan de Wet, his brother Piet and a force of 2 000 men gave Roberts
early trouble by attacking a British garrison protecting Bloemfontein's water-
works on the Modder River. At the subsequent battle of Sanna's Post, the
British lost 600 men, 90 wagons and seven guns. Bloemfontein's water supply
was cut off and within a month 2 000 inhabitants of the British-held town
succumbed to enteric fever.[15]

On 7 May, on the urgent orders of Kruger, Botha arrived at Virginia in the
Free State with 3 000 fellow Transvalers to help in the defence of Kroonstad,
the latest temporary headquarters of President Steyn. In the meantime, De
la Rey had departed to shore up the Boer defences outside Mafeking, leaving
Botha and the main Boer force, now down to only 8 000 following a wave
of desertions, to assemble at the Sand River to try to defend the new capital.

While Botha was making his way to the Free State, the Transvaal Volksraad
met for what many correctly assumed would be the last time. Most MPs
in the field, except for De la Rey and Botha, were present, many of them
coming directly from the war front. Also in attendance in their full finery
were the consuls and attachés of foreign powers. Wreaths lay on the chairs of

Joubert and other notable absentees, and the republican flag, the Vierkleur, was draped across the seat of Cronje, still in captivity on St Helena.

A solemn President Kruger addressed the gathering at length, speaking about the sacrifices the republics had made, the goodwill of foreign governments towards his people, and his hopes for the success of a three-man mission sent abroad in the vain hope of convincing foreign powers to intervene in support of the Boer cause (Hillegas remarks that 'there was hardly one burgher who did not cling steadfastly to the opinion that the war would be ended in such a manner'[16]). Formally confirming the appointment of Louis Botha as commandant-general of the ZAR, he declared the republic's finances to be satisfactory. From now on, the executive committee would take responsibility for conducting the war. A decision had been made to take the fight to the British before they could reach Pretoria. 'There was no talk,' Hillegas reported, 'of ending the war or of surrender.' "Shall we lose courage?", Kruger asked rhetorically. "Never, never, never!" he thundered.'[17]

Orange River Colony

On the banks of the Sand River, outside Kroonstad, Botha and his outnumbered force found themselves encircled by the advancing enemy. Their only alternative to being routed was to keep moving men and materiel around the countryside so as to be able to fight another day. The Boers' ability to steal away without engaging in combat was a constant source of frustration for the more conventional Roberts. Even where they had dug in along river banks, he complained, 'they slip away in the most extraordinary manner'. 'Somehow,' Pakenham quotes him as saying, 'the Boers always save even their wagons and heavy guns without paying the price in casualties. Botha's army is in full flight, yet they march like victors.'[18]

On 11 May, a defiant President Steyn, described by Botha as 'the soul of the war',[19] read the writing on the wall and departed Kroonstad for Heilbron, 96 kilometres to the northeast, which he declared as his new capital. The very next day, Roberts marched into Kroonstad without encountering any resistance. While he lingered there for eight days so as to rest and re-equip his forces, he received the welcome news that Mafeking had been relieved.

On 26–27 May, Roberts and his large force crossed the Vaal River into the

ZAR. The flat terrain and absence of any natural barriers that the Boers could defend meant that the roads to Johannesburg and Pretoria were now wide open. A day later, Roberts announced that the British Crown had annexed the Free State, which would henceforth be known as the 'Orange River Colony', but he backdated the proclamation to 24 May 1900 in honour of Queen Victoria's birthday.

CHAPTER 9

PRETORIA FALLS

Into the Transvaal

Lord Roberts's war machine was now moving onto the Transvaal highveld on either side of the railway line over a 40-kilometre-wide front – 'a massive, unstoppable procession of guns, men and horses' heading for Johannesburg and Pretoria.[1] The Boers had no chance of stopping the juggernaut, but Botha and 3 000 burghers, whose numbers kept dropping as the British advanced, supported by De la Rey and his men from the Free State, managed to force General French's vanguard back across the Klip River, not far from present-day Soweto. After a three-day battle at Doornkop, on the Klipriviersberg, the British cavalry and infantry silenced the Boers' seven artillery pieces and drove Botha and his men from their positions, despite sustaining another 100 casualties themselves.

As the British swept on towards Johannesburg, members of the Transvaal government, including Jan Smuts, seriously contemplated dynamiting the gold mines, which Kruger, FW Reitz and others had always claimed were the root cause of the republic's troubles. Blowing up the mines, they argued, would settle the score at one fell swoop with the British, the Uitlanders, the Randlords (mine owners) and their companies, and might even persuade foreign investors to bring pressure to bear on the British government to end the war.[2] Botha, however, would not hear of it and told Kruger he would resign if the threat to the mines was carried out. With his eyes on the future, he understood – if others didn't – that wealth from the mines would be crucial to the economic rehabilitation of the Transvaal. He gave orders that on no account were the mines to be damaged, at which point Kruger backed down and the mines were left untouched.

On 31 May 1900, a triumphant Roberts marched into Johannesburg to find that most of the Uitlanders, on whose behalf the war had supposedly been fought, had long since left. Sixty-four kilometres away in Pretoria, President Kruger and his government had begun moving 96 kilometres down the railway line to Machadodorp in the east, leaving Vice President Schalk Burger, now free of his military duties, and Smuts in charge of the capital. The flight of their president and figurehead further damaged Boer morale.

Hillegas reported that the impending approach of the British had transformed the Boer capital into a scene of desperation and panic: 'Men with drawn faces dashed through the city to assist their hard-pressed countrymen in the field; tearful women with children on their arms filled the churches with their moans and prayers; deserters fleeing homeward exaggerated fresh disasters and increased the tension of the populace – tears and terror prevailed almost everywhere. Railway stations were filled with throngs intent on escaping from the coming disaster, commandos of breathless and blood-stained burghers entered the city, and soon the voice of the conquerors' cannon reverberated among the hills and valleys of the capital.'[3]

The full weight of responsibility for the war now descended upon the broad shoulders of Louis Botha, by now distinctly heavyset though still vigorous and physically fit. It was *his* task, he reflected grimly, to surrender Pretoria to Lord Roberts.[4] And how could he continue the fight the British, he asked himself, when so many of his burghers had simply given up the uneven battle and gone home? Just as De la Rey had predicted a mere seven months earlier, those who had opposed the war, such as himself and Botha, now found themselves in the forefront of battle long after the loudmouth politicians who had clamoured for war had run away.

Courage returns

Arriving in Pretoria ahead of Roberts, Botha was presented with an executive order directing him to hold up the British advance on the capital for as long as possible. Instructing De la Rey to defend the outer perimeter of the capital, he rode into Church Square on horseback and – from the steps of the Raadzaal – addressed a large and nervous crowd. Furious at the plundering of government property by returning burghers, he demanded the restoration

GL ARCHIVE/ALAMY STOCK PHOTO

WORLD HISTORY ARCHIVE/ALAMY STOCK PHOTO

GRANGER HISTORICAL PICTURE ARCHIVE/ALAMY
STOCK PHOTO

GLASSHOUSE IMAGES/ALAMY STOCK PHOTO

Four key figures in the Boer struggle for independence (clockwise from top left): President Paul Kruger of the ZAR, President Marthinus Steyn of the Orange Free State, General Christiaan de Wet and General Koos de la Rey. The sometimes fraught relations between Steyn, De Wet, De la Rey and Louis Botha are discussed in Chapter 21.

of law and order and appointed a triumvirate of officers to put an immediate end to the looting of magazines.[5]

The next day, 1 June, Botha was among those present at a *krygsraad* of senior Transvaal generals. Shaken by the desertion of so many of their men, those present were persuaded momentarily of the hopelessness of their cause. Smuts wrote movingly of 'the bitter humiliation and despondency of that awful moment when the strongest hearts and stoutest wills in the Transvaal army were, albeit but for a moment, to sink beneath the tide of our misfortunes'.[6]

Kruger was sent a message suggesting that, in view of the collapse of organised resistance in Pretoria, the time had come to open negotiations with the British. The president agreed and proposed as much to President Steyn, but was stunned by the vehemence of the reply. The Free State president, now taking refuge in his fourth capital, Bethlehem, repeated his unwavering opposition to peace talks and virtually accused his ally of cowardice. Now that the war had entered their own territory, Steyn declared, the Transvalers were seeking a 'selfish and disgraceful peace'. If necessary, his Free Staters would fight on alone 'to the bitter end'.[7]

The council of war continued the next morning in the hall of the Second Volksraad, attended by the same group of generals, as well as some younger commanders who had not been present the night before. The mood this time was quite different. From the Free State, an indignant Christiaan de Wet, privy to the contents of Kruger's telegram, had telegraphed Botha to say that his Free Staters had fought with all they had for the ZAR's independence, and that he (Botha) should use his influence with his generals to continue the struggle. All was not lost, said De Wet, even if Pretoria was now in enemy hands. As the Free State had demonstrated, the Transvalers could continue to make life so difficult for the British that they would eventually seek a just peace with the republics.

Inspired by De Wet's never-say-die attitude, a young captain, Danie Theron, derided those who sought peace as 'traitors' and condemned the government for deserting Pretoria. Determination overcame defeatism. After Botha and Smuts had changed their minds and spoken in favour of prolonging the war, the *krygsraad* decided there would be no peace talks and no all-out defence of the capital; instead, there would be a 'fighting retreat' to the east in order to frustrate the enemy.[8]

Roberts takes Pretoria

With only 2000 burghers at his disposal, Botha no longer had any hope of holding up the fast-approaching British or of defending Pretoria against invasion. Heavy artillery fire from the forts guarding the capital, he decided, would merely provide the enemy with an excuse to retaliate and kill or injure scores of people. On 5 June, after declining a demand from Roberts – via an emissary carrying a white flag – that he should surrender the capital, Botha and Lucas Meyer bade farewell to their wives and families, mounted their horses and rode off into the eastern hills a few hours before the British entered the town and hoisted the Union Jack above the Raadzaal. Before also slipping away to join De la Rey's commando, Smuts managed to send by train to Machadodorp over £500000 in gold and gold coin, as well as secret documents, heavy guns, ammunition and other supplies needed if hostilities were to be continued.

Roberts was now in possession of his second Boer capital, and it seemed to him the war was now running to its end. As he had done in the Free State, he issued a proclamation that all burghers who laid down their arms and committed to remaining neutral would be allowed to return to their homes and farms without being taken prisoner. By the end of June, 8000 Transvalers had joined 6000 Free Staters in taking advantage of the offer – some 40 per cent of the Boers' original mobilisation.[9]

Having learnt from experience of the Boers' propensity for fighting back while on the retreat, Roberts sought a meeting with Botha to sound him out about peace. After an exchange of messages via friends of Annie Botha, the two men agreed to meet at Zwartkoppies, outside Pretoria, on 7 June. But, two days later, just as Roberts was about to set out for the meeting, Botha called it off. He had learnt that De Wet was causing mayhem in the Free State by cutting British supply lines; unless Roberts had some offer to make besides surrender, there was no point in talking to him.[10]

Despite the huge disparity in numbers, the re-energised Boers now set about preventing the British from proceeding further eastwards down the railway line. Marshalling a force of 4000 burghers and 30 guns, Botha positioned his men along a series of low hills in the northeastern Magaliesberg, some 30 kilometres from Pretoria, across the rail line to Machadodorp. If it hadn't already dawned on Roberts, he now understood there would be no

Boer surrender. On 11 June, he sent his own force of 14 000 men and 70 guns to attack Boer positions at both ends of their 40-kilometre defensive front.

After two days of fierce fighting, the British succeeded in driving the Boers off the western slopes of Donkerhoek, a key ridge rising above the road and railway line. Once again, a pitched battle came to an inconclusive end in the dead of night, with the Boers stealing away and making for other vantage points from where they could continue to fire away at the enemy. While neither side was defeated at Donkerhoek, the Boers sustained far fewer losses than the enemy's 175 killed or wounded, and their performance in one of the last set-piece battles of the war filled them with fresh heart.[11] An important reason for their improved morale was the confidence they had in their commandant-general's tactical acumen and uncanny 'feel' for the battlefield.[12]

De Wet's example

Christiaan de Wet's successful guerrilla tactics had brought an entirely new dimension to the war. The Free State commandant's bravery and elusiveness demonstrated to his fellow Boers what a small band of determined fighters could achieve against much larger numbers. On 4 June, while Roberts was approaching Pretoria, De Wet and his men bore down upon a British supply column of 56 wagons and 160 supporting troops outside Heilbron and captured the entire column without a shot being fired. Three days later, he and his burghers launched a series of attacks on British garrisons guarding the railway in the vicinity of Kroonstad, taking many prisoners, blowing up supply dumps and destroying bridges, telegraph lines and miles of the single-track railway line linking the Transvaal, Free State and Cape Colony. The British retaliated by burning down De Wet's farmhouse, Roodepoort, near the Renoster River, on the personal orders of Roberts.

Hampered by an accompanying wagon train that restricted their mobility, De Wet and his Free State burghers did not have matters entirely their own way, however. In mid-July, at the Brandwater River basin in the northeastern Free State, some 9 000 Boers, President Steyn among them, found themselves encircled by 16 000 British troops. Steyn, De Wet and the Free State government officials managed to escape, but 4 300 burghers under General Prinsloo were forced to surrender, and in doing so gave up 4 000 sheep, 6 000 horses, artillery pieces and supplies of ammunition.[13] The capitulation debilitated the Free State forces so severely they were unable to offer any meaningful resistance to the British thereafter.

Boer fightback

Outside the Free State, the war now centred on control of the crucial railway line to Delagoa Bay, in Portuguese East Africa – the Boers' only link with the outside world. Botha knew he could not hold off the British indefinitely, so he set about keeping the railway out of enemy hands for as long as possible, while making preparations for the guerrilla campaign ahead. On 18 June, he and his senior officers held a *krygsraad* in the railway hamlet of Balmoral, at which the Boers' change of military strategy was officially confirmed.

The passive, defensive tactics of earlier days would be replaced by hit-and-run attacks on the enemy's supply and communication routes, carried out by pockets of burghers acting independently of one another. The main Boer force, under Botha himself, would operate around the railway in the east, while the Heidelberg, Krugersdorp, Potchefstroom and Rustenburg commandos would attempt to disrupt British communication lines across other parts of the Transvaal. In the west, generals Koos de la Rey and Hermanus Lemmer would mount another offensive behind enemy lines. Botha was authorised by the executive to confiscate any animals, in particular oxen and horses, that might fall into enemy hands.[14]

Having sent General Kitchener to the Free State to restore communication links severed by De Wet, Lord Roberts now found his eastward advance held up by the activities of De la Rey and company in the northwestern Magaliesberg. At Silkaats Nek, De la Rey's daringly successful attack on a British garrison on the wagon road from occupied Pretoria to Rustenburg, in which 23 of the enemy were killed and 189 taken prisoner, was a huge boost to Boer morale.[15]

Last set-piece battle

On 21 July, Roberts and a large force finally set out from Pretoria for Machadodorp, where Kruger and his government had made their headquarters in a train carriage. Within a few days, General French succeeded in occupying Middelburg, 130 kilometres along the railway line. There, Roberts was obliged to pause for almost a month, while at least nine columns of his troops attempted to hunt down De Wet and his fellow insurgents in the Free State. The British commander-in-chief also resolved to await the arrival from Natal of Buller's force of 9 000 men, 42 guns and 761 supply wagons and at least three weeks' worth of provisions, to join forces with French's cavalry.[16]

By this time, the Boers' defensive line stretched for some 80 kilometres to the north and south of the railway line, across the path of the oncoming British. On the Dalmanutha plateau between Belfast and Machadodorp, along the eastern rim of the highveld, the last great set-piece battle of the war took place. The natural advantages offered by the plateau helped to offset the numerical imbalance between Botha's force of 5 000 to 7 000 fighters and 20 guns (including four Long Toms), and Roberts and Buller's combined army of 18 700 men and 82 guns.[17]

Roberts and Buller had decided to attempt a breakthrough of the Boer line at Bergendal, just south of the rail line on the wagon route to the lowveld. For six days, the Boers held out against the British, giving the Kruger government and its sympathisers time to get away to safety towards Komatipoort. On 27 August, at the Bergendal ridge, a weak link in the centre of the Dalmanutha line, 74 members of the republican police (or 'Zarps') endured a three-hour bombardment by Buller's artillery without a single man leaving his post.[18] When the Zarps finally succumbed to a follow-up attack by infantry, 40 of them were dead, wounded or taken prisoner. According to Tim Couzens, the hours-long barrage by massed artillery on such a small area was 'one of the most concentrated and murderous the world had yet seen, and foreshadowed the hell that was to come 14 years later in Flanders and northern France'.[19] Later that day, Botha was forced to order his commandos to fall back to avoid becoming encircled, thus allowing the British to enter Machadodorp and its surrounds. Casualties on both sides were high, with the British suffering some 300 killed, wounded and missing against 78 for the Boers.

As Couzens records, Botha, skilful as ever, had again avoided a knockout blow, and 'fighting of [a] nasty and lethal kind was to continue in the rugged countryside east of Belfast for 18 months to come'.[20]

Believing the war was now over save for some final mopping-up operations, however, Roberts announced by formal proclamation on 1 September that the Transvaal had been annexed by the British Crown. Kruger responded with an edict two days later declaring the proclamation to be null and void. The British commander had been correct to conclude that the conventional war had come to its end. What he had failed to realise, though, was that a new and far more bitter phase of the conflict was about to begin.

CHAPTER 10

Burning Farms

Acts of war

The Anglo-Boer War was unusual in several respects. At various times during the fighting, the two sides communicated with each other by means of messengers waving a white flag. Truces were often arranged to enable each army to reclaim its dead and wounded from the battlefield. The Boers refused to fight on the Sabbath, and the British never sought to take advantage of that. When Joubert died, Lord Roberts, as we have seen, was among the first to commiserate with the family. And shortly before an ailing Queen Victoria died on 22 January 1901 during the war, President Kruger sent her a sympathetic message from exile in Europe.

Letters between the two sides were couched in the most courteous language. Kitchener always sent Boer leaders such as Steyn and De Wet formal notification of his proclamations, and would receive a reply beginning, 'I have the honour to acknowledge receipt of Your Excellency's letter ...' Lord Roberts's written invitation to Botha, on 18 June 1900, to surrender before the British took Pretoria reads as follows:

> Your Honour
>
> I address these few lines in the hope that they may have the effect of inducing your Honour, in the cause of humanity, to refrain from further resistance. The British force under my command so greatly exceeds the Boer army in numbers, that although this war may be prolonged for a few more weeks, there can be but one result. After the gallant struggle your Honour and the Force under your command have made, there can be no

question of loss of honour should you decide to accept the counsel I now
venture to proffer.

I have the honour to be
Your Honour's obedient servant
[Signed]: Roberts
Field Marshal
Commanding the British Army in South Africa[1]

To which Botha replied, in similarly ultra-polite terms, that it was not possible to accept the cessation of hostilities, which he so much desired.

Friendships were sometimes forged in the unlikeliest of circumstances. De
Wet once described General Knox, who was trying to hunt him down, as
'my old friend'.[2] Around Christmas 1900, General Beyers sent an officer to
General French, under a flag of truce, to seek permission to recover the bodies of several of his men who had died in a skirmish. French gave the officer
a bottle of whisky and some cigars to take to Beyers as a Christmas present.
Beyers had nothing to give in return, so he released two British prisoners and
sent them to French in lieu of a gift. In return for General Viljoen's passing on
letters to British prisoners of war, General Smith-Dorrien sent over two boxes
of claret. Viljoen was so pleased he sent Smith-Dorrien an engraved Kruger
gold sovereign in return.[3]

After the British captured both Boer capitals, Kruger, Steyn, Botha, Smuts
and others had no qualms about leaving their wives to reside in Bloemfontein
and Pretoria, knowing they would come to no harm. Roberts even paid a
courtesy call on 'Tant Gezina' Kruger in the Transvaal capital and permitted
her to stay on in the Presidency. Relations between the occupying British
army and Afrikaner residents were surprisingly cordial, with Mrs Annie
Botha occasionally attending officers' concerts.[4]

These 'gentlemanly' acts of war became few and far between, however, after
Roberts decided he would no longer protect and feed the wives of burghers who were out in the countryside carrying on the fight. By mid-winter
of 1900, hundreds of Boer women and children had been left out in the
veld because of the British scorched-earth policy. And on 2 September, the
British commander sent Botha a letter declaring his wish to be rid of the
remaining wives of Boer leaders (including old Mrs Kruger) and insisting

that Botha find accommodation for them.⁵ Roberts backed down after a reply from Botha poured scorn on the suggestion that the wives were passing on information to the British. Annie Botha was allowed to stay on in Pretoria, but Mrs Kruger died a year later.⁶ Roberts also repeated the threat, in his proclamation of 16 June 1900, to destroy all farms in the vicinity of railway lines damaged by Boer commandos.

Botha was outraged: solicitous of wounded enemies and chivalrous to prisoners himself, it offended his sense of justice that wives and children should be made victims of the Boers' honourable struggle for independence. In an angry reply to Roberts, he protested that the British were perpetrating 'barbarous acts' by burning down Boer farms, even those nowhere near railway lines. 'Wherever troops moved out,' he wrote, 'not only were houses burnt down or blown up with dynamite, but also helpless women and children were driven from their homes and deprived of food and clothing without the slightest ground for any such deed.'⁷

Botha's helpless rage was understandable: since Roberts's troops had begun farm-burning in the Free State in June 1900, several hundred Boer homesteads had been incinerated and their inhabitants given a few minutes to gather up their belongings before being sent to hastily established camps. From June to November, as many as 600 farms were burnt to ashes.⁸

This scorched-earth policy, initiated by Roberts and extended by Kitchener, introduced a new and much harsher element into the war. In Meintjes' graphic description: 'As a sheet of flame swept over the country, hapless women and children were herded into concentration camps. For hundreds of miles homesteads were burned down, crops set ablaze and all animals shot and bayoneted, even burnt to death, in a mass execution which planted a bitterness in the hearts of the Boers which was only to deepen as the years passed.'⁹ When Emily Hobhouse's revelations of the horrific effects of scorched earth were published in British newspapers, there was grave disquiet in the ranks of the Liberal Party and around the world.

Roberts's justification for farm-burning – which he did not expect would continue for long – was that the Boers were now subjects of the British Crown; those who continued to resist were rebels to be punished rather than an enemy to be defeated. This short-sighted view worried some of his officers, who thought that the destruction of Boer farms would only help to make the commandos more resolute than ever. One captain concluded at the war's end that 'if the farms had not been burnt, the war would have been sooner over'.[10]

Kruger leaves

By 10 September 1900, the ZAR's executive council had moved further down the railway line to Nelspruit, where, at the urging of Botha and President Steyn, its members decided that President Kruger should go into exile – for an initial period of six months. Determined to carry on the struggle 'for as long as I live', the resolute Steyn refused to go himself. His republic had made huge sacrifices and he could not bring himself personally to abandon the cause.[11] The next day, a tired and saddened Kruger left for Delagoa Bay to await a warship sent for him by Queen Wilhelmina of the Netherlands. He was never to see his beloved Transvaal again. In his absence, General Schalk Burger was made provisional president, but the real leader of the Transvaal was now Commandant-General Botha, whose task it was to reorganise and reinvigorate the Boers' military campaign.

Since the last major set-piece of the war, at Bergendal, the Transvaal Boers had broken up into three columns. One had moved southeast towards Barberton, hotly pursued by General French; a second was fighting off the attentions of General Pole-Carew's troops along the railway line to Delagoa Bay; while a third had gone northwards towards Lydenburg, harried along the way by General Buller. (De la Rey had been dispatched earlier to round up men in the western Transvaal.) The hilly and wooded countryside of the eastern Transvaal was not conducive to pitched battles, however; instead, there were frequent skirmishes between British forces and small bands of Boers.[12]

Botha took personal command of a 5 000-strong commando in the rugged, mountainous area between Machadodorp, Lydenburg and Nelspruit.[13] After falling ill with malaria, he recuperated briefly at Hectorspruit before having to give way to Pole-Carew's column, which was bearing down on Komatipoort. Throwing artillery pieces into the Crocodile River and abandoning large stores of ammunition and railway stock, Botha and 2 000 of his men followed President Steyn's party as it wound its way through the Sabi Valley and up onto the Transvaal highveld. Steyn and 300 commandos had loaded up with reserves of gold and currency and departed on a roundabout route that would eventually take them back to the ravaged Free State.[14]

The British Liberal parliamentarian and author Harold Spender gave a colourful description of Botha's life at this time as 'having all the romance and colour of a Rob Roy, outlawed and yet defiant, chased and yet chasing, conquered by all the rules of the game but still often victorious over his conquerors … We must not imagine it was ever an easy life. These great deeds were not done without sweat and agony. Often these Boer commandos escaped only as by fire. Again and again, they emerged from the jaws of their pursuers, breathless, stripped of their possessions, emaciated with long hunger, ragged, almost foodless. They would go for weeks without regular sleep … All but the most stalwart fell away.'[15]

Cyferfontein

In late October, having trekked for many miles through the northern Transvaal bushveld to evade the British, the leaders of the two Boer governments, President Steyn and General Botha, joined De la Rey and Smuts at Cyferfontein, a secluded farm in the Zwartruggens hills, 120 kilometres west of Pretoria, to hammer out a joint strategy to counter Roberts's farm-burning activities.[16] To these Boer strategists, the sacking and looting of farms by the enemy was both a curse and a blessing. On the one hand, it kept many more burghers out in the field, bent on revenge; on the other, it was inflicting the most severe hardship on Boer families.

As was often the case during the war, relations between the Transvalers and Free Staters at Cyferfontein were far from easy. In Pakenham's view, the fundamental differences in the make-up of the two Boer states – the one a 'sheep and cow' and the other a 'gold' republic – were bound to produce contrary attitudes to war and peace.[17] The absent Kruger's mantle as the uncompromising, iron-willed 'volksleier' (leader) of the Afrikaner people had fallen upon Steyn, who, like De Wet, was unwavering in his hostility to negotiations with the enemy. Steyn's was an ideological struggle to preserve not only the independence but also the purity of Afrikanerdom. If people believed at the beginning of the war that God was with them, he demanded to know, what had changed since then?[18]

For Kruger, Botha, Smuts and company from the much larger and wealthier ZAR, the choice was not as simple. There were the diverging interests of a large part-Afrikaner, part-British and part-cosmopolitan population to consider. As Pakenham writes, 'Death and glory had less attraction for the *volk* in the Transvaal, when a hundred thousand *uitlanders* were waiting to pick up the pieces.'[19]

While Smuts had been converted, temporarily, to Steyn's idealistic and impassioned way of thinking, the more forward-looking Botha continued to agonise over the merits of fighting on vainly and indefinitely, or of trying to save the Transvaal from further devastation. Uppermost in his mind was the deeper moral question of whether he and his fellow male Boers had the right to inflict further suffering upon their women and children. His dilemma was compounded by the disappointing outcome of the October 1900 'Khaki' election in Britain, fought primarily over the 'South African War' issue, in which Salisbury's Unionist government had been re-elected at the expense of Campbell-Bannerman's more pro-Boer Liberals.

Although it was acknowledged at Cyferfontein that continued guerrilla resistance would provoke more farm burnings, those present resolved not only to prolong the war but also to re-enter and invade the two colonies, where the British could not burn farms or inflict reprisals on their own citizens. In Botha's mind, at least, the more successful the Boers' guerrilla tactics, the better the chances of extracting favourable terms for peace.

The Cyferfontein gathering also decided to divide the Boer commandos into separate forces: one column would move down into Botha's old stamping ground, Natal; another, under De la Rey and De Wet, would cross into the Cape Colony in the hope of whipping up Afrikaner support for the Boer cause. There was also talk of resurrecting the plan to blow up the Rand mines, this time as a justifiable act of revenge against Roberts and the mining interests supporting him.

Had the twin offensive planned at Cyferfontein actually materialised, the course of the war might have turned out differently. But soon after their return to the Free State, Steyn and De Wet were ambushed at Bothaville and were fortunate to escape with their lives. By this time, De la Rey and Smuts were already in action raiding British encampments in the Magaliesberg, while Botha and General Viljoen had joined forces to attack British garrisons guarding Belfast, Machadodorp and other stations along the Delagoa Bay railway. To Botha's relief, the plan to disable the mines had to be abandoned.[20]

Roberts departs

Towards the end of the year, Roberts handed over command of British forces in South Africa to his deputy, Kitchener, and departed for Britain, where he received the rapturous welcome afforded to conquering heroes. A 19-gun salute greeted the arrival of his warship at Cowes, from where he travelled to the Isle of Wight for a special audience with Queen Victoria, who raised his title from viscount to earl and made him a Knight of the Garter. It soon became evident, however, that Britain had not yet won the South African War. A thanksgiving service arranged for St Paul's Cathedral had to be cancelled when it dawned on the populace that the apparent end of hostilities was in fact 'a false sunset'.[21]

Despite the occasional setback, December 1900 was a month in which the Boers dared to imagine that the war was turning in their favour.[22] This was partly due to De la Rey's success in inflicting heavy casualties on a British camp at Nooitgedacht, between Rustenburg and Pretoria, and the capture of a British garrison at Helvetia in the eastern Transvaal, and partly by the effectiveness of the Free Staters' invasion of the Cape Colony, which had progressed as far as the Atlantic coast and other Afrikaner strongholds such as Graaff-Reinet and Mossel Bay. The British authorities in the Cape retaliated by declaring martial law in many parts of the colony.

Middelburg

The situation in which the new British commander, Kitchener, found himself was a difficult one. Aided by a sympathetic Afrikaner population, his Boer enemy could range freely over wide-open countryside to blow up railway lines, cut communication links, ambush garrisons and make off with enough heavy guns, ammunition and supplies to be able to prolong resistance indefinitely.[23] But the very nature of guerrilla warfare meant that the Boer leadership had no cohesive battle plan and no long-term objective beyond harassing the British forces until their government sued for peace.

Gleaning from intelligence sources that Botha was more disposed than his fellow generals to peace negotiations, Kitchener decided to seek a meeting with the Boer leader. Using Annie Botha, still living with her children in Pretoria, as a go-between, he invited her husband under cover of a flag of truce to a meeting, which took place at Middelburg, east of Pretoria, on 28 February 1901. The occasion was noteworthy not so much for its predictable outcome as for the distrust it provoked between Botha and his Free State allies.

Before setting off to meet Kitchener, Botha informed De Wet of his intentions, and asked that he and Steyn should come closer to Middelburg in case he needed to consult them. The Free Staters were not happy about the meeting, but De Wet, in his war memoir, makes no mention of any dissatisfaction and merely records that he and Botha had a long talk at Vrede afterwards, and that the two parted 'with the firm determination that, whatever happened, we would continue the war'.[24]

The discussion at Middelburg lasted from 10 am to 3 pm and took place in a cordial atmosphere. Kitchener was impressed by Botha, noting: 'He has a nice unassuming manner, and seemed desirous of finishing the war, but somewhat doubtful of being able to induce his men to accept peace without independence in some form or another. He repeated that he and his people felt bitterly about losing their independence ... He was very bitter about those who had surrendered. Botha is a quiet, capable man and I have no doubt carries considerable weight with his burghers: he will be, I should think, of valuable assistance to the future government of the country in an official capacity.'[25]

Kitchener left Botha in no doubt that independence was out of the question, and that it might actually be dangerous given the state of black/white relations and the after-effects of war – a point the Boer leader was prepared to concede. In response to Botha's list of demands, which included an amnesty for acts of war, payment of the ZAR's debts, the restitution of farms and the exclusion of black races from voting rights, Kitchener asked for an assurance that all commandos would lay down their arms. This was a commitment Botha felt unable to give, unless the Free Staters upon whose cooperation he depended were offered and accepted the identical terms.

Kitchener and Botha obviously got on well together. In the evening, after their talks ended, the British commander invited his visitor to play a game of bridge. Botha demurred, saying he could only play whist. Kitchener said he would teach him bridge and the pair played for some hours, with Botha losing £15 (which he was to repay years later). As the Boers had no playing cards for the long evenings, Botha asked Kitchener to send him some, and in due course received a gift of 50 packs. After the war, Botha became an avid bridge player himself for the rest of his days.[26]

Negotiations fail

Kitchener's attitude, at this time, was conciliatory: he was prepared to be financially generous – provided the Boers accepted the annexation of their republics as being final and not to be haggled over.[27] He also thought the million pounds that Botha had asked for to rebuild and restock farms – no more than one month's expenditure on the war – was a price worth paying. But Sir Alfred Milner, upon whose advice Joseph Chamberlain depended, was not interested in settlement, sensing that total victory was at hand. He trimmed Kitchener's proposals to London to such an extent that the Boers had little incentive to settle.

The British government's terms for peace were communicated by letter on 7 March. Days later Botha formally turned the offer down, without offering any explanation. A disappointed Kitchener blamed the failure of the negotiations on Milner's intransigence, but the truth of the matter was that the Boers were not yet ready to give up on their demand for independence.

Botha informed his burghers of the failure of the Middelburg negotiations by circular letter from Ermelo, in which he said: 'The spirit of Lord Kitchener's letter makes it very plain to you all that the British Government desires nothing else but the destruction of our Afrikaner people and the acceptance of the terms contained therein is absolutely out of the question. Virtually the letter contains nothing more, but rather less than what the British Government will be obliged to do should our cause go wrong ... Let us as Daniel in the lion's den, place our trust in God alone, for in His time and in His way, He will certainly give us deliverance.'[28]

As Edgar Holt notes, the contrast between Kitchener and Milner became ever more apparent after the failure of the Middelburg talks. Kitchener, the soldier, was anxious to end the fighting and prepared to make all reasonable concessions; Milner, the civilian administrator, wanted the British army to go on fighting until the Boers had no choice but surrender.[29]

CHAPTER 11

THE WAR DRAGS ON

The blockhouse system

The new British commanding officer, the ferociously hard-working and driven General Herbert Kitchener, was tired of the war in South Africa and hoped to move on to become commander-in-chief (or perhaps viceroy) in India.[1] The failure of the Middelburg negotiations, and his disillusionment with Milner, made him embark on an even more uncompromising strategy to bring an end to the Boers' guerrilla activities. To impair the mobility of the enemy, he ordered the building, across the veld, of an intricate web of at least 8 000 tin-and-stone blockhouses situated some 900 metres apart and linked by barbed wire, telegraph and telephone lines. These mini-fortresses extended across almost 6 000 kilometres (enclosing over 80 000 square kilometres) of the Transvaal and Free State, and were guarded by 50 000 troops and 16 000 African auxiliaries.[2]

This blockhouse system considerably reduced the open spaces available to the Boers, whose attacks became more sporadic and less effective. Kitchener also sent four separate troop columns to funnel the Boer commandos, in particular that of De Wet, into ever-narrowing strips of territory. His refusal to take any more displaced families into the so-called concentration camps, leaving them in the veld for the burghers to look after, made matters even worse for the embattled Boers.

The zeal with which these restrictive measures were applied as well as the pitiful condition of Boer women and children in the camps – where thousands were dying of dysentery, measles and other epidemic diseases – brought about another wave of revulsion worldwide. In Britain, the Liberal leader Henry Campbell-Bannerman, well briefed by Emily Hobhouse, characterised

Kitchener's tactics as 'methods of barbarism', but the British commander was unfazed. One of his responsibilities, he argued, was to safeguard the families of Boers who had already surrendered and, in some cases, gone over to the British side.

Philip Botha killed

In March 1901, Botha was devastated to learn of the death of his elder brother Philip – among the Boers' most well-regarded generals – at Doornberg in the northeastern Free State. Such was the shock that he refused ever to speak about his loss.[3] It would have added to his growing belief that the war against the British had become an exercise in futility. Another who felt the same way was Annie. Like her husband, she could see only one outcome of the conflict and bridled at the senselessness of the bloodshed and suffering that would precede it. On the occasion mentioned earlier, she travelled for three days to see Botha to bring him a new proposal from British headquarters to consider. The strong argument of Annie, with whom he had a close and loving relationship, would have weighed heavily on his mind.[4]

Early in May, Botha convened a *krygsraad* of Transvaal generals. The mood was one of pessimism; burgher desertions were continuing apace, stocks of ammunition were running low, and hopes of foreign intervention were dwindling. Those in attendance decided to ask Kitchener for permission to send a small delegation to Europe to consult Kruger about negotiating peace. President Steyn was informed of the meeting by letter and reacted with predictable outrage, accusing the Transvalers of leaving his Free Staters in the lurch. Surprisingly, Kitchener turned down the request on the tenuous grounds that Kruger was no longer ZAR president and that he (Kitchener) could only negotiate with the Boer leaders in the field.[5] But he approved the sending of an enciphered telegram to Kruger, the contents of which would have been quickly decrypted by British intelligence.

Such was the vehemence of Steyn's opposition to negotiations, however, that it was decided to hold another joint war council of the two governments, which took place on a farm near Standerton, in the eastern Transvaal.[6] As usual, Boer morale rose with even the faintest indication of a change in fortunes. Three successful guerrilla actions against the British in a fortnight, resulting in the seizure of supplies of weapons, food and ammunition, as well as an uncompromising message from Kruger to trust in God and never to give in, persuaded those present at the meeting to resolve once again to fight on. Smuts was at last given permission, after much pleading, to mount his own expedition into the Cape Colony.

Into Natal again

In May, Annie Botha left Pretoria for exile in Europe, leaving nine-year-old Louis (Jnr) to join his father on commando. She took with her a lengthy report on conditions in the republics to be given to Kruger.[7] An ill-judged proclamation by Kitchener to the effect that Boer officers who failed to surrender by 15 September 1901 would be banished permanently from South Africa provoked Botha into renewed defiance. Hastily assembling a force of 1000 men from four southeastern Transvaal commandos, he made his way in heavy rain across the border to Scheeper's Nek, near Utrecht, in Natal. At nearby Blood River Poort, he won another brilliant tactical victory, luring a 16000-strong column of khakis under the command of Colonel Hubert Gough into a trap and inflicting 44 casualties (20 killed, 24 wounded), taking 235 prisoners, and relieving the enemy of a large stock of horses, arms and ammunition.[8]

Roy Digby Thomas vividly describes how, time after time, Botha narrowly evaded capture as he was harried from town to town: 'He and his closest followers suffered hunger and thirst. They were deprived of regular sleep, and lacked the clothing to protect them from the highveld winter. For months they existed on what they could scavenge from the countryside.'[9] The British farm-burning policy deprived them of support from Boer farmers and added to their hardship.

More important than his tactical acumen, says Digby Thomas, was Botha's personal relations with his followers: 'Despite the privations, he managed to turn himself out in neat clothes, looking handsome and assured. His kindness towards others was legendary and he made his men feel he really cared for their well-being … If anyone had a problem, he knew he would receive a sympathetic hearing … The burghers adored him. Many would have done anything for him.'[10]

Cold and wet September weather and the exhaustion of their horses forced Botha and his men to rest for a few days in the vicinity of Utrecht, enabling Kitchener to rush reinforcements to northern Natal to bar the commando's further progress. After being repulsed by two well-defended British posts at Itala Mountain and Fort Prospect, Botha's drenched and bedraggled men were forced to abandon any thought of crossing the Tugela or invading Zululand, and fell back towards the Transvaal again, attacking some British troops on Botha's farm at Vryheid on the way. The retreating Boers were also able to capture a 36-wagon supply convoy, which provided them with much-needed food and clothing.[11]

Although his foray into Natal ended unsuccessfully, Botha's response to Kitchener's proclamation brought home to the British that the war was by no means over. Kitchener still required thousands of troops to counter the combined guerrilla activities of Botha along the Natal border, De la Rey in the western Transvaal, Smuts in the Cape Colony and De Wet in the Free State. The war was now two years old and its substantial cost – to an impatient British government and public – had become unacceptable.

Last battle

On 25 October, the peripatetic Botha was fortunate to escape capture when his laager on a farm near Ermelo was surrounded by 2 000 British troops, with eight guns. The British commander, Colonel Rimington, came upon the Boer encampment in the early hours of the morning, only to watch as Botha, his young son and companions rode off into the distance. In his haste, Botha had left behind his Bible and hymn book, his son's hat and some personal papers, all of which were returned in due course by Rimington, to whom Botha wrote a cordial thank-you note. Once again, the commandant-general had demonstrated to his men the truth of his oft-repeated maxim: 'No Boer need ever be captured if he doesn't want to be.'[12]

Botha's last major battle of the war took place a few days later, at Bakenlaagte, south of present-day Witbank, where his burghers joined forces with Commandant Hendrik Grobler's commando to rout a British force led by one of Kitchener's most successful officers, Lieutenant Colonel GE Benson, hitherto the scourge of the Boers in the eastern Transvaal. Benson's 'flying column' would often march for up to 64 kilometres at night to attack the commandos in their laagers at dawn, forcing them to saddle up in the early hours to avoid capture.[13] Botha had demanded that the activities of Benson and his 'restless column' be brought to an immediate end.[14]

On 30 October, Benson's long resupply column of over 300 wagons, 800 horses and 1400 men was making its slow way via the farm Bakenlaagte to Balmoral, on the Delagoa Bay railway line, when its rearguard became bogged down in misty and rainy conditions and was set upon by Botha's men. Benson sent back reinforcements and positioned men and guns on a nearby ridge, which became known as Gun Hill. Though he and 280 troops fought with great bravery to defend the hill against superior numbers, they were overrun by Botha's men, losing 231 men killed or wounded.[15]

Benson himself was wounded and died the next morning, to be deeply mourned by Kitchener. The Boers, who had lost more than 50 of their own, declined to follow up with an attack on the main British camp at Bakenlaagte because of the presence on the farm of 25 Boer families.[16] Reporting to the War Office in London, Kitchener wrote: 'If a column like Benson's, operating twenty miles outside our lines, is not fairly safe, it is a very serious matter, and will require a large addition to our forces if we are to carry on the war.'[17]

No 'whites only' war

Though there had been a tacit understanding, before the war, that the conflict would be a 'white man's' war, in which black people would not be recruited as armed soldiers, as the war dragged on the agreement was honoured more in the breach than in the observance. It could hardly have been otherwise in a country in which more than four-fifths of the population was black. Both sides made extensive use of black African and coloured auxiliaries, employing the skilled as transport drivers, blacksmiths, wheelwrights, carpenters, farriers and even intelligence gatherers, and the unskilled as labourers to dig trenches, look after horses, guard equipment or carry out menial tasks in the military camps.[18]

More and more black people were drawn into the fighting as the war dragged on, especially on the British side as the need for manpower rose during Kitchener's anti-guerrilla campaign. Unlike the Boers, the British were able to pay wages for services rendered. Caught between two fires, many blacks chose to enter the war in an attempt to escape poverty, find better-paid work or settle scores with the Boers who had taken away their land and livelihood. By the war's end, there were an estimated 30 000 volunteers serving in the British army, many of whom were 'scouts' paid to provide information about commando movements.[19]

The Boers also relied heavily on the support of some 10 000 black or coloured *agterryers* (attendants on horseback), who served as gun bearers, ammunition carriers, dispatch riders or personal servants. In the field, these attendants shared the clothing and food (and sometimes even the tents) of their masters, and in times of desperation were given arms and pushed forward into the front line as combatants.

From early in the war, however, the more remote areas of the Transvaal had been a no-go area for Boer families and fighters because of black hostility. In the western Transvaal, the Kgatla tribe from across the Bechuanaland border were in control of large swathes of territory – with the approval of the British. To the north, the British helped to defend black tenants who had taken over former white farms against attacks by guerrillas. The Boers, for their part, dealt ruthlessly with any black people known or suspected of aiding the British.

Kitchener's scorched-earth policy led to the displacement of black as well as white families. By the end of the war over 115 000 black refugees had been settled in the concentration camps, which became a source of cheap labour for the British army. Conditions in these overcrowded, insanitary camps were even worse than in the Boer camps, with over 14 000, or one in ten, inhabitants dying of disease.

With the Boers often having to survive by plundering black homesteads for food and provisions, resistance intensified and became ever more violent. In order to evade their British pursuers, the commandos had to range across tribal areas whose inhabitants either offered armed resistance or informed on them. Both sides took the law into their own hands, and atrocities were frequent. Towards the end of the war, inter-racial conflict, to quote Nasson, 'was rising beyond politically tolerable levels'.[20]

There were many appalling examples of this conflict, on the one hand the summary and sometimes mass executions by the Boers – throughout 1901

– of armed and unarmed black Africans suspected of working for or support-ing the British,[21] and, on the other, the butchery at Holkrans in the Vryheid district in May 1902, where a Zulu impi, in retaliation for confiscation and labour conscription, speared 56 Boers to death in a battle in which almost a hundred of their own warriors were killed or wounded. The 'unbearable state' of black/white relations in the republics was one of the chief reasons for the Boers' eventual acceptance of a peace settlement.[22]

'Hensoppers' and 'joiners'

A further cause of deep concern to the Boer generals was the growing num-ber of defections from their ever-shrinking ranks. After the annexation of the Free State and Transvaal by the Crown, almost 14 000 burghers had laid down their arms and taken an oath of neutrality: they could see no point in carrying on a fight the Boer republics could not possibly win. Their oppo-sition was both active and passive. The passive retired to their farms, kept their heads downs and did no damage to the Boer war effort; the active, known as 'joiners', attempted to bring the war to an early end. The most prominent joiners were Andries Cronje and Piet de Wet, both brothers of serving Boer generals.

The republican governments refused to recognise the right of any citizen to opt out of the war; commandos who came across burghers not doing their duty would often force the latter back into military service. Even passive 'hens-oppers' (hands-uppers) were regarded as traitors and treated with contempt by Botha and his fellow Boers. Many were treated harshly – court-martialled, sentenced to death for treason and espionage, and shot by firing squad.

Soon after assuming command, Kitchener sought to encourage negotia-tions by forming 'Burgher Peace Committees' out of influential Boers who had already taken the oath of neutrality. The purpose of these committees was to persuade commandos still in the field of the hopelessness of continuing the struggle and of the wisdom of surrender. Out of them arose two units, the National Scouts in the Transvaal and the Orange River Colony Volunteers in the Free State, which abandoned neutrality, donned khaki uniforms and fought on the British side.[23]

By the end of the war, some 2 000 of these Scouts were deployed on patrols or engaged in active combat; another 2 500 were engaged in providing ancillary services to the British army. They brought the number of hensoppers who had surrendered to 26 per cent of those eligible for military service or 33 per cent of the 60 000 burghers who had originally joined a commando. The growing rift in Afrikaner ranks was another reason for the Boer leaders eventually agreeing to negotiate.

Botha's contempt for joiners who had gone over to the enemy may be gauged by his heated response to the 80-year-old former president of the ZAR, MW Pretorius, who became a virtual joiner when, at the request of Kitchener, he tried to persuade the Boer commandant-general to surrender. He reported on his return that Botha had scolded him for carrying messages from the British. If it had been somebody else, Botha would have had me shot, said Pretorius. Botha gave the elderly man a message to take back to Kitchener: 'If he sends a Boer again, we will shoot the messenger ... we do not want peace, since we are fighting for our independence and will keep on fighting. Tell Kitchener that he controls the railway lines and we the rest of the country. We are not interested in peace.'[24]

CHAPTER 12

PEACE AT LAST

Into Swaziland

The early days of 1902 brought little relief to Louis Botha and his beleaguered commandos. General Bruce Hamilton had taken up Benson's mantle as the bane of the Boers in the eastern Transvaal. Kitchener had given Hamilton 15 000 troops, in 12 columns, to drive Botha and his men towards the Swaziland border. The extension of the blockhouse system to the east of the former ZAR had seriously restricted the commandos' movements, presenting Botha with the dilemma of how to disperse his forces sufficiently widely to evade capture but still exercise control over their activities. Once again, the Boer commander amazed his men with his uncanny anticipation of enemy intentions and his judgement: 'Without maps and without formal training, he was able to calculate the size of the pursuing British columns, their rate of progress and where they would camp. Time and again he slipped out of a deadly encounter when it seemed inevitable he would be cornered.'[1]

A noteworthy Boer victory over the enemy at Bankkop, east of Ermelo, on 3–4 January, during which 28 New Zealanders were captured, was marred by the battlefield loss of one of Botha's most trusted lieutenants, General JD Opperman.[2] Other minor successes in the field were offset by the effectiveness of Hamilton's nocturnal raids, in which many burghers were taken prisoner. To evade Hamilton, Botha was forced to retire eastwards to the hills of Vryheid and into Swaziland, where he spent the next month on the run, eluding his pursuers.

In Swaziland, Botha demonstrated his firm refusal to tolerate any behaviour that violated his personal code of conduct. On receiving a complaint from the Swazi regent, Labotsibeni, that the British had occupied the small town of Bremersdorp (now Manzini), he sent one of his generals, Tobias Smuts, to investigate. Smuts put the small British unit guarding the town to flight, but to the dismay of his men ordered everything in Bremersdorp, including buildings and provisions, to be razed to the ground.[3]

Botha felt that Smuts had dishonoured a promise that he (Botha) had made to the Swazis, and stripped his fellow general and friend, an honourable and much-admired man, of his rank. To Botha, a gentleman's agreement was binding; once he had given a promise, he would not go back on it and expected others to do the same. To his credit, Smuts accepted the decision and remained loyal to Botha to the end of the war. As Meintjes observes, Botha's word of honour meant more to him than any personal attachment and was the key to understanding some of his more contentious decisions in the years ahead.[4]

Last victories

The British were now dead set on bringing the Boer resistance to an end. While Hamilton pursued Botha in the eastern Transvaal, various British commanders were sent after De la Rey in the west. In the Free State, four columns of troops tried to corral De Wet and his men. The elusive Free Stater was actually caught twice and escaped each time, on the second occasion managing to get away in the company of President Steyn. But 800 of his men, including his own son, were captured, along with livestock and wagons. On 4 March, De Wet and Steyn narrowly evaded their pursuers yet again and fled to join De la Rey in the western Transvaal.[5]

One after another, British commanders sent to apprehend the elusive De la Rey returned empty-handed. In late February 1902, at Yzerspruit, south of Klerksdorp, De la Rey ambushed a British column, inflicting heavy losses and helping himself to much-needed supplies. Hearing the news of the Yzerspruit disaster, Lord Methuen unwisely decided to lead a column from his headquarters at Vryburg to Lichtenburg (in the western Transvaal) to intercept De la Rey as his commando headed north.[6]

On 7 March, at the farm Tweebosch, on the Little Harts River, the British army was dealt one of its heaviest defeats in the guerrilla war, losing over 200 men killed or wounded and giving up over 800 prisoners. On hearing that

Methuen himself had been wounded and taken prisoner, De la Rey sent him in his own wagon to seek better medical treatment in Klerksdorp than the Boers were able to provide. Each side then helped the other to clear the dead and wounded from the battlefield. Because the Boers were unable to accommodate so many prisoners, De la Rey ordered that the khakis be given rations and released. Yet, as Bossenbroek reveals, the 'Lion of the West' had also a less chivalrous side. Among those captured were eight Cape coloureds who had rampaged through a Boer farm the night before the battle. They were made to dig a mass grave, then blindfolded and shot.[7] Mercy, one regrets to record, was reserved for white men only.

Negotiations begin

While the fighting carried on into 1902, the air was thick with rumours of peace talks. The Dutch prime minister, Dr Abraham Kuyper, had written to London offering to mediate between the Boers and Britain – a proposal that was formally declined. When Kitchener received copies of the relevant correspondence from London, he forwarded them to Acting President Schalk Burger, who immediately asked for safe passage to the Free State in order to confer with President Steyn. Caught unawares, the Free State leader reacted angrily, but felt he had no choice but to condone Burger's willingness to parley in order to present a united republican front.

Discussions between the two governments began on 9 April at Klerksdorp, in the western Transvaal. Burger, Botha, De la Rey and FW Reitz led the Transvaal delegation, and Steyn, De Wet and Barry Hertzog that of the Free State. It was Botha, supported by Burger, who spoke out most strongly in favour of a negotiated peace, not out of defeatism – he averred – but because he feared the unequal struggle might result in the extinction of Boer-Afrikanerdom.[8] Although Steyn, now crippled by disease and half-blind, had been among the very last in 1899 to consent to war with Britain, he was still opposed to any surrender unless independence for the republics was guaranteed. Despite their differences in approach, the two governments agreed nonetheless to put a set of proposals before Kitchener as a basis for negotiation.

Pretoria's stately Melrose House, built by a wealthy British businessman in 1886 and requisitioned by Roberts to serve as his headquarters, was the venue for the meeting between Kitchener and the Boer delegation. During the talks, Steyn assured Kitchener that the people of both republics sincerely desired peace but were determined also to realise the objective for which his people had fought. Does that mean you wish to retain your independence? a bewildered Kitchener asked, to which Steyn replied, 'Yes, so that the people may not lose their self-respect.'[9] Kitchener could only respond by saying, 'Men who have fought so well cannot lose their self-respect.' Wishing to keep the discussions going, however, he undertook to put the Boer delegation's proposals before the British government.

On Monday 14 April, Kitchener formally advised the Boer representatives that London had turned down their demand for independence, whereupon the discussions resumed but this time with the Boers' archenemy, Lord Milner, in attendance. The Boer leaders told the British they had no mandate to concede independence: according to the constitution of each republic, this was a matter that could only be decided by the people.

Who then were 'the people'? To the Boers, it was obvious: certainly not those Afrikaners who had taken the oath of neutrality or become joiners; they were represented now by the British. Steyn argued vehemently that the only people who could fairly claim to represent the Boer republics were the burghers still fighting in the field. Rather surprisingly, Kitchener and Milner agreed.[10] It was decided, therefore, to adjourn the negotiations until the commandos were able to nominate, from their ranks, 30 delegates from each republic to come together in May, at Vereeniging. Until then, hostilities would continue.[11]

To Vereeniging

The period between the Pretoria and Vereeniging meetings was one of the strangest of the entire war.[12] Consulting burgher commandos scattered across South Africa – in Smuts's case, in the farthest reaches of the northwestern Cape – was no easy task, and Boer messengers had frequently to cross British lines waving flags of truce or carrying safe-conduct passes. Any of these go-betweens who were mistakenly taken prisoner were immediately released. Legend has it that De Wet himself was once mistaken for a messenger and let go before he was identified.[13] Yet, as the two sides drew closer together, the fighting went on: on 11 April at Roodewal, near Lichtenburg, the last significant clash of the war took place between General Kemp's western Transvaal commandos and General Ian Hamilton's 11 000-strong force. The outnumbered Boers came off worst, losing 43 men killed, including Commandant FJ Potgieter, and 50 wounded, against a toll of 12 men dead and 75 wounded on the British side.

On a chilly morning in mid-May, 60 representatives of the Boer people came together in a tented camp on the banks of the Vaal River at Vereeniging. By this time, the constant, unrelenting pressure on the commandos had exacted a severe toll. Kitchener's scorched-earth tactics and blockhouse system, combined with sweeping offensives across the veld, were overwhelming the Boers. The burghers were at the end of their tether, and for many the conclusion of the war could not come soon enough. Deneys Reitz, who had travelled back with Smuts to a meeting of Transvaal commandos prior to Vereeniging, graphically described their plight: '... nothing could have proved more clearly how nearly the Boer cause was spent than these starving, ragged men, clad in skins or sacking, their bodies covered with sores from lack of salt or food ... Their spirit was undaunted but they had reached the limit of physical endurance and we realised that if these haggard, emaciated men were the pick of the Transvaal commandos, then the war must be irretrievably lost.'[14]

On 15 May, the meeting at Vereeniging began with reports from the various commandos of the dire circumstances in which they found themselves. The divisions between Transvalers and Free Staters were as wide as ever, but with one significant difference: President Steyn was too ill to take an active part in the discussions, so the 'bittereinder' (bitter-ender) leaders were slightly less inflexible than usual.[15]

Discussion began in deep earnest on the second day: De Wet spoke briefly in favour of prolonging the conflict until the Boers were forced to surrender (in which case it would be possible to resume hostilities later), but Burger, with Botha's support, argued passionately that it made no sense to go on fighting. 'Can we let the people be annihilated for the sake of honour and fame for ourselves?' he demanded to know.[16]

After listening patiently to many speeches for and against prolonging the war, Botha rose once again to address the meeting, knowing he might be condemned for speaking frankly but determined to tell the truth as he saw it. 'We know that differences of opinion are to be found everywhere and on every question,' he said. 'When, therefore, a man differs from those who think this war can and ought to be continued, we must not ascribe his opinion to discouragement, weakness or cowardice … Whatever our private opinions may be, we must stand together although we differ.'[17]

He then outlined the reasons why the tide had turned against the Boers – the blockhouses and barbed wire, the scarcity of food in the field, the lack of ammunition and the pitiful condition of their horses, and, with the massacre at Holkrans still fresh in the mind, the alarming hostility of the blacks. Warming to his theme, Botha lamented the plight of Boer women and children, of whom nearly 30 000 had already died in the concentration camps, and the shame of those burghers who had gone over to the other side: 'If we continue the war, it may be that the Afrikaners against us will outnumber our own men … so what is there left to hope for? The question for us to answer is this: Are we, after fighting for two years, going forwards or backwards? My own conviction – founded upon the views expressed by my commandos and the speeches I have listened to at this meeting – is that we are not gaining but losing ground. There is nothing in my opinion more evident that during the last six months the tide has been setting steadily against us – in favour of the enemy.'[18]

When Botha sat down, Koos de la Rey got to his feet, with the eyes of every delegate upon him. To their surprise, the indomitable old general had changed his mind, and was now in wholehearted agreement with Botha. De la Rey's words made the deepest impression upon the assembled company: 'It is argued that we must fight to the bitter end. The commandant-general has asked whether that bitter end has arrived. I think each man must decide that for himself. It must be borne in mind that everything – cattle, goods, money, wife and child – has been sacrificed. There are men and women who wear nothing more than plain skins on the naked body. Is not this the bitter end?'[19]

De la Rey's impassioned appeal altered the tenor of the discussions. The next day, it was resolved to send to Pretoria a delegation consisting of Botha, De la Rey and Smuts representing the Transvaal, and De Wet and Hertzog the Free State, to put a set of proposals before Kitchener and Milner. By that night, the delegation was in the former ZAR capital.

To the Boer negotiators at Melrose House, it was clear that the British proconsul and his military commander had entirely different objectives: Milner, the civilian, wanted the war to continue until the Boers were 'begging on their knees', while Kitchener, the warrior, was prepared to concede an honourable peace.[20] Both men were adamant, however, that self-government for the Boers was not negotiable. As the talks threatened to go nowhere, Kitchener made a crucial intervention: without Milner's knowledge, he drew Smuts aside and said that, in his opinion, a Liberal government would come to power in Britain in two years' time and would be more likely than the Tories to grant the Boers their independence.[21]

With this prospect to encourage them, the Boer delegation agreed to reconsider the terms that Kitchener had offered Botha at Middelburg, but with three additional concessions: rebel Afrikaners in the Cape would be given amnesty; financial compensation of £3 million instead of £1 million would be paid; and, crucially, the question of voting rights for Africans and coloureds would be deferred until after self-government had been achieved.[22]

Once these proposals were formally endorsed in London – over Milner's privately expressed reservations – the five Boer leaders returned to Vereeniging on 28 May to consider the ultimatum they had been given: there was to be no more haggling over terms; just a 'yes' or 'no' answer. The commando representatives had three days to decide whether it was to be war or peace.

Three choices

Schalk Burger reopened the discussion by saying the Boers now had one of three choices: to continue the fight; accept the British peace terms; or simply surrender. Smuts and De la Rey spoke in support of Botha, who was in favour of the second option, but the Free Staters continued to hold out. At this point Steyn, shocked at De la Rey's change of heart and saddened at the way the discussions were going, resigned and left the conference, appointing De Wet as acting president and giving him the following advice: 'If the Transvalers should decide to make peace and if you should find it futile to resist any further – then give in. We cannot continue the war with a handful of Free Staters. So we are not to blame. We have fulfilled to the letter our agreement with the sister republic. Without the Transvaal, it would be folly for us to

Boer and British officers at Vereeniging during the peace negotiations, 1902.
Seated are (left to right) General Christiaan de Wet, General Louis Botha,
General Herbert Kitchener and Colonel Ian Hamilton.
In the back row (left to right) are Colonel Henderson, Van Velden, Major Watson,
H Fraser, Captain Maxwell and H de Jager.

PICTORIAL PRESS LTD/ALAMY STOCK PHOTO

continue the struggle on our own.'²³ One of the reasons for Steyn's departure was his unwillingness to put his name to any peace treaty.

Discussions among the delegates continued for two days until early on the morning of 31 May, when Botha and De la Rey went over to De Wet's tent and persuaded him, with time running out, to allow the British proposals to be put to a vote. By now, the conclusion was foregone. That afternoon, 54 delegates voted in favour of peace and only six – three Transvalers and three Free Staters – were against. Amid a deathly silence, Kitchener's representatives, two British officers, were summoned to the tent to be informed by Botha, as spokesman, that the Boers accepted the British government's terms. Shortly before midnight, the formalities at Melrose House were concluded. Schalk Burger was the first to sign on behalf of the Boers, and Milner the last to sign for the British. On 31 May 1902, the Anglo-Boer War came to an end.

The so-called Last Gentleman's War was often that in name only. Though there were acts of courtesy and chivalry on either side, there were numerous incidents that contravened the established rules of warfare: Boers had shot British soldiers, and black people suspected of collaborating, out of hand, while British troops, protected to some extent by martial law, had summarily executed Boers who had donned British uniforms, sometimes because they had no clothes of their own. If truth be told, the Anglo-Boer War was a dirty war, often waged beyond the control of military high-ups, and it found the African and coloured people caught in the middle.[24] Rayne Kruger summed it up succinctly: 'The Boers said the war was for liberty. The British said it was for equality. The majority of the inhabitants ... gained neither liberty nor equality.'[25]

*

Louis Botha's conduct at Vereeniging drew praise from all sides, even from those who, like Ds JD Kestell and JBM Hertzog, did not agree with him. Hertzog, later to become his most bitter political enemy, said this of Botha: 'I shall always respect Commandant-General Louis Botha; for he has shown himself to be possessed of a heart that feels all these things (the brunt of the war), while he has the courage to tell his people, and us, exactly how matters stand.'[26]

Many of the Boer leaders at Vereeniging could not face having to return to their commandos to explain that, after so much suffering, the republics had lost their independence. Botha was not among them. Addressing his men on a hillside near Vryheid, he expressed his gratitude for their faithful service. 'It oppresses me that I can do nothing else for any of you, and that I can give no more than thanks,' he said. 'One consolation remains to all of you: you can go now and rest a little. As for me, my real work only begins at this hour. The day when rest will be mine, will be the day when they lower me into the grave. The sacrifices we had to make were terrific; but we are going to see a greater South Africa.'[27]

CHAPTER 13

DEALING WITH MILNER

Scars of war

On the last afternoon at Vereeniging, Botha won approval for a delegation of himself, De la Rey and De Wet to travel to Britain and Europe to raise money for the post-war reconstruction of the ravaged republics. In Spender's words, they were going to London 'with a touch of that rather pathetic faith in the central power which brought the citizens of Ancient Rome to Caesar'.[1] On the Continent especially, the three hopefuls were to be give a lesson in realpolitik.

Before leaving, Botha had to settle several unresolved matters with the governor of the Transvaal, his *bête noire*, Lord Milner. These included the surrender of Boer arms and ammunition, the repatriation of prisoners of war from St Helena and Ceylon, and the disbanding of the concentration camps. He also had to visit Standerton in order to recover his farm Varkplaas, now renamed Rusthof, which was to become his new family home.

In a public speech in Durban, he raised eyebrows among Afrikaners by openly declaring his faith in a better future for South Africa as part of the British Empire. His visit to the city enabled him to reunite with his scattered family, which had suffered grievously during the war: two of his sisters had been ejected from their burning farmsteads at a moment's notice and a sister-in-law and her children had experienced the agonies of life in a concentration camp. His eldest brother, Philip, had died of his wounds in the war; another brother, Chris, was alive but stricken with a fatal disease; and his youngest brother, Theunis, had been a prisoner of war on St Helena. Annie was still away in Europe, with their two baby sons, one of whom he had not yet seen.

Despite their despondency, Botha and Burger issued a heartfelt joint appeal to the Boer-Afrikaner people: 'Let us now take each other by the hand for the other great battle which lies ahead of us, the well-being of our people, and set aside all feelings of bitterness, and let us learn to forget and to forgive so that the deep scars made by this war may eventually be healed.'[2]

On either side, these scars ran deep. A conflict that the British had predicted would be over by Christmas of 1899 and cost an estimated £10 million had lasted for almost three years and cost almost £220 million – 12 per cent, in 1900, of Britain's GNP.[3] From beginning to end, Britain had deployed some 450 000 troops in South Africa,[4] against 60 000 to 70 000 burghers in the field. At least 22 000 British, 34 000 Boer and more than 15 000 black lives had been lost. On the Boer side, the losses and damage to infrastructure, homesteads, farms, livestock – and to Afrikaner self-esteem – were incalculable. Around 230 000 whites and blacks had been interned in the concentration camps, of whom more than 46 000 are known to have died.[5]

Pleading for help

On 30 July 1902, the three Boer leaders – dubbed the 'Glorious Trio' by the popular press – set sail for Britain aboard the RMS *Saxon*, fortified by a rousing send-off from cheering crowds in Cape Town. Accompanying his father was the ten-year-old Louis Botha, who, after 18 months on commando, was used to running wild, and had to be handed over to De la Rey to be kept in check. To while away the long hours on board, Botha played bridge and deck quoits and De la Rey played draughts, while De Wet remained in his cabin for most of the voyage writing his war memoirs.[6]

The Boers' brave fight had captured the British public's imagination, and the excited crowd gathered at the dockside in Southampton on 16 August gave a welcoming roar to the three generals as they disembarked onto English soil. The Anglo-Boer War had been the first war to be systematically captured by movie cameramen,[7] and the Glorious Trio's visit to Europe featured in 'bioscopes' throughout the UK and South Africa in 1903.[8] (Four years earlier, the film *Savage South Africa,* modelled on Buffalo Bill's Wild West, was the prime attraction at the Greater Britain Exposition at Earl's Court.) A decade later, Louis Botha was one of the first South Africa politicians whose profile was much enhanced by cinema newsreels, especially the 'African Mirror', produced monthly from 1913 by the American IW Schlesinger's African Theatres Trust.[9]

On arrival in England, Botha received the sad news of the death of his old mentor and friend, Lucas Meyer, in Belgium a few days earlier. Depressed by the news, he and his two companions declined the invitation of Lords Roberts and Kitchener to attend the spectacular Coronation Naval Review at nearby Spithead, and departed by train for London, where they were met by throngs of curious spectators at Waterloo Station and outside their hotel off the Strand. A day or two later, they were taken by special train and carriage down to Cowes for a secret – and extremely cordial – meeting with King Edward VII aboard the royal yacht.[10]

Departing England in pouring rain after a short stay, the trio were unprepared for the near-hysteria that greeted them on their arrival in the Netherlands. The British were not popular on the Continent, where there was strong opposition to any expansion of their Empire. At The Hague, Botha had to stress rather pointedly, 'We have not come here to rejoice. We are the delegates of a most unhappy people; and we are unhappy because we have done our duty; because we have defended our liberty and our independence.'[11]

While in Europe, Botha launched an emotional appeal 'to the civilised world' for money for Boer widows and orphans, in words that gave grave offence to the colonial secretary, Joseph Chamberlain: 'Our dwellings, with the furniture, have been burned or destroyed, our orchards felled, all agricultural implements broken up, mills destroyed, every living animal driven off or killed – nothing, alas! was left to us. The land is a desert. Besides the war has claimed many victims, and the land resounds with the weeping of helpless widows and orphans.'[12]

Botha's purpose in paying a quick visit to the Netherlands and Belgium was primarily for a joyful reunion with Annie and their young children, as well as to attend Lucas Meyer's funeral and consult with President Kruger before returning to England to meet Chamberlain at the Colonial Office. The meeting with Kruger, by all accounts, was harmonious, despite mischievous attempts by the popular British press to suggest that the old president had upbraided Botha for signing away the independence of the Transvaal.[13]

On their return to London, the trio ran into an uncompromising colonial secretary, peeved not only by their enthusiastic reception but also by virulent attacks on him by pro-Boer quarters in England. In response to reports from Europe that the peace terms at Vereeniging might be revised, a studiously polite Chamberlain offered the visitors a few minor concessions but flatly refused to consider an increase in the miserly amount of £3 million he had promised by way of compensation.[14]

From London, the three Boer generals returned to the Continent to continue their fundraising efforts, meeting as usual with much sympathy but little by way of financial help: European governments and financiers took the view that rebuilding the Boer republics was the wealthy Empire's responsibility, not theirs. As they were now British subjects, the Glorious Trio had to mind their public utterances so as not to cause undue offence to their new masters.

Good wishes, but little else

At times, Botha allowed his emotions to get the better of him. In Brussels, he declared bitterly: 'We have come to understand the tactics of our enemies. They used two: first their concentration camps and then the burning of farms and the devastation of the country. Alas, we did everything to preserve our independence, but how could we resist a people who had decided to exterminate our race? The commandants said they could not leave their men to die of hunger, and the women of misery; and they preferred the peace which was offered them to certain death. I have no heart to speak long of the sufferings we have endured …'[15]

In late October, laden with good wishes, honours and encouragement, but very little money (about £103 000), the trio returned to London, where an article under Botha's name in *The Contemporary Review* of 1 November attracted widespread attention. In it, Botha argued that Britain's interests would be best served by being generous in rebuilding the former Boer republics. It made no sense, he claimed, for Britain to spend large sums on keeping troops in South Africa when she should rather be financing reconstruction. No colony, he pointed out, could be governed against the wishes of the population. His advice to the British government was to help the Boers, 'not simply as an act of humanity, but as a matter of high policy'.[16]

His message fell on receptive ears. Five days later, Botha listened from the gallery of the House of Commons as Chamberlain proposed that the cost of liquidating the war should be increased from £3 to £8 million and announced his intention of visiting South Africa in order to see whether that sum would suffice. The increase in compensation was approved unanimously, so the Glorious Trio's visit to Britain, at least, had not been entirely in vain.[17]

The stress and tension of the previous few months had taken their toll on Botha, who fell ill and postponed his return trip to South Africa. His convalescence allowed him to meet leading British politicians, among them the Liberal politician David Lloyd George and the Liberal Party leader, Sir Henry Campbell-Bannerman. He also took De la Rey and De Wet along with him to call on the King, who invited them to dinner at Buckingham Palace. Edward VII had come to admire the Boers, and was aware that he would need their loyalty in the future. He offered each of the trio a knighthood, an offer that was politely but firmly declined. On 13 December, the trio boarded a ship bound for the Cape, to prepare for the arrival of Joseph Chamberlain, making the first-ever visit to an imperial outpost by a colonial secretary.[18]

Need for unity

The long voyage home gave Botha time to reflect on the role he had been called upon to play in the public life of the Transvaal colony. With Kruger in exile, he had become, at the age of only 40, the de facto leader of his people. An optimist by inclination, he believed – or persuaded himself – that out of the devastation and destruction of the past something positive might emerge. But that would require, above all, the unification of the white population of South Africa. A united South Africa, in turn, would need the protection and economic support that only a great power such as Britain could provide. Having entered into a binding agreement with the imperial government, the Afrikaner – and in time all the inhabitants of South Africa – could derive undreamt-of benefits from membership of the Empire. Bearing no deep-seated animosity towards the British himself, Botha tended, most unfortunately for him, to underestimate the strength of anti-British feeling among many of his fellow Boer-Afrikaners.

He sorely needed allies to help persuade others of the advantages of the imperial link, and in Koos de la Rey and the brilliant Jan Smuts he had two strong-minded men he could rely on. While abroad, Botha had kept in touch with Smuts by letter, and as soon as he was back in Pretoria, he called on him to help with preparations for Chamberlain's visit. Downcast and disillusioned after the war, Smuts was sorely in need of a new challenge and a new leader to follow. 'He had fallen in behind Rhodes, and then behind Kruger. Now he fell in behind Botha,' wrote HC Armstrong.[19]

The singular political partnership that grew up between these two former Boer generals was to last until Botha's premature death 17 years later, 'reinforced, amidst all the stresses and of that creative and harrowing time, by bonds of mutual trust, loyalty and love such as seldom, if ever, united two political leaders'. The two men complemented each other perfectly. Smuts, introverted and cerebral, excelled at putting pen to paper, while the more outgoing and emotional Botha was less inclined to do so. Smuts was a better debater and public speaker, but Botha also had a first-class political brain and a much easier rapport with people. The pair's modus operandi while in office, Hancock writes, was first a discussion, followed by a draft produced by Smuts, then further discussion, after which Smuts would prepare a document for Botha's signature. During the Milner administration, there was scarcely a memorandum or document signed by Botha that Smuts had not been asked to draft for him.[20]

An arrogant visitor

Joseph Chamberlain arrived in Durban on 26 December 1903 and was soon up in Pretoria to meet a 100-strong delegation of Boer-Afrikaners, led by Botha, with Smuts as the spokesman. Botha was determined to be pleasant to the visitor, knowing that 'Foxy Joe' and his fellow Conservatives were likely to be out of power before long. Smuts, on the other hand, took an instant dislike to Chamberlain, who refused to countenance any further changes to the terms agreed at Vereeniging. The colonial secretary's 'line of reply' to the list of Boer grievances, Smuts complained in a letter to a friend in England, had been 'insulting'.[21]

Chamberlain showed no inclination, during his short sojourn, to interfere with Milner's administrative methods or arrangements. He did agree, however, to underwrite a £35 million loan from the mining companies to rebuild the infrastructure of the Transvaal and Free State, as a quid pro quo for permitting the mine owners to import Chinese workers to replace the inadequate supply of 'native' labour on the mines.[22] Their opposition to the prospect of adding another foreign element to South Africa's already troubled racial mix was one of several reasons for Botha, Smuts and De la Rey to turn down an invitation from Milner, at Chamberlain's request, to take a seat on the colony's new Legislative Council. Despite a tempting salary of £500, the trio had little hesitation in declining to join what they regarded as an ornamental body and no substitute for proper responsible government. Botha maintained his opposition to the nominated legislature for the next two years: he wanted no part of any government that had not been properly elected.[23]

The colonial secretary eventually departed for home, leaving his unpopular proconsul in sole charge of post-war reconstruction in South Africa. Among Milner's immediate priorities was the repatriation of more than 150 000 Boer prisoners of war and inmates of concentration camps, the resettlement of 100 000 blacks from the camps, as well as the restoration of the railway network. To assist him, he brought in a group of brilliant young graduates from Oxford University, including Patrick Duncan, Lionel Curtis, John Buchan and Geoffrey Dawson. The group, which was dubbed 'Milner's Kindergarten', was to make a significant contribution to the rebuilding of South Africa.

It was not only the Boers who found Milner's dictatorial style of government irksome, however. Returning Uitlanders, many of whom knew the Transvaal far better than Milner, and who still thought the war had been fought for their benefit, had little time for his 'benevolent autocracy' and were impatient for the spoils – and public preferments – of 'victory'. As their gratitude to the British government gradually diminished, they began to castigate the Milner administration for being 'expensive, wasteful, aloof and over-regulating'.[24]

On the stoep

Quietly, Botha bided his time. When not at Rusthof, he lodged in a boarding house in Pretoria and then in a house of his own, purchased with a loan from the mining magnate Abe Bailey. As in Kruger's day, his front stoep became the meeting place of a constant stream of callers – widows, orphans, unemployed and disabled soldiers – to whom he offered a sympathetic ear, guidance, counsel and financial assistance from the funds collected in Europe.

AR Colquhoun, who was to become the first administrator of Southern Rhodesia (today Zimbabwe), gave this lively but rather churlish and not entirely accurate portrayal of Botha in 1904–1905: 'An eloquent speaker in Dutch, he is in touch with European thought, and is as far removed from the "peasant farmer" type in mind as he is in appearance. He is a great ally of the Dutch Reformed Synod, and is constantly called on to perform such services as laying foundation stones. His faults are curiously un-Boer-like. He talks a great deal in public, being apparently unable to resist the temptation to make a speech; he is a little too anxious to fill the public eye. One is constantly reminded that he is practically a *parvenu* in politics having gained his present position as leader of the Boers chiefly by the elimination of stronger personalities during the war.'[25]

There was great indignation on the stoep, and among Boer-Afrikaners generally, as the governor's true intentions became transparent. Besides encouraging immigration to South Africa in the hope that Englishmen would eventually outnumber Afrikaners, and implementing measures to 'anglicise' the civil service, Milner foolishly insisted that English rather than Dutch should be the medium of instruction in state schools. These measures – particularly the last-mentioned – struck a highly sensitive nerve: military defeat by the British was now to be followed by cultural domination.

Milner's unpopularity among Afrikaners obscured many of his administration's positive achievements, most notably in redeveloping agriculture – a matter dear to Botha's heart.[26] However, Milner had been operating on the mistaken assumption that the end of the war would bring about an economic boom in the Transvaal. Instead, the opposite occurred: drought, a weak gold price and popular discontent conspired to cause a slump. Under pressure from the powerful mining interests, an increasingly desperate Milner – although aware of the political risks – gave his assent to the plan to import several thousand indentured Chinese labourers in order to lower production costs on the mines. In so doing, he hastened his own recall from South Africa, and gave Botha and Smuts the political opportunity they had been waiting for.

CHAPTER 14

INTO POLITICS AGAIN

Rebuilding

While tending as best he could to the needs of his people, Botha also had to attend to his own finances, much depleted after nearly three years of war. Under the new British administration, the Vryheid district had been returned to Natal from the Transvaal, and he and his wife no longer had any desire to go back to their once cherished but now ruined farm, Waterval. His claim for compensation for losses incurred in the war came to £20 000; when he was awarded only £900, he sent the cheque back in disgust.

Botha was now a true Transvaler, and Rusthof was the new family home. As a pre-war landowner, he was able to borrow money to re-establish a farming business, and eventually to grow his land holdings in the Standerton district to a sizeable 10 000 acres (over 4 000 hectares). Physically still full of energy, he bought up quantities of the barbed wire the British army had brought with them, made fences out of it and stocked his paddocks with cattle and horses of the best quality. Having the Platrand railway station on a neighbouring property was a help, as he was able to send milk and produce by train to Johannesburg every day, and before long his farming enterprise was profitable. He planted trees, built dams and together with Annie erected another large and comfortable sandstone farmhouse on Rusthof.

Botha was also able to indulge his speculative bent, buying and selling properties at a profit. According to his friend and biographer, FV Engelenburg, had he not had such a deep concern for the future of his people, he could have become extremely rich. In politics, his business acumen combined with his leadership experience to give him advantages that most of his opponents simply did not possess.[1] (While Botha was comfortably off, a life in politics prevented him from accumulating great wealth. Married in community of property, on his death he left an estate valued at £67648.[2])

When, during 1903, it became apparent that Milner was intent on allowing Chinese labour into the Transvaal to work on the mines, Botha decided it was time to re-enter the political arena. Earlier, he had undertaken to give the governor notice of his political intentions, and this he duly did in a letter drafted by Smuts, in which he said he would be failing in his duty if he did not give his fellow burghers an opportunity to express their views about some of the important issues of the time – among them mine labour, the status of coloured people and education. 'We therefore propose to hold some meetings at the more important centres during this and the following months ...' he told Milner.[3]

The first of these meetings was held at Heidelberg on 2 July 1903. Three resolutions were passed: the first denounced the plan to import Chinese labour as 'a capitalist plot'; the second demanded equality of Dutch with English, especially in schools; and the third protested the imposition of a debt upon the Transvaal without legislative consent – 'no taxation without representation'. In Hancock's words, this was 'the first fusillade in the fight for self-government'.[4]

Also present at the Heidelberg meeting was Emily Hobhouse, the doughty Englishwoman who had become a heroine to the Boers for her campaign against conditions in the concentration camps. Seated on a white horse, Botha caught the attention of every eye as he led an entourage of eight generals, a posse of mounted men and a cavalcade of conveyances and people on foot into the market square. The mood was sombre, and the British visitor was deeply moved by the dignity of the occasion and the sight of so many impoverished burghers listening intently to their former commandant-general. After the meeting, Botha invited his audience to a garden party, at which they were able to meet the celebrated Miss Hobhouse in person.[5]

Alien Chinese

To Botha and his fellow Afrikaners, the introduction of thousands of unmarried Chinese – with their alien customs, inability to speak a European language and need for special food – herded together in semi-confinement and sending their earnings out of the country, was an exercise in folly. He was well aware of the economic importance of the gold-mining industry – it had been he, after all, who had protected the mines during the war – but, after his past experience of the rapid growth in Indian numbers in Natal, he was far more concerned about further complicating 'the racial tangle'[6] in South Africa than the short-term profitability of the mines.

In September, he wrote formally to Milner's labour committee to assert that the shortage of black labour on the mines was a temporary problem requiring a less risky remedy than the importing of Chinese workers. He and Smuts went to see the governor to persuade him of the strength of Afrikaner opposition to the plan, but the obdurate Milner, under severe pressure from the mine owners, would not pay heed. By the end of 1903, the beleaguered governor was under attack from both Afrikaners and Uitlanders: to the former, 'Milnerism' had become the epitome of British oppression and his 'Chinese cure' the defining issue of his governorship.

In February 1904, 15 prominent Boer-Afrikaner leaders in the Transvaal, among them Botha, Burger, De la Rey and Smuts, sent a cable to the new colonial secretary, Alfred Lyttelton, protesting at Milner's plan to bring in the Chinese. When Lyttelton tactlessly replied that he could not accept their claim to represent Transvaal Boer opinion, Botha realised the moment had come to mobilise and form a new political party.[7]

On 12 February 1904, the Transvaal's Legislative Council passed the necessary ordinance and soon Chinese labourers began arriving in droves to work on the mines. (By July, their number had reached almost 50 000.) To Botha, Smuts and company, the dismissive attitude of the Colonial Office and the governor to their representations was an insult. A conference of burghers at Fordsburg was followed by a three-day convention of 160 people in Pretoria, where a committee, steered by Botha and including Smuts, was appointed to lay the foundations for a new party. Six months later, Het Volk (The People) was formally established on the premises of the newspaper *De Volksstem* in Pretoria.[8]

The death of Kruger

On 14 July 1904, President Kruger died at Clarens, on Lake Geneva, in Switzerland. At the end of the war, the old patriarch had been prevailed upon by the Glorious Trio to remain in exile. Besides not wishing to subject himself to British rule again, the wily Kruger knew how helpful the image of a tired and lonely father-figure, kept apart from his people against his wishes, might be to the reawakening of Afrikanerdom.[9] His last advice to his *volk* (people) was a message to Botha and the nascent Het Volk movement: 'He who wishes to create the future must not lose track of the past … Seek all that is to be found good in the past, shape your ideal accordingly and try to realise that ideal for the future … Never forget the grave warning in the words "divide and rule" and never let it be applied to the Afrikaner people.'[10]

Now recognised, by common consent, as the Boer leader upon whom Kruger's mantle had descended and the personification of Afrikanerdom's rebirth after the war, Botha took personal charge of arrangements for the old president's funeral. Queen Wilhelmina again came to the Boers' assistance by providing a ship to carry Kruger's body back home, and Botha himself accompanied the funeral train on its 1600-kilometre journey from the Cape to Pretoria, stopping along the way wherever crowds of people gathered to pay homage to their fallen leader. At the funeral, leading Kruger's cortege through the streets of Pretoria, along which the Vierkleur fluttered, were the Boer heroes made famous by the war – Botha, Schalk Burger, Koos de la Rey and Christiaan de Wet. According to Meintjes, 'the emotion unleashed [at the funeral] contributed to an awakening of Afrikaner nationalism which cannot be exaggerated'.[11]

Growing in stature

Botha's stature among his fellow whites at the time is well described by Smuts's biographer, HC Armstrong: 'He lived spaciously, all his doors open, and to him came everyone who wanted advice or was suffering under a grievance. And like Kruger, and with some of Kruger's patriarchal benevolence, Botha received them all. He had time to spare for everyone. The stoep of his house was always crowded with men and women, mainly ruined farmers from the veld, with their children, who came for help and trusted Botha with a pathetic trustful helplessness. He had the art moreover, even if he had to send them away, of being able to make them feel they had gained everything by coming to see him.'[12]

Het Volk set out to be a party of conciliation and coexistence between former enemies, its primary aim the forging of unity among whites. To Botha, however, reconciliation entailed much more than merely rebuilding relations between Boers and Britons: it required also the healing of the bitter rift within Boer-Afrikaner ranks between those who had fought for independence and those who had given up the battle or (like Christiaan de Wet's own brother) gone over to the enemy's side. Overlooking and forgiving the activities of the hensoppers and the National Scouts must have been extremely difficult for any Boer general, and it is a measure of Botha's far-sightedness and generosity of spirit that he was able to prevent his own resentment from getting in the way of what he perceived to be the Afrikaner people's long-term interests.[13]

At the founding congress of Het Volk, he said the following: 'Let us put back the past so far that it no longer has any power to keep us apart. Less than a year ago we were in opposite camps – we of the same house passed each other without a handshake. Tonight we are gathered in order to consider the fortunes of one and all ... Let us do all we can to heal the breach, then we shall again become great. Let the name of "Handsupper" and "National Scout" be excised from our vocabulary. The honour of the people is too great and delicate to be tarnished by such stains.'[14]

Though the response of the delegates was decidedly unenthusiastic, one of those who nodded his approval was Koos de la Rey.[15]

Mutual dislike

Het Volk's core demand was self-government, not only for the Transvaal but also for the Orange River Colony, where a similar political movement, the Orangia Unie, was launched in July 1905. The latter's co-founders were ex-president Steyn, Abraham Fischer, Christiaan de Wet and the man soon to emerge as Botha's bitterest political opponent, the Free State's legal representative at Vereeniging, JBM (Barry) Hertzog.

Hertzog, like Smuts, was Cape-born and had been educated at Victoria College (Stellenbosch), but, unlike Smuts, had furthered his law studies in Amsterdam (rather than Cambridge). His family had moved to the Orange Free State when he was a lad, and before the age of 30 he had become a judge.

He was legal adviser to Steyn and De Wet during the Anglo-Boer War, and was a Boer general in his own right.

Intellectually, Hertzog was of a similar bent to Smuts, whom he always respected even though they differed politically for most of their lives. But he had a visceral dislike, unfortunately, of Botha, and his ill-feeling was warmly reciprocated by the older man. Botha's vision of the future was of a united white South Africa in which it did not matter whether one was Afrikaner or English. Hertzog's vision was much narrower: a country in which both white races lived side by side while retaining their separate identities, languages and cultures. Hertzog was a much better hater than Botha, and the two men, both patriots who loved their country, grew to regard each other with loathing. (Years later, in September 1919, Governor-General Sidney Buxton wrote to Milner, by then colonial secretary, noting that Hertzog remained very bitter about Botha to the end of the latter's life: 'It is notable that since he has returned (he did not return in time for the Vote of Condolence) he [Hertzog] has not said one word either inside or outside the House in reference to Botha's death. He was a brother in arms during the war, a joint signatory at Vereeniging and for two years, a member of Botha's cabinet.'[16])

As Meintjes reflects, if only Hertzog and Botha had been able to work together, the nascent South Africa would have benefited immeasurably. 'But the Afrikaner is an individualist,' writes Meintjes, himself an Afrikaner, 'who does not easily bow the knee to anyone, and once there is suspicion and personalities have clashed [as they did at Vereeniging], he finds it easier to break away than to make friends. It underlies much of Boer history, the breaking away, the founding of new republics, the trekking on ...'[17]

Botha continued to vex Hertzog and his Free Staters with his frequent appeals to whites to reach out to one another in a spirit of unity. On one occasion, he declared: 'My sincere hope is that it may please the Omnipotent Father to imbue with unanimity all the white inhabitants of South Africa, so that one nation may arise from them fit to occupy a position of dignity among the nations of the world, where the name of Boer will be greeted with honour and applause.'[18] On another occasion, he said, 'Forget that there are two races – in order to combine in one nationality.' To Afrikaners like Hertzog, exhortations such as these were anathema.

The Lyttelton constitution

Sensing that the Liberal Party in Britain might soon win power and grant self-government to the former Boer colonies, Milner conspired with the colonial secretary, Lyttelton, to foist a new constitution on the Transvaal, which made provision for a form of limited representative government under Milner's guidance. The Lyttelton constitution came into formal existence on 31 March 1905, but was never to be implemented because opposition to it was so strong. Het Volk forged links with the most prominent grouping of English-speakers, the Responsible Government Association, to ensure that the constitution was never put into effect. The agreement that was struck between the two sides, however, required concessions from Het Volk in the Transvaal that were never demanded of Orangia Unie, in particular on the sensitive question of language policy in schools. Yet on key issues, such as the vote being limited to white males only and the demand for full self-government, the two parties were as one.

By then, Milner had come to realise that he had outstayed his time in South Africa and sailed home to England, to be replaced as governor by Lord Selborne, a more conciliatory Conservative aristocrat who shared Botha's interest in land affairs and farming.[19] The departing proconsul remained convinced that Britain was asking for trouble by granting self-government to the Boers. To a friend, Sir HF Wilson, he wrote: 'From my point of view, all that has happened during the past eighteen months is wholly deplorable. People here – not only liberals – seem delighted and think themselves wonderfully fine fellows to have given South Africa back to the Boers. I think it all sheer lunacy.'[20]

CHAPTER 15

COMING TO POWER

Labour shortage

If Botha and Smuts had foreseen the benefits of the temporary importation of Chinese workers into the Transvaal, they might not have been so vehement in their denunciation of the Milner administration's plan. Politically, the fallout that reverberated around Britain over the 'slave-like' conditions imposed on the indentured Chinese helped to bring the Liberals to power there in 1905, thereby hastening the advent of self-government for the two former Boer republics two years later. Economically, Chinese labour helped to restore profitability to the mines. However, there was a high price to be paid in social costs for both the Transvaal and the unfortunate Chinese.

The war had driven some 129 000 unskilled black mineworkers out of the Witwatersrand into the rural areas, and gold production had dropped dramatically. If the devastated colony was to recover economically, the gold mines had to become productive as quickly as possible. An important reason for unskilled worker dissatisfaction was that monthly wages had fallen during the war years from 43 shillings to 30. So the quickest and most expedient way for the Milner administration to reduce the manpower deficit was to allow the mine owners to seek alternative sources of cheap labour.

The solution was found in Asia, where the Russo-Japanese War of 1904–1905 had driven poverty-stricken agricultural workers out of their jobs in Manchuria. Recruited by the Chinese Engineering and Mining Corporation – among whose directors was one Herbert Hoover, later to become the 31st president of the US – almost 64 000 labourers were brought to South Africa on three-year contracts between 1904 and 1906.[1]

'Chinese slavery'

Working conditions for the Chinese labourers were abysmal: confined to poorly equipped mine compounds, they were handed the most difficult and dangerous jobs on the underground stopes, and given stiff punishments – including floggings, fines and imprisonment – should their productivity drop. Their resistance to these dire circumstances took the form of desertion and, occasionally, violent crime, which the authorities had difficulty containing.

In the British election of 1905, Campbell-Bannerman's Liberal Party raised the cry of 'Chinese slavery' in a British colony under Conservative rule to damaging effect. Former colonial secretary Joseph Chamberlain went so far as to ascribe his party's loss at the polls not so much to such factors as post-war exhaustion or taxes or tariff reform as to the plight of Chinese workers on South African mines.[2]

Although the cost of imported Chinese labour, including recruitment charges and transport, was actually higher than that of employing Africans, the skill of the Chinese in mining lower-grade ore at ever-deeper levels, as well as the lower price of dynamite now that Kruger's monopoly had ended, helped to restore the mines rapidly to profitability. Black labour began to flow back to the Witwatersrand and by 1906 the mines were in full production again, providing employment for 18 000 whites, 51 000 Chinese and 94 000 Africans. Gold output had gone up in value from £12.6 million in 1903 to £27.4 million in 1907, while South Africa's share of global output had risen to 32.32 per cent.[3] The Transvaal could now claim to have the most productive gold mines in the world.

Notwithstanding this marked improvement in mineral output, Boer-Afrikaner resentment of the Chinese presence continued to simmer, and in due course brought the exercise to an end. Yet the impact of the Chinese on developments in South Africa was dramatic and far-reaching. In Sarah Gertrude Millin's opinion, besides driving the Conservatives out of power in Britain, these migrant workers brought forward the granting of independence to the Transvaal (followed by the Free State). Not only did the Chinese change the fortunes of parties and people, she wrote, 'they changed the fate of South Africa and perhaps even of the British Empire ...'[4]

Smuts in London

The new Liberal government in Britain had barely settled into office before Smuts was in London, sent by Het Volk in early 1906 to press the case for responsible government for the former Boer republics. After a cordial meeting with Winston Churchill, during which the newly appointed under-secretary of state for the colonies inquired of his visitor whether he had ever heard of a conquered people being given back their country so quickly, Smuts presented Churchill with a memorandum, approved by Botha and entitled 'Points in Reference to the Transvaal Constitution', for consideration by the British cabinet. Smuts went on to several other Liberal luminaries, among them Lloyd George and the prime minister, Henry Campbell-Bannerman. A second meeting with Campbell-Bannerman shortly before Smuts left for home was to alter the course of South African history: 'I put a simple case before him that night in 10 Downing Street,' Smuts recorded later. 'It was in substance: do you want friends or enemies? You can have the Boers for friends and they have proved what quality their friendship may mean. I pledge the friendship of my colleagues and myself if you wish it. You can choose to make them enemies, and possibly have another Ireland on your hands. If you do believe in liberty, it is also their faith and their religion. I used no set arguments but simply spoke to him as man to man, and appealed only to the human aspect which I felt would weigh deeply with him.'[5]

'I could see Campbell-Bannerman was listening sympathetically,' Smuts told his biographer and friend, Sarah Gertrude Millin. 'Without being brilliant, he was the sort of sane personality – large-hearted and honest – on whom people depend. He reminded me of Botha. Such men get things done. He told me there was to be a cabinet meeting [the] next day and he said, "Smuts, you have convinced me."' 'That talk,' said Smuts, 'settled the future of South Africa.'[6]

At a meeting of the British cabinet the next day, 8 February, in an address described by Lloyd George as the 'most dramatic, the most important ten-minute speech ever delivered in our time',[7] Campbell-Bannerman persuaded his col-leagues to set aside their fears and place their trust in the Boers. The cabinet decided there and then to revoke the Lyttelton constitution and send a royal commission to Pretoria to settle the question of responsible government without delay. Kitchener's pre-Vereeniging prediction to Smuts that the Liberals would be more sympathetic to the Boer cause than the Conservatives had proved prescient.

Botha, as might be expected, was euphoric at the British government's decision. For the rest of his life, both he and Smuts felt indebted to Campbell-Bannerman, who did not live long enough to savour the outcome of his magnanimity. On the British premier's untimely death in 1908, Botha sent the following cable to London: 'Have learnt with deepest sorrow of the passing of C-B, in whom the Empire loses one of its wisest statesmen and the Transvaal one of its truest friends. In securing self-government for the new colonies, he not only raised an imperishable monument to himself, but through the policy of trust he inspired the people of South Africa with a new feeling of hopefulness and co-operation. In making it possible for the two races to live and work together harmoniously, he has laid the foundation of a united South Africa.'[8]

Revisionist historians of Empire now regard Campbell-Bannerman's decision as more of a party-political tactic than a generous gesture. According to Ronald Hyam, 'the clue to Liberal policy was expediency, not magnanimity, and it was put into effect by a gamble rather than a gesture'.[9] That view finds support from Hermann Giliomee, who asserts that the Liberals were eager to extricate themselves from the mess of Milner's Chinese labour policy and happy to have Britain's vital interests in South Africa secured without having to dominate the region.[10]

Ridgeway Commission

The royal commission, led by Sir Joseph West Ridgeway, sent out to prepare the ground for an election in the Transvaal, began its work in May 1906. Delimitation – the fair apportionment of seats between urban and rural constituencies – was the main issue to be settled. Botha, who brought Smuts along as interpreter to meetings with the commission, did not have high hopes of Ridgeway and was not surprised when his commissioners produced a constitution designed to ensure 'a British majority but not a mining majority'.[11] He and Smuts had other ideas, needless to say, and took to the hustings without further delay.

Four parties contested the February 1907 election for the Transvaal's new Legislative Assembly: Het Volk; two pro-British parties – the 'Responsibles' led by Milner's attorney general, Sir Richard Solomon, and the 'Progressives', led nominally by mining leader Sir George Farrar but spearheaded by the energetic Percy FitzPatrick – and a minor party representing white labour interests. Two issues were uppermost during the campaign: British 'domination' and Chinese labour.[12]

Realising that Het Volk would need the support of English-speakers, Botha toured the *platteland* (country districts) preaching a message of reconciliation and goodwill between the two white groups. Now able to travel by motorcar, he spoke in town after town and in most constituencies.[13] Often with him on the campaign trail was the revered Oom Koos de la Rey, who trusted Botha implicitly and believed – mistakenly, as it turned out – that his former military commander shared his ideal of an independent republic, free of Britain's yoke.

Success at the polls

Back in 1905, Botha had shrewdly concluded an electoral pact with Solomon's pro-self-government Responsibles, whereby Het Volk undertook to tone down its opposition to Chinese labour on condition the Responsibles withdrew their support for Milner's education policy, and accepted the restriction of the franchise to white males. The more die-hard of the pro-British parties, the Progressives, on the other hand, warned against the dangers of Boer domination and campaigned for closer imperial ties.

Despite the efforts of the Ridgeway Commission to be fair but also to produce an election result favourable to British interests, precisely the opposite occurred.[14] Het Volk took 37 seats, giving it an absolute majority in the new legislature over the Progressives (21 seats), the Responsibles (6 seats) and Labour (3 seats). Botha himself stood for election in Standerton and easily won the seat against a young English farmer. Many moderate English-speakers, tired of racial divisions, declined to 'vote British' and gave their support to Het Volk instead. Despite the party's unexpectedly good showing, however, the governor, Lord Selborne, saw fit to appoint a majority of Progressives to the new upper house, the Senate.[15]

The election result gave Selborne no choice but to send for Louis Botha and invite him to form a government. Het Volk's victory 'restored supremacy to the Boers, less than five years after a war fought with the avowed object of wresting that supremacy from them'.[16] There had been some talk of the hard-working Smuts becoming premier, but he stood back in favour of Botha, aware that Het Volk's performance was largely due to the popularity of its leader. As Smuts wrote to the party organ, *Die Volksstem*, in support of an appeal for funds to make a special presentation to Botha: 'I agree that no one more than General Botha is entitled to gratitude and recognition. The victory of the people's party at the polls is chiefly due to his never-flagging endeavours, which began on the day peace was proclaimed, in the cause of welding the inhabitants of the Transvaal into a compact, lasting organisation; to his common sense and well-considered counsel; to his moderate policy and his work for cordial racial co-operation. These outstanding merits deserve worthy acknowledgment.'[17]

On 4 March 1907, Botha and a cross-party cabinet, several of whom were English-speakers, were sworn in by Selborne. Before the ceremony in the old Raadzaal in Pretoria, where Botha had once jousted with Kruger, he was heard to murmur to a friend: 'May the Lord help me to bear the responsibility.'[18] Besides being prime minister, Botha took upon himself the portfolio of agriculture, while Smuts became colonial secretary and minister of education. Botha's former rival for the premiership, Sir Richard Solomon, was appointed as agent general in London and before long the Responsibles were subsumed into the ranks of Het Volk. Smuts wrote to the veteran Cape politician John X Merriman to say, 'On a policy of racial peace, we carried many English constituencies with us, and I wish that we should continue that policy night and day.'[19]

A striking feature of the new administration was the warmth of the relationship that grew up between the British governor and the new prime minister. At heart both gentleman farmers, the pair grew to greatly respect and admire each other. Overcoming his dismay at Het Volk's success at the polls – which he knew would give rise to fears and second thoughts in London – Selborne wrote privately to an uneasy King Edward VII to reassure him about Botha, describing the premier as 'a born leader of men, with plenty of moral courage, a man of natural dignity of manner and reserve, who does not wear his heart on his sleeve, and will not go enthusing with English Radicals, who, being a great Tory by nature (as all Boers are), he will probably dislike.'[20]

Steyn's suspicions

In May 1906, not long after Smuts's return from London, he and Botha paid a visit to ex-president Steyn in the Orange River Colony. After a long sojourn in Europe, Steyn's physical condition had improved, enabling him to resume his former prominence in the affairs of the colony. With his encouragement, Orangia Unie was established in Bloemfontein two years after the founding of Het Volk and the new party swept the boards at an election held in November 1907. Ill health precluded Steyn from becoming physically active in politics again, so the well-respected Abraham Fischer became prime minister of the Free State, with JBM Hertzog as his law adviser and attorney general. His several years of exile had not allayed the unforgiving Steyn's suspicions of the British, nor his resentment of conciliatory Transvalers such as Louis Botha.

The Transvaal's new prime minister hardly had time to catch his breath before he was summoned to London to attend the Imperial Conference of 1907. At the formal opening of the Legislative Assembly shortly before Botha left, Governor Selborne announced that his new administration had decided that the employment of Chinese labourers was to cease 'at the earliest possible moment'.[21] Notwithstanding the benefits to the mining economy, Botha had made up his mind that for political reasons the Chinese had to go. Repatriation took much longer than expected, however, because of resistance from the mine owners, and it was not until 1910 that the last Chinese worker left South Africa.[22]

Although it was not really necessary for Botha to attend the largely ceremonial Imperial Conference, he deemed it advisable to go to an event that turned out to have a significant impact on his thinking. In London, he met and got along well with Campbell-Bannerman, who told him over dinner in a Holborn restaurant that this was the very place at which he had made his famous speech during the Anglo-Boer War about 'methods of barbarism'.

Among those back home who were uneasy at the Transvaal premier's departure was Steyn, who confided his misgivings in a letter to Merriman: '... it would be better if Botha did not lay the loyalty butter on so very thick'.[23]

It must be said that Botha did, on occasion, lay on the loyalty butter with a spatula. At a function in London attended by Campbell-Bannerman, he declared, 'Today, although a South African, I stand here as a British subject, a son and a brother of our great British Empire ... I am a soldier, and I did my duty then as a soldier, but I am ready to do that same duty today on behalf of the British Empire.'[24]

CHAPTER 16

THE REFORMER

Lauded in London

Botha was disarmed by the warmth and splendour of the reception he was given in Britain. Five years earlier, he had been put up in an unpretentious, out-of-the-way hotel in London; now he was an honoured guest of the British government and the equal of the leaders of Dominions such as Canada and Australia, who had gathered under the imperial crown. Enthusiastic crowds greeted his appearances in public and he found himself lionised by London society, from King Edward VII downwards. The great and good who met Botha, so different from the stereotypical Boer of their imagination, were confounded by his easy-going charm and impressed by his remarkable memory for the faces and names of people he had met.[1] Among those whom Botha met in London was the under-secretary of state for the colonies, Winston Churchill, who brought his mother to a grand banquet in Westminster Hall. On being introduced to Lady Churchill, who was standing beside her son, Botha paused and said, 'He and I have been out in all weathers.'[2]

Behind the façade, however, he was deeply conflicted. On the one hand, the Peace of Vereeniging was a binding agreement that had to be honoured in spirit and letter, especially as the imperial government[3] had delivered on, and in some respects had exceeded, its undertakings. But memories of the war crowded in and he was uneasy about the adulation showered upon him by those who had inflicted such suffering on his people. He was uncomfortable with all the pomp and ceremony, knowing that photographs of him enjoying British hospitality and showing up at official functions in knee breeches and silk stockings would be offensive to many Boers who had fought alongside him. It took a long and intimate talk with King Edward, who told him how much he appreciated the difficult circumstances in which Botha found himself and assured him of the respect and friendship of the British people, before his uneasiness began to diminish. As he told a friend afterwards, he felt as if a great weight had been lifted from his mind by his conversation with the King.[4]

During his two-week stay in Britain, he was made a privy counsellor, awarded an honorary doctorate in Dublin and given the freedom of the cities of Manchester and Edinburgh. Impressed by the kindness and courtesy he received on all sides, he gave what Harold Spender describes as 'a generous return'.[5] In meeting after meeting, he pledged the loyalty of the Transvaal to the Empire, and reiterated that British interests would be safe in the hands of his cabinet. Surprisingly, he never overcame his nervousness about speaking in English and would always reply to toasts and speeches in Afrikaans, which had to be translated for his listeners.

One of those to be impressed by Botha at the Imperial Conference of 1907 was the rising Liberal politician and president of the Board of Trade, David Lloyd George, who described the Transvaal premier as a born leader of men. 'The great head,' Lloyd George wrote later, 'the steady, dauntless, understanding eyes full of fire and light, the deep husky commanding voice – as I sat opposite for him for hours I found myself drawn to gaze upon him. I thought of him leading his men in a charge and I felt I would rather be on his side than facing him. Afterwards I heard him speak in his own tongue. There was power, directness, conviction in his voice and manner. One could understand the sway he exerted over his rugged and valiant commanders and why they followed him into battle without reckoning the odds. He was a more magnetic speaker than either Milner or Smuts.'[6]

Friend of Jameson

Like the Deity, history often moves in mysterious ways. Also in London to attend the Imperial Conference was Dr Leander Starr Jameson, rehabilitated via an extraordinary set of circumstances and now the premier of the Cape Colony. A hero to many British jingoes, Jameson had served a short prison sentence before being pardoned for his misadventure in the Transvaal in 1895–1896. Undaunted, he had returned to the Cape and become leader of

DC Boonzaier's caricature of the unlikely friendship between
Louis Botha and Dr Leander Starr Jameson (from De Burger, *1915).*

BRENTHURST LIBRARY

the pro-British Progressive Party, and then prime minister of the colony from 1904. Botha, who was ten years younger, had never met him before.

Despite Jameson's atrocious reputation among the Boers, Botha found that he quite liked the man. Besides, it was important for reconciliation in South Africa that good relations should exist between Cape Town and Pretoria.[7] In discussions during the Imperial Conference, he found himself siding with Jameson in supporting freedom and equality for the Dominions and pleading unsuccessfully for a combined South African supreme court as a precursor to unification. Engelenburg records that their contact in London led to 'a measure of mutual consideration and understanding of each other's intentions from which shortly many benefits for South Africa were destined to flow'.[8]

On most other matters pertaining to the Dominions, Botha kept his own counsel, honouring his undertaking to Steyn not to commit South Africa in any way. Jameson's biographer, Colvin, confirms that 'although the Transvaal premier gave his political benefactors silence, he gave them nothing else'.[9] Back in South Africa, however, there was incomprehension in many circles that he and Jameson had become friends. Meintjes judges this to be the point at which Botha's popularity began to wane among his own Afrikaner people: 'Conciliation was all right perhaps, but Jameson was beyond the pale.'[10]

Other matters

During his time in London, Botha pressed the Colonial Office hard to rein-state Swaziland as a protectorate of the Transvaal (as it had been of the old ZAR), but his efforts were unsuccessful. Lord Selborne believed that a semi-independent status for Swaziland, similar to that of Basutoland (today Lesotho), should suffice until all the 'native' protectorates could become part of a united South Africa. Selborne's view found support in London, and in Transvaal opposition circles as well.[11] In the City of London, Botha took the opportunity to meet representatives of the gold-mining industry, concerned as always about labour costs. He undertook not to repatriate a single Chinese before the departee had been replaced by a black labourer, but beyond that firmly refused to commit himself.[12]

His confidence that he had done the right thing in coming to Britain may be gauged from his account of a conversation with Arthur Balfour, the former Tory prime minister. Balfour said to him, 'Well, Botha, you have done it; you have got your constitution. What will come of it?' Responded Botha, 'I believe that in five years I shall return to this country to ask for the confedera-tion of South Africa.' 'That is impossible, incredible,' said Balfour. 'We shall see,' was Botha's confident reply.[13]

Despite Steyn's prediction that Botha would return from London empty-handed, the Transvaal premier won the promise of another £5 million loan for reconstruction, to be underwritten by the British government. Mischief-makers in opposition ranks in the Transvaal alleged that this was a 'bribe' by the Liberals to hasten the exodus of Chinese from the mines, an unfounded accusation echoed in the British parliament by the Tories. It was neither the first nor the last time that the sensitive Botha's reputation was made to suffer from rumour and slander.[14]

Opposition at home

The path of the peacemaker, Botha realised on returning from London, was strewn with stones. Once again, the most extreme reaction came from the Free State, where Christiaan de Wet had been expressing his views in letters 'full of bitter criticism'.[15] Another Free Stater, a backvelder named Breytenbach, also incensed at Botha's courting of the English, accosted the premier in his office in Pretoria and tried to blackmail him into paying a large sum of money to conceal that years earlier he had supposedly paid Botha £2000 to obtain a share in one of Kruger's dynamite concessions. Botha stood his ground and called in the head of the police, a Major Fuge, and had the man arrested. Shortly before his trial, Breytenbach attempted to run away by train, but was observed by Botha, who happened to be on the station platform seeing off his sister. After a message had been sent along the line, the train was stopped and Breytenbach taken into custody. He was brought to trial and sentenced to three years' hard labour. The outcome of the trial was a relief to many of those who had doubted Botha, but not to some of the older Boer-Afrikaners who 'never quite forgave him the favours of the British public'.[16]

An immediate test of Botha's standing among his own people was the grand reception given by Annie in Pretoria on the couple's return from London. Fears that Boer-Afrikaners might stay away were confounded when hundreds turned up to see the Union Jack flying side by side with the Vierkleur, and to hear 'God Save the King' being played for the first time at an official function. The event was a bold declaration of intent by Botha: an affirmation of his belief in reconciliation between Boer and Brit and a show of defiance to his critics. Having given his word, he was not a man to go back on it.

Cullinan diamond

A political furore erupted later in the year when the Transvaal government decided to present the priceless Cullinan diamond to Queen Alexandra, wife of Edward VII. The huge gemstone, the largest diamond in the world, had been found in 1905 in the partly state-owned Premier mine. In August of 1907, Botha proposed that the government should purchase the 40 per cent of the diamond it did not own and present the jewel to the King as an expression of loyalty and a gesture of thanks for Britain's granting of self-government to the Boers. His motion, which he hoped might be unanimous, was approved by 42 votes to 19. Curiously, the most vocal opposition to the gift came from pro-British sympathisers inside and outside the legislature – in Engelenburg's words, the very men who 'posed as the guardians of British prestige in our country'.[17] In the Free State, needless to say, the trio of Steyn, De Wet and Hertzog were appalled.[18]

The King's advisers in the Liberal government advised him not to accept the diamond because the Transvaal could not afford it and because of the public outcry in Britain and South Africa. But the monarch, who had not been well disposed to the Boers until he met Botha, was persuaded by his son, later George V, to accept the gemstone, which he duly did with much enthusiasm a year later.

By coincidence, on 19 August, 1907, the day on which Botha's proposal was approved in the Transvaal legislature, the British parliament voted to guarantee the aforementioned loan of £5 million to the new administration in Pretoria. A large part of the money was earmarked for Land Bank capital. As the faithful Engelenburg comments drily, it was remarkable that several ardent 'patriots', who had displayed their disgust at Botha's gesture of loyalty to the 'English', never hesitated for a moment in applying for a Land Bank loan.[19]

His staunch ally

Botha could not have withstood the stress he was under without the unstinting support and exceptional administrative abilities of his second in command in the Transvaal government, Jan Smuts. Also a firm believer in the necessity of reconciliation as a prerequisite for the unification of South Africa's four colonies, Smuts understood that such an outcome could only be achieved in close collaboration with the British.

Singly, neither he nor Botha could have been as effective as they were in political tandem. Botha was highly persuasive on the hustings; Smuts did much of the hard work behind the scenes. A famous, and inaccurate, British cartoon depicted the six ministers of the Het Volk cabinet, all with the face of Smuts. Its caption read: 'The controlling influence of General Smuts in the Cabinet is so apparent that the government may be said to be concentrated on him alone.'[20]

This was unfair on Botha: Smuts, by his own admission, would never have achieved the results he did without the support, guidance and tact of the man eight years his senior. Each felt the need for the other in public life. 'What Smuts was able to accomplish thanks to his trained intellect, Botha achieved through sheer intuition.'[21] No petty jealousies ever affected their relationship and there was never any doubt about the sincerity of their friendship. As Smuts wrote of Botha, 'He had a natural sympathy that enabled him to get extremely close to others and to read their characters with marvellous accuracy. It gave him an intuitive power of understanding and appreciating men which was very rare.'[22]

Facing down the mine owners

From his encounters in London, Botha had realised that his new government's immediate priority was the recruitment of thousands of black workers to replace the Chinese, as the imperial government was insisting. To do this, he would have to face down the powerful mining companies, which had been used to getting their own way under the Milner and Selborne regimes and were threatening to close mines if Botha dared to carry out the British government's wishes.

Help came from an unlikely quarter – the immensely wealthy South African-born Randlord, Sir JB Robinson, who had always kept his distance from the rest of the mining fraternity. Robinson promised to help repatriate the Chinese and, if necessary, to assist the Transvaal government to run the mines with the help of white and black labour. The mine owners rapidly took stock: if the government began to run some mines, where might it stop? And, in that case, what would be left for their shareholders?

As Harold Spender notes, 'Capital is not always as brave as it looks. Faced with loss of profit, its courage dwindles.'[23] The mine owners quickly capitulated, the Chinese began going home, and the recruitment of almost 200 000 black workers for the mines began. Most of the black workers who replaced the Chinese were Mozambicans, whose working conditions were no better. Historians such as Charles van Onselen point out also that importing Chinese labour had enabled the mine owners to bring down wages, which accounted for the reluctance of black South Africans to return to the mines after the war.[24] But by bringing the most powerful private interests in the Transvaal to heel, Botha had demonstrated to anyone who doubted him that he intended to be master of his own house.

Reforming the Transvaal

The next most immediate task was reform of the civil service, overmanned and in the hands of Milner's Kindergarten. Botha did not do as Steyn and Hertzog had done in the Free State, namely, alienate the English sector by driving out English-speaking civil servants and summarily replacing them with Afrikaners. Instead, he kept the best of the imported officials, dismissed the rest and over time replaced them with capable Transvalers.

After taking steps to improve the quality of the civil service, he next turned his attention to the state's defence. Milner had abolished the system of commandos and field cornets and replaced them with a large and costly body of armed policemen.[25] Botha reinstated the field cornet system for home defence, but thought it wise to muster recruits slowly and not provide them with arms. As a precaution, he requested the imperial government to keep its remaining 30 000 troops in South Africa to help maintain the peace.

Conscious of his own lack of formal schooling, he gave Smuts the task of reorganising the Transvaal's education system. Within a few months, the Education Act of 1907 was on the statute book, recognising the rights of both language groups and introducing free primary education for all white children.

Farming was another matter dear to Botha's heart, so dear that he kept the agriculture portfolio in his own hands. Unlike some of his supporters, he had gone along with Milner's plans for revitalising Boer farms and replenishing supplies of stock and seed.[26] He sent promising young Afrikaner farmers to Europe and America to study the latest farming methods and bring them back to the highveld. He also settled, in the countryside, landless and unemployed *bywoners* (tenant farmers), who had become a serious social problem after the war.

Looking back on Botha's three years as Transvaal premier, the avowedly partisan Engelenburg describes them as 'a brilliant accomplishment'. He and his cabinet colleague restored a measure of economic and political health to the Transvaal and reinforced the mineral-rich colony's predominant position on the subcontinent. The next step was political unification.

In the 1907 election, Botha had pointed out the wasteful extravagance of the current system and urged the people of South Africa to unite as Australians and Canadians had done. The old Boers, he declared, were the pioneers of the Transvaal and should also be pioneers on the question of 'federation'.[27] In taking the initiative on this great issue, Botha knew he could count on the support of a man to whom he had become close – the British governor, Lord Selborne.

CHAPTER 17

UNIFICATION

The case for union

To most political leaders in South Africa's four colonies, unification made good sense. Four governments, four parliaments and four railway, customs and legal systems were a recipe for waste and conflict. Two of the colonies, the Transvaal and the Free State, had no outlet to the sea and were in the hands of the Cape and Natal when it came to customs and freight charges. The Transvaal had begun to retaliate by making increased use of the Rand–Delagoa Bay railway, and by threatening to withdraw from the intercolonial customs agreement.

There were many obstacles in the way of closer union, however. The richest colony, the Transvaal, was reluctant to bear the financial burden of the others. The Afrikaners of the Free State were fearful that a unified country would be dominated by English interests, while Natal feared the opposite – that any union would be run by Afrikaners such as Botha and Smuts. And liberals in the Cape were concerned that their colony's limited non-racial franchise would be unacceptable to the former republics.[1]

The only certainty, perhaps, was that unification was not a good idea unless and until all four colonies were self-governing and able to take their own decisions, rather than have a future foisted upon them by imperial inter-ests.[2] As early as 1906 – in anticipation of self-government for the Transvaal and the Free State – the likes of Botha, Steyn, Smuts and Merriman had been in communication with one another about forging closer ties. Yet it was Jameson, in the Cape, who set the unification ball rolling by formally requesting the governor of the Cape and the Transvaal, Lord Selborne, for his views. The subsequent 'Selborne Memorandum', written by members of

Milner's Kindergarten, recommended a much closer association of the four colonies, for without it South Africa would never enjoy peaceful or effective governance. The memorandum had a powerful effect on English-speakers in particular.[3]

In 1907, after Botha and Jameson had returned from the Imperial Conference in London, Smuts wrote on behalf of himself and Botha to Merriman, who was poised to succeed Jameson as premier of the Cape. 'The problem of federation is a great thing for our political intellects to wrestle with,' said Smuts, 'and will lift South Africa out of the rut of selfish commercialism in which it is now stagnating.'[4] From the Free State, Steyn also wrote to Merriman: 'Botha and Smuts seem to favour unification. In fact the more one thinks about it, the more you become convinced that that is the only kind of union we ought to accept.'[5]

Despite preliminary talks between the leaders of the four colonies, convened by Botha and held at his house in September 1907, it took a breakdown of the Railway and Customs Conference in May 1908 to bring matters to a head. Spender exaggerates only slightly when he describes the situation as perilous: 'So deep were the divisions of the delegates and so strong the pressure of local interests that not even the prospect of possible disaster to the peace of South Africa could bring them to renew their understanding.'[6]

Fortunately, wiser counsel quickly prevailed. Aware of the consequences of failure, and realising that a solution acceptable to all was unattainable, the conference delegates passed two resolutions: the first proposed a closer union between the four colonies, and the second called for a National Convention to bring this about. The four colonial parliaments almost fell over one another in their eagerness to approve the proposals and select delegates for a convention to be held, without delay, in Durban.[7]

The National Convention

Delegates to the National Convention were determined in proportion to each colony's white population: 12 for the Cape, 8 for the Transvaal, 5 for Natal and 5 for the Orange River Colony. There were also three non-voting representatives from Rhodesia. Of the 30 attendees from South Africa, 16 were English-speaking and 14 Afrikaners. Among the leading politicians present were Jameson and Merriman from the Cape, Botha and Smuts from the Transvaal, Moor from Natal, and the Free State trio of Steyn, Hertzog and De Wet. Presiding over the gathering was the chief justice of the Cape, Sir Henry de Villiers, with the widely respected Steyn as his deputy.

Four imperial warships (with guns and fireworks) lay at anchor in Durban Bay as the Convention opened in the City Hall on 12 October 1908. After a brief inaugural session in Natal, the assembly moved on to the Cape in early 1909, and later to Bloemfontein. One of its first resolutions was to keep the proceedings secret in order to encourage participants to speak freely.

The Transvaal delegation, comprising five Het Volk members (including Koos de la Rey) and three Progressives (Sir Percy FitzPatrick among them), had prepared the ground carefully, and took along a support staff of 19 secretaries and advisers. Botha and Smuts had already persuaded the Progressives of their sincerity about reconciliation, and the upshot was genuine unanimity among the Transvalers as to the ends they would pursue.[8]

The omission of any representatives of the other races, according to the historian Leonard Thompson, rarely broke the surface in the Convention: 'The delegates were representatives of their colonies not of their races ... and for the most part they acted colonially.' The Convention must be seen against a background of conflict and confrontation among racial and ethnic groups, especially during the preceding century.[9] During the discussion over the franchise, deep-seated differences emerged between the colonies, and between individual delegates.[10]

Much of the preliminary work on the constitutional question had already been done over the previous months by Smuts, in correspondence with Merriman. The two were in agreement that South Africa should be united – like Australia and Canada – under the British Crown, but, unlike those two Dominions, should have a unitary constitution, which would be more flexible and less expensive than rigid federalism and preclude any interference by British politicians.[11]

Smuts was convinced that union was not only desirable but also attainable – a view shared by Merriman (as well as Steyn). The only issue on which he and Merriman were not in agreement was the franchise. Merriman favoured the Cape's limited franchise, which denied the vote to poor and ignorant white men but granted it to men of colour who were educated and owned property. Smuts (and Merriman) well knew there was no chance of a qualified franchise that excluded some whites at the expense of blacks being acceptable to the northern colonies, so the compromise proposed was that each colony should carry its existing franchise arrangements into the Union.

The human factor

It was Botha, however, who recognised that the human factor was crucial to the success of the Convention. Leaving the technical and jurisprudential issues to Smuts, and financial questions to the Progressives' HC Hull, he set out to dispel the mutual suspicion among delegates and foster a spirit of harmony. To all and sundry, he preached reconciliation and moderation, and practised it consistently. Some weeks into the Convention, Jameson, the standard-bearer for 'English' interests, wrote to his brother Sam: 'Generally, we are going better than I expected. All cooing like doves, Botha is the great factor and plays a capital game of bridge. He, Steyn and I are great pals – so the world wags ...'[12]

Later, he added: 'Botha continues the most satisfactory and far the biggest of the lot. Of course, there is the slimness [cleverness] to look out for, but he has less of it than any of his confreres, and far less than our pseudo-English ... Steyn, too, is quite a surprise and he and Botha are the two factors for a decent British settlement. Strange, but true. Funny that my main pals to get things [done] are Botha, Steyn and perhaps Christiaan de Wet.'[13]

The Natalians, especially, were fascinated by Botha, who had spent his formative years in their midst. At a municipal dinner in Durban in honour of the delegates, he amused his audience by recounting how, less than a decade earlier, he and his commando had been prevented by Commandant-General Piet Joubert from driving down to the Natal coast and 'eating bananas at the seaside'. Years later, in recognition of Botha's efforts as a peacemaker without peer at the Convention, Durban became the first city to erect a statue in his memory.[14]

Using his disarming personality to soothe delegates' fear of the mighty Transvaal contingent, Botha took a leading role in the key debates around the constitution and the franchise. Speaking on Merriman's proposal for uniting the four colonies into a legislative union under the British Crown, Botha said that although the Transvaal possessed great wealth, it longed for 'one flag, one people, one God'. He promised that the colony would be prepared to pool its mineral assets for the benefit of a united South Africa and entrust its future to a parliament representative of the whole of the country.[15]

Botha always spoke in Afrikaans (which had evolved by now from Cape Dutch), his words at the convention translated by his faithful secretary, Dr WE Bok. He strongly supported a unitary rather than a federal state, defended the Afrikaners' language rights, and was particularly forceful on the vexed franchise question. The vote should be given to white men only, he argued. If the Transvaal and the Orange River Colony had to disenfranchise whites at the expense of other races, there would be no union. Here, he found support from Natal, whose 100 000 whites were outnumbered by a million Zulu. After lengthy debate, the Convention adopted his (and Smuts's) proposal to leave the franchise question as it was in the four colonies, except that any bill altering the Cape's non-racial franchise would require a two-thirds majority in both houses of the national parliament.

An expensive compromise

The issue that threatened to derail the convention, however, was not the franchise but the choice of capital city for the new Union. Before the delegates moved to the Cape from Natal, they had appointed a commission to try to ward off a looming deadlock. When no progress was forthcoming by the end of January 1909, it was Smuts once again – in consultation with Botha – who came up with the solution: Cape Town should be the legislative capital, Pretoria the administrative capital and Bloemfontein the judicial capital of a united South Africa. This expensive and inconvenient compromise – which required civil servants to move between Cape Town and Pretoria each year – is part of the price the country continues to pay, more than a century later, for unification.

The most dramatic moment at the Convention was Steyn's intrusion into the language debate. Speaking in English, the ailing Free Stater moved many delegates to tears by pleading for 'race hatred' to be expunged, declaring that 'the equality of the languages is the symbol of the equality of the races ... If this had been realised in South Africa a hundred years ago, the history of this country would probably have been quite different.'[16]

On 3 February 1909, the Convention adjourned, having produced a draft constitution that required ratification by each colonial parliament. The day before, Botha had sent a letter for publication to *Die Volksstem*: 'Tomorrow, after signing the draft Constitution, we break up. The eight Transvaal delegates have done their best, and were unanimous all along the line. We did not approve of everything, but, taking all things together, are satisfied. I think the Constitution is a workable one; it will soon be published. We ask your help in order to explain, and recommend, it to the public. If you do not see your way to support us, do not commit yourself until you have spoken to either Smuts or myself. I feel convinced, however, that you will back us up in order to have Union, and to establish a South African nationality. The work was hard; we are feeling done up. After a lot of trouble, we decided to make Pretoria the seat of a united government, with Parliament sitting at Capetown. You will see, therefore, that Pretoria and the Transvaal are greatly privileged. This compromise is as much as we could obtain. Let us honestly support the covenant; it is an honourable understanding.'[17]

On 9 February, the draft constitution was made public, and referred to each of the colonial parliaments for ratification. While the Transvaal and the Orange River Colony found the draft acceptable, the Cape parliament began tinkering with the apportionment of seats between town and country, and it took the combined efforts of Jameson and Botha to save the situation. Natal insisted on putting the proposed constitution to a referendum of whites, who in due course voted for it by a majority of three to one. In Bloemfontein, in May, the draft was formally accepted by the Convention, to be sent to the imperial government in London for approval.

Politically aware Africans, coloureds and Asians, unrepresented at the Convention, reacted with anger and hostility to the draft constitution, arguing (rightly) that it would entrench the theory and practice of inequality between white and black.[18] African newspapers vehemently rejected the franchise provisions and warned of 'a future filled with hatred and even violence'. Some months earlier, in March 1909, a convention of African groups from all four colonies (a forerunner of the African National Congress) had met in Bloemfontein and resolved to send a delegation to petition the British government in London if the National Convention did not heed their pleas.

London 1909

Two separate delegations left for London in June 1909: the official party of 19 led by Sir Henry de Villiers and including Botha, Smuts, Hertzog and Jameson; and a second, unofficial grouping from the Cape, led by the liberal William Schreiner and comprising African spokesman Dr Walter Robusana, the newspaper editor John Tengu Jabavu, coloured leader Dr Abdullah Abdurahman and others. Assisted by the Indian activist Mohandas Gandhi, the Schreiner delegation made a valiant attempt to persuade the Liberal government in Britain to extend the 'native franchise' to all four provinces of the proposed Union, but failed to make any impression on a Colonial Office anxious to be rid of direct responsibility for South Africa.

In London, the radical British journalist and Boer sympathiser, William T Stead, had a lengthy discussion with Botha, Abraham Fischer (prime minister of the Orange River Colony) and Hertzog over 'the question of the natives'. Stead found the three men immovable on the matter of the franchise. Botha pointed out that the constitution actually extended the rights of blacks, because it enabled black voters in the Cape to legislate for the whole of South Africa for the first time. Stead agreed that this might be so, but warned that 'that very fact might encourage other colonies to disenfranchise the natives in the Cape Colony'.[19]

The August 1909 edition of the *Review of Reviews* carried a long article based on the editor's interviews with a cross section of South African opinion in London. In it, Stead quoted Abraham Fischer's reason for not bowing to critics of the franchise proposals: 'What you ask as to … an alteration of the draft Union Act on a matter which the Convention thought of material importance, and resolved after maturest deliberation, is practically impossible. Acceding to your request would at this juncture mean wrecking union; this none of us are prepared to do, including, I hope, yourself.'

Stead was unpersuaded. He ended the article by quoting Botha's opinion that 'natives' were not fit for the vote and that no self-respecting white man would sit beside a coloured man in Parliament. This outraged Stead, who wrote that he would rather sit beside a Dr Abdurahman or Tengo Jabavu in any Parliament than with certain white men he knew in South Africa. But his strictures were of no avail. 'It was,' Martin Plaut records, 'a case of accept the Bill as it stood or leave it. Nothing would be changed.'[20]

For British MPs (and newspaper editors) at that time, a far more pressing issue than South African unification was the constitutional stand-off between the House of Commons and the House of Lords over Lloyd George's ground-breaking social welfare budget. Liberals and Conservatives who took part in the debate adopted a bipartisan approach to the South Africa Act, with only marginally different emphases. Many MPs felt guilty about abandoning black South Africans to the mercy of whites, but consoled themselves that Britain would retain control over the protectorates of Basutoland, Bechuanaland and Swaziland.[21] In the Commons, Liberals expressed regret at the 'colour bar' in the constitution, but, as the deputy colonial secretary, John Seely, explained, it had been impossible to find a formula to provide for a uniform franchise in all four South African colonies. If, on the other hand, conciliation between the white races were to break down, the effect on the 'native' races would be disastrous.[22]

For the Conservatives, Alfred Lyttelton commended the South Africans for avoiding the disastrous errors the Americans had made, and for facing up to the fact that 'the black races are not the equal of the whites'. The patrician Arthur Balfour agreed: 'To suppose that the races of Africa are in any sense the equals of men of European descent, so far as government, as society, as the higher interests of civilisation are concerned, is really, I think, an absurdity.'

Prime Minister Herbert Asquith, successor to Campbell-Bannerman, summed up the dominant mood of regret, overlaid by a strong dose of wishful thinking: 'Any control or interference from outside … is in the very worst interest of the natives themselves … I anticipate that, as one of the incidental advantages which the Union of South Africa is going to bring about, it will prove to be a harbinger of a native policy … more enlightened than that which has been pursued by some communities in the past.'[23]

In a subsequent letter to Botha, Asquith wrote: 'There is nothing in our conduct of affairs during the last four years on which we look back with so much satisfaction as the full and free grant of self-government to the Transvaal and Orange River Colony, which has rendered possible that which at our advent to power seemed an unreliable dream – the Union of South Africa.

'I am glad that we were able to secure the passage of the Act of Union without amendment through both Houses of Parliament.

'Let me add that we feel a deep sense of gratitude to yourself and your colleagues for the splendid and single-minded patriotism with which you have devoted yourselves to the great task of reconciliation and union.'[24]

British newspapers were ecstatic at the prospect of Boers and Brits burying the hatchet and forging a new unity in faraway South Africa. The comment in the *Westminster Gazette* was typical of many: 'If anyone five years ago had predicted that in the year 1909 General Botha and Dr Jameson would have been sitting together on the steps of the Throne, while the Colonial Secretary presented to Parliament an Act of Union in the joint name of British and Boer, he would have been thought a mere visionary … The British Empire has its critics, but we may at least claim for it that only under its flag could this particular chapter of history have been enacted.'

Act of Union

And so the Union of South Africa Act made its way, unamended, through the British parliament: 31 May 1910 – chosen for its symbolic significance – was set as the day upon which the new constitution would come into effect. For the Tories, Balfour declared the Act to be 'the most wonderful issue out of all those divisions, controversies, battles, bloodshed, devastation and horrors of war and of the difficulties of peace.'[25] Schreiner and his colleagues, by contrast, predicted – presciently – that over time the Act of Union would become an Act of Separation.

With the benefit of a century of hindsight, the historian RW Johnson makes this apt observation: 'The creation of the Union was either a great betrayal, or a necessary step in the transformation of South Africa from "a polyglot assortment of underdeveloped territories into a single modern state with a developing industrial base and infrastructure".'[26]

It all depends on one's point of departure.

CHAPTER 18

PREMIER OF THE UNION

Taking the waters

While in London, Botha met regularly with Prime Minister Asquith, who treated him with the deference due to the man he thought likely to become South Africa's first premier. Asquith offered Botha a peerage, an invitation that was declined no doubt because of the derision it would arouse among Boer-Afrikaners back home. On 24 July, Botha was present – along with Selborne, Jameson and Natal premier Frederick Moor – at the swearing in of John X Merriman as a privy counsellor.[1] Two days later, he and the other three premiers met at the Colonial Office to prepare instructions for the new Union's governor-general. Given a choice between Herbert Gladstone and Sydney Buxton – the former a Liberal home secretary, the latter president of the Board of Trade – Botha opted for Gladstone, whose famous father, William, had commanded the respect of the Boers in the pre-war years. Gladstone duly became South Africa's first governor-general and high commissioner, to be followed a few years later by Buxton.

Despite the adverse effect that the numerous banquets were having on his digestive system, Botha took the opportunity to entertain the full British cabinet to a dinner to celebrate the Act of Union.[2] With little opportunity for the vigorous exercise he was used to, he had grown into a heavily built, imposing, moustachioed figure. Feeling out of condition, he heeded the advice of friends and 'took the waters' at Bad Kissingen, a spa town in northern Bavaria, where he shed 30 pounds (13.6 kilograms) of excess weight.[3]

After his cure, Botha went to Paris and then on to a famous merino stud farm at Rambouillet to buy rams for his department of agriculture. Engelenburg, who helped to arrange the visit, tells how Botha chose a dozen three-year-old rams out of a flock of around 150, and then narrowed the selection down to three. At this point the farm manager consulted his stud book and realised he could not possibly sell the chosen three, as they were the pick of his flock. When Botha remonstrated, the flustered manager explained that when he was told to expect a visit by a famous Boer general, he never guessed the visitor would be an exceptionally clever sheep expert. After the price was raised, the manager reluctantly surrendered the three rams, but would not permit Botha to run his eye over the two-year-olds in the stud. Once complimented by Engelenburg on his skill in judging sheep, Botha replied that he had always been a farmer at heart: 'They may call me a politician or a statesman – but in reality I am a farmer, and nothing else.'[4]

From France, Botha journeyed to the Netherlands to buy Friesian cattle, and then spent a weekend in Scotland in the unlikely company of Dr Jameson. The hyperactive Cape premier was out to persuade Botha of the need for a 'best man' government for South Africa drawn from all parties, no doubt hoping for a place in the cabinet for himself. Botha flirted briefly with the suggestion before rejecting it as impractical. Those firmly against it included Steyn and Merriman, both of whom found Botha's liking for Jameson's company quite inexplicable. In 1911, Steyn wrote to Merriman saying, 'Some persons seem to forget so quickly … I cannot understand this sudden friendship for Jameson. Though I am quite willing to credit Jameson with his moderation, in the Convention and since, I yet feel I dare not forget that to him and the cosmopolitan horde behind him, we owe all the suffering …'[5]

Gladstone's choice

Governor-General Gladstone arrived in South Africa on 17 May 1910, with a free hand to choose an interim ministry to run the country from June until September, when a general election would be held. With Steyn, who had many supporters, out of the running for health reasons, the choice of prime minister lay between Botha and Merriman.

Merriman, recently elected as Cape premier in the place of Jameson, was well qualified for the position. At the age of almost 70, he had been a parliamentarian and administrator for 42 years, was recognised as a master of public finance, and had served in five cabinets. An avowed anti-imperialist, he had travelled to London while a minister in WP Schreiner's Cape government to try to prevent the Anglo-Boer War. In 1904, he helped form the South African Party (SAP) in the Cape in opposition to Jameson's pro-British administration and played a leading role in the run-up to, and during, the National Convention. A strikingly tall and thin figure with a sharp tongue and quick-fire manner of speaking, Merriman was a paradoxical politician: a liberal who fought imperialists such as Rhodes, Milner and Jameson as vigorously as he did Afrikaner nationalists and racists. As the leader of the oldest colony – liked and trusted by politicians across the political spectrum, including Free Staters such as Steyn and Hertzog – and by far the most experienced politician in the country, Merriman had good reason to expect the premiership to be his.

In the other corner was the formidable figure of Louis Botha, the preferred choice of Downing Street because of his performance as Transvaal premier and – thanks to his moderation and amiable nature – of almost the whole of the Transvaal and Natal, as well as FS Malan's Afrikaner Bond in the Cape. To the British government, anxious to make amends to the Afrikaners, it was obvious that the economic vitality of the Union depended on the fortunes of the Witwatersrand mines, and Botha had already demonstrated his dominance of the mining magnates over the issue of Chinese labour. Thompson comments that, in a more mature society, the Transvaal premier's lack of education, the brevity of his parliamentary and administrative experience, and his indifferent health would probably have disqualified him from the highest political office. These shortcomings were offset, however, by his exceptional personal charm and the presence at his side of the indefatigable Smuts.[6] On 21 May, having spent two days taking soundings from a cross section of politicians in the Cape, Gladstone invited Botha to form a cabinet to administer South Africa *pro tem* from 1 June. In typical fashion, the first person Botha invited, by letter, to join his interim administration was John X Merriman.

Merriman, however, had become disillusioned with Botha, and in a terse reply declined the appointment. Along with his Free State friends Steyn and Hertzog, the Cape premier was increasingly suspicious of Botha's intentions vis-à-vis the British, and was disgusted by the Transvaal's presentation of

The veteran Cape politician John X Merriman, flanked by
Louis Botha and Jan Smuts.

the Cullinan diamond to the King, as well as by Botha's friendship with his (Merriman's) *bête noire* in the Cape, Jameson. In a letter to Steyn, Merriman gave vent to his frustrations: 'I have no respect for Botha's political knowledge, my experience on the Convention and since has shown me enough to convince me that we should constantly differ, and in this way weaken and render nugatory good government. Much as I like Botha as a man and admire him as a partisan leader in the field, that does not blind me to his political shortcomings. The whole of his tortuous intrigue with Jameson and the cowardly silence he has kept on that matter, the extravagance of his administration ... to say nothing of the tactics of the steamroller and the caucus which dominate Transvaal politics, all convince me that service under such a chief would – holding the views I do – be an act of political dishonesty.'[7]

In time, as we shall see, Merriman had cause to revise his opinion of Botha, who courageously went public on his relations with Jameson in a landmark speech in Pretoria in mid-June. Saying that 'his friend Jameson' had made a strong case for a coalition cabinet, Botha said he had decided that South Africans would not accept it: 'Talk of coalition, to our people, is as a red rag to a bull.'[8]

Soldiering on as a 'humble musket-bearer' and often dissident voice on the back benches of the new parliament, Merriman gradually began to revise his poor opinion of Botha and, in the early days of the Great War of 1914–1918, became thoroughly disillusioned with Hertzog instead. After South Africa had taken Britain's side against Germany, Merriman declared publicly that Botha was the only man who could, and did, keep the Union on the right track. That put an end to Merriman's long friendship with Steyn.[9]

Botha up close

Few men had as much first-hand knowledge and experience of British and South African journalism and politics as BK Long, the Dominions editor of *The Times* in London, and later a member of the Cape colonial and Union parliaments. In his biography of the mining magnate Drummond Chaplin, Long gave this perceptive sketch of Botha: 'A pervading charm lighted his personality. Not very tall; slow in his movements, almost clumsy, he had the face of a countryman and the heavy walk of an habitual horseman. To look at, there was little captivating about him, except the radiance of his smile. But in talk some secret fascination seemed to radiate from him, strangers were caught in it almost instantly and never forgot, after a few minutes easy conversation, how intense and rapid their liking for him had been. His intimates loved him. To serve him was – for civil servants, for army officers and

*JBM Hertzog, the fiery former Boer general, served in the first Union cabinet
but opposed Botha's policy of reconciliation.*

ARCHIVE PL/ALAMY STOCK PHOTO

men, for all who waited on him or worked for him on his lands – a labour of
deep affection. He had strong sympathy and was quick-moved to emotion;
though not to anger.'[10]

1910 election

Botha drew his first cabinet from the ruling parties in each of the four colonies: the Cape was given four ministries, the Transvaal three, the Orange
Free State and Natal two each. Merriman's old friend in the Cape, JW Sauer,

was appointed to the important post of minister of railways, HC Hull of the Transvaal was made finance minister, Smuts was given no fewer than three portfolios – interior, mines and defence – while Hertzog became minister of justice. Botha himself combined the premiership with the ministry of agriculture. Taking advantage of the prevailing mood of optimism, he brought together a group of men broadly representative of white South African opinion, many of whom had been at war with one another less than a decade earlier. It was an open secret, however, that with Hertzog as a minister, the cabinet was not united on two key aspects of policy – conciliation and education.

With his interim ministry in place, Botha set about building up a South African Party – a coalition between Het Volk in the Transvaal, Orangia Unie in the Free State, the Afrikaner Bond and the SAP in the Cape — in time for the September general election. He and his key lieutenant, Smuts, toured the country urging Afrikaners and English-speakers to stand together and bring about a nation of 'South Africans', bound together by race rather than language or class.[11] Botha's new party platform acknowledged that the Union was a member of the Empire, supported European but not Asian immigration, proposed that 'native' policy should be a non-party issue, and stood against the power of urban capitalists.

The main opponent in parliament was the Unionist Party, led by Jameson (and later Sir Thomas Smartt), a coalition of Transvaal Progressives, Cape Unionists and the Free State Constitutional Party. Natal had no political parties before 1910, but many Natalians supported the Unionists, who were mainly English-speaking conservatives, staunchly pro-British and sympathetic to the interests of the mining companies. A third party was Labour, under Colonel FHP Cresswell, mainly English-speaking, representative of white workers and openly segregationist.

Supported by most Afrikaners and a large number of English-speakers, the SAP won the September election easily, gaining 67 seats to the Unionists' 39, Labour's 4 and 11 to Independents. The election's most stunning surprise, however, was Botha's own loss to Sir Percy FitzPatrick in Pretoria East. He attributed his defeat and the loss of another five Transvaal seats to English-speaking reaction to the policies of 'Hertzogism'.

'Hertzogism'

While minister of education in the Orange River Colony, JBM Hertzog had become the bogeyman of English-speaking South Africans because of his policy of compulsory bilingualism in elementary schools. Unlike his counterpart Smuts in the Transvaal, who had decided that every child should be given early schooling in his or her home language, Hertzog went much further by enforcing Dutch on the minority of English-speakers in the Free State and dismissing unilingual teachers and inspectors imported under the Milner administration. To the English-speaking community of the Free State and particularly of the Transvaal, who had fondly expected the defeat of the Boers to result in English unilingualism across the whole of South Africa, the slightest suspicion of being compelled to learn Dutch aroused wholly irrational fears of Afrikaner domination. Notwithstanding the provision for language equality in the Union constitution, the controversy that Hertzog's attitude aroused in the English-language newspapers, says Engelenburg, 'tore the abnormal nervous system of the South African nation to tatters'.[12]

Botha was in a cleft stick. The row over Hertzogism had given its architect such prominence that the Free State would not have tolerated his exclusion from the cabinet. On the other hand, taking Hertzog into the cabinet would lose Botha many English votes. Deciding that the latter was the lesser of two evils, Botha made it clear that his own preference – Hertzog or no Hertzog – was for equal rights for both languages, mother tongue as the medium of instruction, and no compulsion as to the use of either language. At the same time, he refused to order that Hertzog's controversial Education Act be repealed.[13]

Losing his seat

Botha threw himself energetically into the election campaign, issuing a manifesto on 14 June and following it up with speeches across the country. Yet, for some unexplained reason, he allowed his party's whips to persuade him not to take a safe seat at Standerton, and rather to challenge the Unionists' popular Sir Percy FitzPatrick in Pretoria East, the constituency in which he (Botha) had lived for the past few years. FitzPatrick was not expecting to be opposed and was amazed to learn that his opponent in the election was to be the prime minister, a man he regarded as a colleague and a friend.

No convincing explanation has ever been advanced for Botha's decision to contest Pretoria East. Perhaps he felt that, as leader, it fell to him to demonstrate the dominance of the SAP over the Unionists, who had argued so strongly for a 'best man' government for South Africa. Or perhaps he was overconfident that he could force FitzPatrick to seek election elsewhere. Whichever the case, the Pretoria East election became a high-profile, bitterly contested affair. Botha roped in his wife and family, and even the unlikely figure of the recently freed Zulu king, Dinuzulu, to campaign for him, and was so sure of victory that he made arrangements for a celebratory banquet on election night and a victory parade. Great was his surprise and disillusionment, therefore, when FitzPatrick squeaked home by a mere 96 votes, amid what AP Cartwright describes as 'a tumult of shouting as Pretoria had never heard before in peace or war'.[14] Adds Cartwright, 'the genial Louis Botha whom everybody knew disappeared, and in his stead was a crestfallen and disappointed man, who shook hands with FitzPatrick but could not congratulate him'.[15]

Botha took his rejection by the voters of Pretoria badly. Defeat – says Engelenburg – tempted him to consider resignation. Aware that the atmosphere of goodwill at the National Convention had dissipated and that the old fault lines in South African politics were re-emerging, he thought briefly about retiring from politics altogether and returning to his first love, stock breeding, but as usual his sense of duty overcame him. Taking a safe seat at Losberg, a constituency close to Potchefstroom, he braced himself for the task that lay ahead. At the age of 48, Louis Botha was feeling the effects of the continual strain 'of which he, more than anyone else, was the victim'.[16]

A grave responsibility

As Spender describes it, the task facing Botha as prime minister was daunting. He had to reconcile two races recently divided by a bitter war; to combine the administrations of four provinces which were 'notoriously and conspicuously conflicting'; to maintain control over a black population three times as numerous as whites and govern them 'with justice and sympathy'; and, lastly, to keep a balance between Boer agriculturalists and the great industries of the Rand, with their competing demands for cheap labour. In a nutshell, 'Botha now found himself the ruler of a country which was a veritable whirlpool of shifting racial and social currents; perhaps the most puzzling country to govern of all the lands of this distracting globe yet occupied by white men. Well may he have taken a grave view of the responsibilities that lay ahead of him.'[17]

The English writer H Hamilton Fyfe, who travelled the length and breadth of South Africa shortly after Union, made the following assessment of the new premier in a book published in 1911, entitled *South Africa Today*: 'General Botha is a man with elements of greatness in his character, but without the tact and training required to carry him comfortably through the troubles of managing a difficult Party. He has so far got through them, but it has frequently been pain and grief to him. His health has suffered. There is little doubt that he would be happier on his farm, or as Minister for Agriculture without any further responsibilities.'[18]

It was a downhearted and reluctant prime minister, thus, who departed for Cape Town in November 1910 to attend the opening of the first Union parliament. The late Edward VII had been succeeded as King Emperor by George V, who was represented – in a flag-bedecked and festive Cape Town – by his uncle, the Duke of Connaught. Entering into the spirit of the occasion, Botha and Annie moved formally into Groote Schuur, the grand house on the slopes of Table Mountain bequeathed by Cecil John Rhodes to South Africa's future prime ministers. Describing his impressions of the momentous occasion to readers of *The Times* of London was the journalist and author Basil Williams, who wrote of the new prime minister:

> Unquestionably, General Botha is South Africa's leader. He has proved himself a gallant, a resourceful and a courteous captain, during three long years of war. Though he won no overwhelming victories, he was great as the embodiment of that slow tenacity which served the Boers so well. The habit of command, which he acquired in war, he has never since abandoned, and all who approach him acknowledge it to be his right. It is not that he is brilliant or has ever expressed strikingly original ideas. But he is a man of sound judgement and extraordinary tact in weighing the human element in a problem. He is a farmer, and has something of the slow finality that comes to the best farmers from watching the slow and sure processes of nature. He has also some of the defects of a man long

'The Idol' – DC Boonzaier's depiction of South Africa's first
prime minister as the Buddha (from Rand Faces, 1915).

BRENTHURST LIBRARY

accustomed to command; he is impatient of opposition and is apt to take
it with childish petulance as an insult against himself. As a parliamentary leader this will prove his chief weakness, for parliamentary criticism
being still new to him, he is more inclined to circumvent than to meet it.
Besides his petulance, he has a vein of almost childlike simplicity. When
a great work is done, as in the last Convention, he rejoices like a boy at
play. Childlike is also his loyalty to friends and causes and his inability to
understand what seems disloyalty in others.[19]

The prime minister's strengths and weaknesses were to become more apparent, and more pronounced, in the fraught times that lay ahead.

CHAPTER 19

Signs of Trouble

Releasing Dinuzulu

The first caucus meeting of the Union's new governing party gave a hint of the intrigues about to beset the SAP from within. Botha had nominated the well-regarded speaker of the Transvaal parliament, General Christiaan Beyers, as the first Speaker of the House of Assembly. Merriman, on the other hand, thought the Cape Speaker, Sir James Molteno, had a better claim. And, seeing that the Transvaal already held most of the key cabinet portfolios, even some Botha supporters felt that not every important post should go to a northerner. The Free Staters, whose default position was resentment of Botha's Transvaal, supported Merriman, and Molteno duly became the government's nominee for the speakership. Beyers, in his heart a Hertzog man, was not best pleased.

Botha took seriously the promise he had made to the British government always to bear the interests of the South Africa's 'native' population in mind. As proof of his good intentions, one of his first acts as Union premier was to release his old acquaintance the Zulu king, Dinuzulu, from his imprisonment by the Natal government in the wake of the Bambatha Rebellion of 1906 and the uprisings that had ensued. Running what he knew would be a political risk, Botha had Dinuzulu taken from prison at Newcastle, placed on the farm Rietfontein in the Middelburg district of the Transvaal, and given a pension to live on.

Botha had taken the precaution of first eliciting the support of WP Schreiner, who had campaigned determinedly for the Zulu monarch's release.[1] 'You know I am a friend of Dinizulu [sic] and make these proposals in his interest. You are also a friend of his and I wish to have your approval and goodwill in the matter,' he wrote. Schreiner sent Botha an appreciative message by return, saying, 'Trust your known and valued friendship for him to ameliorate his condition and so win abiding goodwill of all best Zulus.' Spender records that a deputation of the King's wives came to the Botha farm to express their gratitude for Dinuzulu's release, and were treated to tea and sandwiches.[2]

The opening session of the Union's parliament was devoted to passing the legislation required to put unification into practice. Among the trickiest issues was the allocation of powers and tax revenues from central government to the provinces. The Free State's presence in the Union gave Hertzog a national platform from which to denounce the capitalism of the Randlords and object to immigration from Britain on the grounds that it would lower Afrikaner workers' wages.[3] By now, Hertzogism had become synonymous with anti-imperialism and anti-British sentiment. Whereas Botha made a habit of not using inflammatory language to denounce his parliamentary opponents, from the benches beside him Hertzog was uninhibited: 'By lies, distortion and false representation, Jameson and his party were endeavouring to flood South Africa with racialism,' he claimed.[4]

To London again

In May 1911, Botha had to leave South Africa for London once more to attend the four-yearly Imperial Conference. The long sea voyage meant a prolonged absence, which gave opponents of reconciliation ample opportunity for mischief-making. Among them, rather surprisingly, was the outspokenly pro-Boer Emily Hobhouse, by this time in poor health. Deeply disillusioned with the British establishment, she castigated Botha (as well as her good friend Smuts) for being so subservient to 'monarchical flummery'.[5]

Subservience, however, was not in Botha's nature, and nothing – not even mockery for having to dress up to attend the imperial court – was to divert him from his aim of establishing the Union's proper role as a fully fledged Dominion within the Empire. Personally, he was far from well: overwork and an attack of ptomaine poisoning had left him feeling weak and nauseous, and his weight had billowed to around 120 kilograms.[6] After a second visit to take the waters of Bad Kissingen, he felt better, but again found himself the focus of all eyes at receptions, banquets and ceremonial events to mark the coronation of George V. Spender records that the romance of Botha's rise to power had nobles and society hostesses falling over themselves to entertain him and Annie in their great houses; universities in England and Scotland presented him with honorary degrees; and Glasgow gave him the freedom of the city.[7]

Once again, he was offered various imperial honours, but agreed to accept only one: an honorary generalship in the British Army, which had never before been offered to anyone outside the ranks of royalty. 'Social life reaches its peak this month – unfortunately for us,' Botha wrote to Smuts in early June. 'Dinner, lunch, church service. Coronation Day – all commands in uniform and one feels so unhappy in the uniform, which is not only uncomfortable but also dear and stiff and I can tell you it is all very difficult.'[8]

For the rest of the month, he continued to grumble about the high prices in London, the discomfort of his uniform and the seven or eight hours of boredom he would have to endure in Westminster Abbey during the coronation. But when the ceremony was over, he declared himself glad to have been there, describing it as 'particularly beautiful; it was brilliant in the highest degree and well-regulated. I and my wife had good seats in the Abbey. The ceremony lasted seven hours … You will understand my feelings in a stiff heavy uniform all that time, but one must admit that they understand how to make this sort of thing beautiful, tasteful and brilliant, and so orderly too …'[9]

At the Imperial Conference, Botha found himself having to firmly oppose attempts by the leaders of New Zealand (especially) and Australia to create an Imperial Defence Council, with full powers of control over the Dominions. 'I have never heard of a more idiotic proposal,' he wrote to Smuts.[10] Joining forces with Sir Wilfrid Laurier of Canada to quash the proposal, Botha said in a speech: 'The premature creation of such an Imperial Council would tend to make the connection onerous and unpleasant to the Dominions. Let us be aware of such a result. Decentralisation and liberty have done wonders. Let us be very careful before we in the slightest manner depart from that policy.'[11] Reporting later to Smuts, he wrote: 'We [Laurier and I] have destroyed root and branch the proposal for an Imperial Council of State or Parliament and we have succeeded in keeping the Conference as a roundtable affair.'[12]

While Botha was away, the SAP's mouthpiece in the Transvaal, *Die Volksstem*, informed its readers that South Africa would not have to take part in any imperial war, a view it attributed to the absent prime minister. From London, Botha felt it necessary to issue an immediate contradiction: 'There is no such thing as optional neutrality,' he cabled. After his return to South Africa, he went on the record again, confirming that 'should the unhappy day ever dawn when the common Fatherland is attacked, Dutch and English Afrikaners will be found defending the Fatherland to the very last.' That was not what the Hertzogites wanted to hear.[13]

In London, Botha had been able to take forward a scheme for the defence of South Africa that he had first discussed with Britain's leading defence strategist, Lord Haldane, back in 1907. Lord Methuen had subsequently been sent out to discuss with Botha and Smuts the role the Union might play in the defence of Empire. The plan was taken further at the Imperial Defence Conference in 1909, and finalised in 1911.[14] A subsequent meeting at the War Office helped to frame the South Africa Defence Bill, which was quickly passed into law by the Union parliament. The Defence Act of 1912 made provision for a small Permanent Force, a larger, part-time Active Citizen Force and a general reserve of citizens. Military training was compulsory for those eligible, either in Defence Force units or in 'rifle clubs' based on the old commando system. With great energy, Smuts (aided by the ex-Speaker, General Beyers) immediately set about building up the Union Defence Force (UDF) to enable the country to participate in the defence of Empire.

Guest of honour

One of the many grand occasions Botha attended in London was a luncheon held in his honour by the Eighty Club. Four years earlier, Campbell-Bannerman had been in the chair when Botha solemnly thanked the British premier for the grant of self-government and promised that the Boer republics would prove worthy of the confidence placed in them. Now, Campbell-Bannerman was dead and Lloyd George occupied the chair. Replying to the toast, Botha was able to attest to the success of the Liberals' great initiative: within four years, the granting of independence to the Transvaal had led to the Union of South Africa. 'We only ask for time,' Botha said, 'and to be left alone; and then we shall show you what wonders we can do in that part of the British Empire ... There is only one message I have to bring from

Botha in court dress.

CLASSIC IMAGE/ALAMY STOCK PHOTO

South Africa, and that is the offer of the hand of brotherhood, friendship and of love of our people towards yours.' This straight and simple speech, says Spender, was received with 'a hurricane of applause'.[15]

Though Botha's conversational English was more than adequate, he always insisted on having his words translated by his secretary, Dr Bok. He would sometimes complain, according to Meintjes, that his own speeches were more Bok than Botha, but never deviated from a practice that puzzled his listeners, and on one occasion caused a hilarious incident. In 1911, British politicians were on high alert for physical attacks on their person by militant suffragettes.

At a public dinner where Botha was the guest of honour, he had just uttered a few sentences in Afrikaans when Dr Bok popped up behind him to translate.

The toastmaster, unaware of who Bok was, assumed this to be a suffragette-inspired attack and dragged him physically from the main table. There was much excitement and confusion before the unfortunate Bok was able to continue with the English version of Botha's speech, which the audience found difficult to listen to as they tried to suppress their laughter.[16]

The fruits of Botha's work at the conference, according to Engelenburg, who was with him in London, only became known later when an account of the deliberations was published. In the meantime, newspaper readers in South Africa were titillated by reports and pictures of their prime minister, dressed to the nines, enjoying the highlights of the London season. The sight of Botha in knee breeches and silk stockings at the court of King George, says Engelenburg, 'had a remarkable effect on the temper of his compatriots, many of whom are always inclined to think the worst of their leaders. To them, the silk stockings were a symbol of national treason.'[17]

Botha's absence from South Africa came to an end on 29 August 1911, when he arrived in Cape Town after being away for almost three months. His health having improved, he was in better spirits and pleased with what he had been able to achieve in London. The Afrikaner Bond in the Cape welcomed him at a luncheon, and his faithful constituents in Losberg greeted him with 'a procession of carts and carriages a mile long'.[18]

Jameson goes home

By late 1911, Dr Jameson had tired of South Africa and written from London to his lieutenant, Sir Thomas Smartt, to say that he would 'not be coming back to politics'. A few days later, he addressed Smartt again, saying, 'I am surer than ever that I am doing the right thing in the interests of the party as well as my selfish self [by] replacing the incompetent self by the competent you.'[19] The Unionists made several attempts to delay Jameson's resignation, but the party leader made his last speech in parliament on 15 February, protesting against anti-English measures in education and the civil service, which were 'in conflict with the spirit of the Africa Act'. He described Hertzog as 'a John the Baptist with an ideal, but the vehemence of this ideal had made him forget the bargain to which the two races had come at the Convention'. 'Let them not try to make South Africa bilingual in a single year. If you feed a child on jam in moderate quantities, he will like it, but if you push a pot down his throat he will probably never eat jam again,' he warned.[20]

On 10 April 1912, Jameson paid his farewell respects to Botha, a man he had looked up to and whose policy of reconciliation he had staunchly supported. In Parliament after Jameson's departure, Botha spoke with feeling about the loss of his opponent: 'From the day I first met him, a strong friendship arose between us and today that friendship is even stronger.' After praising Jameson's character and his work, Botha said in that simple way that went to the hearts of men: 'I conclude by wishing him God's blessing.'[21]

Not everyone, it must be said, viewed Jameson in so generous a light. The Scot may have fitted into Botha's all-encompassing vision of a united (white) nation, but he had altered the course of South African history and left in his wake a trail of disaster and a legacy of bitterness. As Botha was to learn, there was a price to be paid for claiming Jameson as a friend.

In the early days of Union, the principle of collective cabinet responsibility was not so firmly entrenched as to prevent a strong-willed cabinet member from saying and doing contentious things on his own account.[22] While in London, Botha had been angered to hear of an unsuitable judicial appointment made by Hertzog without consultation and came regretfully to the conclusion that there was no place in the cabinet for both himself and his minister of justice.

Yet it was not Hertzog, but the minister of finance, Hull, who caused the first open rift in the cabinet and party. The former leader of the Transvaal Responsibles had no ideological differences with his colleagues but was a stickler for probity, and found it intolerable that Sauer, as minister of railways, should incur heavy expenditure without having obtained authorisation from either the treasury or cabinet. In May 1912, Hull handed in his resignation and almost caused a mutiny among Cape members of the government.[23]

The loose-tongued Hertzog took immediate advantage of the absence of collective unity to address the issue always uppermost in his mind – that of 'nationhood'. At Nylstroom, and in subsequent speeches at Smithfield and De Wildt, he insisted that the new Union should be based on the absolute equivalence of English and Dutch. There were two separate but equal 'streams', he asserted, along which the nation's life flowed, and which should come together in the interests of South Africa before those of Empire.[24] This otherwise defensible proposition was undermined by the intemperance of Hertzog's language, from which any spirit of fraternity was absent. He denounced his English-speaking opponents, including the respected new Unionist leader, Sir Thomas Smartt, as 'foreign adventurers' and 'bastard sheep', and poured cold water on his own government's policy of conciliation.[25]

The angry and contemptuous tone of Hertzog's De Wildt speech, on 7 December 1912, in which he declared he 'did not know what conciliation means',[26] was directed ultimately at one target – the prime minister. For Botha, who had made conciliation his watchword, this was the last straw. In equally uncompromising language, he declared that Afrikaners had lost the war forever and now had to forge a future 'completely merged in a new nationhood'.[27]

There could no longer be room for both these strong-willed and determined politicians in one and the same party.

CHAPTER 20

SCHISM

Fault on both sides

The schism in Afrikaner ranks had its origins much earlier than 1910, but after Union it became centred on the personalities of generals Botha and Hertzog, and to a lesser extent Hertzog and Smuts. Over the years, Botha and Hertzog had developed an intense distaste for each other, which was never the case with Smuts and Hertzog. (It had actually been Smuts who persuaded Botha to take Hertzog into the cabinet.) The fault lay on both sides. As DW Krüger writes, Botha was firm in his refusal not to depart from the great principle of one united nation, but was not always careful to avoid offending the sensibilities of Afrikaners, and at times was strangely blind to the emotions of his old republican supporters. Hertzog, on the other hand, fearing that Afrikaners would lose their identity in Botha's united South Africa, showed an equal lack of tact in the way he went about protecting that identity, seeming to take delight in arousing the fury and resentment of English-speakers.[1]

Within the ranks of the SAP government, two aspects of official policy vis-à-vis Britain were raising Afrikaner eyebrows: a proposal to encourage British immigration, and a willingness to contribute to the upkeep of the Royal Navy at a time when South Africa needed to build its own naval defences. There was even more unease when Botha uttered words of praise for Cecil Rhodes at the dedication of a memorial to the great empire-builder on the slopes of Table Mountain. Was Botha the man they had thought he was, many die-hards began to wonder.

Hertzog scented an opportunity, and in a series of provocative speeches suggested that South Africa's interests were being sacrificed on the altar of Empire. His anti-imperialist strictures at Nystroom were rapturously received by his Afrikaner audience, but in predominantly English-speaking Natal the outrage was palpable: 'The whole of Natal feels insulted by it,' Botha wrote to Smuts from Pietermaritzburg on 1 October, 'in newspapers, clubs, streets, houses or wherever one goes. There is unprecedented excitement which, as you can understand, is causing us harm. Yesterday I met our party here, and believe me they also feel so strongly that one can hardly speak to them. Whatever I say and do I get only one answer; they are regarded as "*uitlanders*".'[2]

For all his moderation, Botha was not one to turn a blind eye to open provocation or personal insult. Smartt had appealed to him to put an end to Hertzog's improper behaviour and Merriman joined in the condemnation of his Free State colleague and friend's Nylstroom speech. Backtracking only slightly, the wily Hertzog apologised to Smartt at Smithfield and said at Vrededorp that he revered Botha and would not have his job at any price. But that could not undo the harm done to the SAP's efforts to recruit English-speaking voters in the eastern Cape and Natal. Botha was angry.

The last straw

Hertzog's fiery speech at De Wildt was the straw that broke the camel's back. When an outraged Sir George Leuchars, one of two ministers from Natal, resigned rather than continue to serve in the same cabinet as Hertzog, Botha decided it was time to act. With the rest of the cabinet behind him, he invited Hertzog to do as Leuchars had done, and, when the Free Stater declined, submitted his own resignation to the governor-general. Knowing that he was the only choice as premier, Gladstone invited Botha to form a new cabinet, which he promptly did, this time excluding both Leuchars and Hertzog from its ranks.

All the while, Abraham Fischer, Hertzog and Botha himself had been in regular contact with ex-president Steyn. The elderly Fischer told Steyn that while he disagreed with his cabinet colleagues who claimed that Hertzog's actions were neutralising all of the good done by Botha, the Free Stater's manner – 'though perfectly innocent in intention, was, as regards tact and tactics, unfortunate and uncalled for'.[3] This was hardly news to Steyn, who had been following events closely and had been told by Hertzog that 'he had given

Botha rope for a twelve-month so that the premier might comfortably hang himself'.[4] Fischer appealed to Steyn for counsel and was advised to follow Hertzog, but was persuaded by others in the SAP to remain in the cabinet. He was to pay dearly for doing so by being condemned, in the Free State, to a lonely old age.

Although supportive of Hertzog, Steyn did his best to prevent a final breach between his lieutenant and the prime minister. On 6 January 1913, he telegraphed Botha from his farm, saying, 'Because of the heat arrived here more dead than alive yesterday. Can I do anything without sacrificing Hertzog to prevent cleavage?'[5] His ill health made worse by the crisis in Afrikanerdom, Steyn's condition deteriorated further and he found it difficult to swallow. His doctors advised a period of rest, and the ex-president kept out of politics until April, when he made the impractical proposal that Botha should resign and he and Hertzog agree to serve under a different prime minister.[6]

By now, it had become obvious that a 'fundamental and irreconcilable divergence'[7] had arisen between the two groups within Afrikanerdom: one proposed partnership within a commonwealth of free British states as essential to the Union's economic future; the other looked for salvation to a sovereign state under a republican regime, outside the Empire. Occupying the middle ground between the ultra-Afrikaners and English jingoes was a preponderant section of moderate Afrikaners and English-speakers, 'of whom Botha was the soul, and the South African Party the outward manifestation'.[8] Put simply, the clash was between one political leader trying to turn out good South Africans and another trying to turn out staunch Afrikaners.[9]

A new party

The exclusion of Hertzog from the national cabinet gave rise to widespread indignation in Afrikaner circles, especially in the Free State. President Steyn had never disguised his sympathies for his long-standing political colleague, nor had men such as Christiaan de Wet, Ds JD Kestell and others of a similar mind elsewhere in the country who had lost confidence in Botha as the Afrikaners' leader. They had convinced themselves – if no one else – that the prime minister was committed to putting the interests of Britain before those of South Africa.

On 28 December 1912, thousands of Afrikaners gathered around Paul Kruger's statue in Pretoria to honour Hertzog as a champion of the Afrikaans language. In a fiery and widely quoted speech, De Wet said he would rather live on a '*mishoop*' (dungheap) than live in a palace among strangers. Referring to English-speakers, he said: 'It is all very well to say that we have to live side by side, but it does not mean that we have to get under one blanket.'[10]

Hertzog's exclusion from the cabinet was, as Spender notes, by no means a disaster for him: 'It gave him martyrdom, and martyrdom was the best seed-ground for a new party if he wished to form one.'[11] For a while, the ex-minister remained a member of the SAP and carried on as if nothing had happened. More pressing matters had diverted the nation's mind from Afrikaner *broeder-twis* (dispute between brothers), including the 'native' threat, Smuts's difficulties with the Indians and a violent strike by gold miners in Johannesburg. Besides that, none of Hertzog's supporters wished to be held responsible for a final break with the SAP, a prospect as painful to them as it was to Botha.

During the 1913 parliamentary session, however, Hertzog resumed his attacks on the prime minister within the party caucus and referred to him in the House of Assembly as a '*papbroek*' (coward). Only five members of the House stood by Hertzog, but at the Free State congress of the SAP in May, Botha's omission of Hertzog from the cabinet was condemned by 47 votes to one. In the Transvaal, by contrast, support for Botha from the likes of De la Rey and others remained firm.[12]

In July, a final attempt was made by friends of both men to bring the two together, but it was too late. At the annual congress of the SAP in Cape Town in November, after Botha had won a vote of confidence by 131 votes to 90, Hertzog rose to his feet and led his supporters out of the hall, followed by De Wet waving his hat in the air and calling out loudly 'Adieu'.[13] Early in 1914, at a conference in Bloemfontein, a new organisation under Hertzog's leadership – the National Party – came into being, with a founding slogan of 'South Africa First'.

The SANNC is established

Two years earlier, also in Bloemfontein, another political movement had been inaugurated, destined over time to have an even greater influence on the course of South African history than Hertzog's National Party and its white successors. Some 60 prominent African community leaders – excluded from formal politics by the creation of Union and dismissive of the notion that their interests could be served by well-meaning whites – assembled to form the South African Native National Congress (SANNC), which duly became the African National Congress (ANC) in 1923. Middle-class products of mission school education, the delegates established an organisation to promote national unity and protect and advance the interests of black people. In white political circles, and in mainstream newspapers, little attention was paid to this significant occasion.

'Native policy', as always, was determined by white economic interests, especially those that depended upon the availability of black labour and ready access to land. Its most far-reaching instrument, the Natives Land Act of 1913, had a profound impact on the lives of black people and aroused the most resolute opposition to its provisions. The Act grew out of the segregationist proposals of the Milner-appointed Lagden Commission (1903–1905) and the Native Affairs Committee of 1912, headed for a time by Hertzog. The Lagden report had recommended that, if friction was to be avoided, whites and blacks had to be permanently kept apart in politics and land ownership.[14] Land should be demarcated into separate white and black areas, and in urban areas 'locations' set up to house Africans. The influence of the Lagden Commission, as Meredith points out, was to elevate the segregationist practices throughout southern Africa, as well as most of colonial Africa, to 'the level of a political doctrine'.[15]

The 1913 Land Act took the Lagden recommendations much further than was originally intended. The Act aimed to get rid of those features of African land ownership and sharecropping to which white farmers objected, to ease congestion in the tribal reserves, and to facilitate the recruiting of labour for the mines. The Act made provision for the ownership and occupation of land by whites and blacks across South Africa, and defined the nature of African land tenancy. A schedule to the Act stipulated which parts of the country were to be regarded as 'native areas'. These 'scheduled areas' – the existing reserves, tribal locations and black-owned land – amounted to some 9 million hectares, less than eight per cent of the Union's land area. A commission appointed under the Act subsequently recommended the 'release' of additional land to Africans to bring their share to 13 per cent, but such was the outcry from whites that the recommendation had to be abandoned.

There is no gainsaying the devastating effects the Land Act has had, down the years, upon the lives of black South Africans. Richard Msimang, UK-trained solicitor and brother of ANC stalwart Selby Msimang, concluded that the Act had three interrelated outcomes: first, it brought about a loss of black land and a curtailment of blacks' security of tenure; second, it resulted in a loss of black property, mainly cattle, confiscated by whites; and third, it converted African people 'overnight' into a class of labourers.[16]

Botha's own segregationist beliefs bore a striking resemblance to those upon which the National Party's homeland or 'Bantustan' policy came to be based some 40 years later. Like most white politicians of the time, he believed that black people should live and exercise their political rights in the traditional areas set aside for them, which included the Transkei, Zululand, parts of the Transvaal and the High Commission territories of Basutoland and Swaziland. His views were deeply paternalistic, but to his way of thinking fair-minded and reasonable, and necessary if racial tensions and conflict between blacks and whites were to be averted.

It is worth noting, as CFJ Muller does, that black leaders of Botha's time did not object so much to the *principle* of territorial separation as to the provisions of the Act, which barred Africans from buying land and enabled white farmers to eject blacks from farms on which they had lived for generations.[17] Botha and the SAP government could count themselves fortunate that the SANNC, led by the moderate John Dube, chose peaceful protest – petitions, delegations and the like – rather than violent resistance as the way of expressing opposition to the Land Act and ensuing discriminatory legislation.

Trouble on the mines

In July 1913, a strike by white miners on the Witwatersrand mines that turned violent overshadowed Botha's political troubles with the fractious Hertzogites. A relatively trivial dispute over working conditions at the New Kleinfontein mine outside Benoni grew into a tense stand-off between mine owners and white mineworkers over the recognition of a trade union. A subsequent mass meeting of miners in central Johannesburg erupted into mob violence, which the police were quite unable to control.

Smuts, as minister of both mines and defence, was forced to call in imperial troops to quell the unrest, for there was not yet any South African army to speak of. In the rioting, shops were looted, the Johannesburg railway station set alight and the office of *The Star* newspaper, regarded as the mouthpiece of the mine owners, burnt down. Twenty-one people died and 47 were injured.

With the strike out of control and most mine owners having fled the city, Botha and Smuts courageously drove unarmed through the streets of Johannesburg to the Carlton Hotel to negotiate face to face with the strike leaders. They were recognised immediately, and a seething crowd gathered outside the hotel as the negotiations took place inside. Realising that they were powerless against the multitude, the two SAP leaders had no option but to concede to demands for a reinstatement of those dismissed at New Kleinfontein and an investigation into the miners' grievances.

While the strike leaders returned to their offices to consider the proposed settlement terms, Botha and Smuts left the hotel without an escort. Their car was forced to a halt, and the pair could have been killed at any moment by the enraged mob. According to Engelenburg, a furious Botha shouted at the strikers who stopped the car: 'You can shoot; we are unarmed. But know this, that we are here to make peace for you people. And if we are shot, all that is finished.' He and Smuts were allowed to proceed unhindered.[18]

The settlement of the dispute, known as the 'Bain Treaty', was a victory for the miners and a humiliation for the government, and particularly for Smuts, who said afterwards that signing the document was one of the hardest things he had ever had to do. He vowed that never again would he find himself in a similar situation; next time, he and the government would be fully prepared.

A second and potentially more serious strike broke out only a few months later. It began among white coal miners in Natal, spread to railway workers in Pretoria and then to gold miners on the Witwatersrand, after which a general strike involving some 20 000 workers of all races was declared. This time, Smuts was ready. He called up units of the newly mobilised UDF, ordered burghers in the rural districts to protect railway stations and other strategic points, and sent General Koos de la Rey and his men into Johannesburg to train their guns on Trades Hall, the strikers' headquarters.

Realising they were outgunned, the strikers quickly capitulated. This was not enough for Smuts, however, who took the law into his own hands and rushed nine immigrant trade union leaders by special train to Durban, where they were put on a ship bound for Britain. Labour politicians were outraged, but the country breathed more easily. Smuts, and Botha, had demonstrated once again their bravery under fire, and shown they were not to be trifled with. In parliament, Smuts pleaded successfully for indemnity for his actions and argued the need for emergency measures. Not long afterwards, a Riotous Assemblies Act found its way onto the statute book.[19]

Dealings with Gandhi

Another contentious issue that flared up in 1913–1914 was Indian immigration, a matter that Botha deputed Smuts to handle on the government's behalf. In 1911, a Bill to limit the influx of 'Indians and other Asiatics' into the new Union had been promulgated, but was subsequently withdrawn because of opposition from the Viceroy of India, who thought it was too discriminatory, and from Free Staters, who regarded it as not discriminatory enough.[20] The new Immigration Act of 1913 aroused furious violent reaction among Indians, prompting their leader, the lawyer Mohandas Gandhi, to employ what would become his world-famous tactic of *satyagraha* (passive resistance) and to demand the repeal of all laws in South Africa that adversely affected his people.

The subsequent arrest and imprisonment of Gandhi and his followers provoked such tumult that the government appointed a commission to investigate their grievances, and Smuts met face to face with Gandhi on several occasions. In June 1914, the two men reached a compromise agreement that recognised certain Indian rights and brought an end to passive resistance. To the government's relief, Gandhi departed South Africa after a stay of over 20 years, never to return. 'The saint has left our shores,' a relieved Smuts declared, 'I sincerely hope for ever.'[21]

War looms

By far the greatest predicament confronting Botha and the governing party in 1914, however – against which all other quandaries paled – was the extent to which South Africa should involve itself in the war threatening to break out in Europe. Since the early days of the century, tensions had been simmering as the British, French, German, Russian, Austro-Hungarian and Ottoman empires fought either to protect their possessions or extend their influence on the Continent, in the Middle East and around the world.[22] As these empires looked increasingly towards Africa and parts of Asia for supplies of raw materials, an arms race developed which eventually propelled the world to war.

One direct outcome of the bad blood spilt over the Jameson Raid, and the Kaiser's inflammatory telegram to the Boers, had been the Anglo-German naval arms race. The Germans had concluded, from Britain's entanglement in South Africa, that it was not possible to build an empire without a strong naval fleet. Since the second Anglo-Boer War, each side had been building up its navy, and particularly the number of dreadnought battleships, in order to gain a decisive advantage on the high seas. As early as 1910, a far-sighted member of Milner's Kindergarten, Philip Kerr, observed that 'a solution to the rivalry between the great military power of Europe and the great sea power of the world is the most difficult problem which the Empire has to face'.[23] 'The British Empire is now fighting for its existence,' declared Britain's minister of war, Lord Kitchener.

It took a wholly unexpected incident – the assassination of the Austrian archduke, Franz Ferdinand, heir to the throne of the Austro-Hungarian Empire, by a Bosnian Serb in the city of Sarajevo – to set off a chain reaction that split Europe into two armed camps and plunged mankind into the deadliest and most destructive war the world had known.

For the fledgling Union of South Africa, and Louis Botha, the conflict could not have come at a more inconvenient time. Unlike the other Dominions, South Africa in 1914 was still a nation divided against itself, ill-equipped and unprepared to be drawn into any imperial quagmire. To take his country to war on the side of the British, moreover, who little more than a decade earlier had inflicted such grievous harm on the Boer-Afrikaner nation, would mean that Prime Minister Botha stood little chance of completing the great task of reconciliation upon which he had set his heart, and upon which he had staked his entire political future.

CHAPTER 21

GOING TO WAR

A narrow escape

We have Winston Churchill to thank for an account of Louis Botha's movements shortly before the outbreak of the Great War in August 1914. Botha and Annie were in the northern Transvaal, on their way back from a visit to Northern Rhodesia (today Zambia), and had booked passage on a German ship due to sail on 3 August from Beira to Delagoa Bay, and then on to Cape Town. On that very day, in London, Churchill was walking away from the Houses of Parliament when he ran into the South African cabinet minister Sir David Graaff. 'What do you think is going to happen?' asked Graaff. 'I think it will be war,' replied Churchill, 'and I think Britain will be involved. Does Botha know how critical it is?'[1]

That night Graaff cabled Pretoria, saying, 'Churchill thinks war certain and Britain involved', or words to that effect. In Pretoria, Smuts sent the telegram on to Botha, who promptly cancelled his voyage to the Cape. Were it not for this timely message, Botha later told Churchill, he would actually have been aboard a German vessel when war was declared and might have been detained and taken to Dar es Salaam in German East Africa, to where the ship was immediately diverted.[2] 'The Prime Minister,' wrote Churchill in characteristically colourful style, 'the all-powerful national leader of South Africa would have been in the hands of the enemy at the very moment when large areas of the South African Union were trembling on the verge of rebellion. One cannot measure the evils which might have come upon South Africa had such a disaster taken place.'[3]

Botha was back in Pretoria on 4 August when Britain declared war on Germany for having invaded neighbouring Belgium the night before. An immediate decision now had to be made about South Africa's participation in the war. The fledgling UDF, made up mostly of civilian conscripts and volunteers, was only two years old, and the country itself had foes 'within and without her gates'.[4] Many of the white population were openly anti-British and thus pro-German.

Constitutionally, neutrality was not an option for any Dominion. On the same day that war was declared, Botha cabled the British government to say that South Africa would undertake its own defence if the imperial troops garrisoned around the country were needed elsewhere. On 7 August, the British accepted the offer, but added a presumptuous request: would the UDF be prepared to invade German South West Africa (today Namibia) in order to capture and disable a network of radio transmitters at Windhoek, Swakopmund and Lüderitzbucht that were in communication with German naval shipping on the high seas? If South Africa could not help, other imperial forces would have to be called in.

For Botha and the SAP government, the choice of whether or not to go on the offensive was agonising. Could, or should, the Union go to war against Germany on the side of a country against which the two Afrikaner republics had waged a bitter struggle little more than a decade before? On the other hand, could South Africa afford to sit by and let other Dominion forces (perhaps even troops from India) take the initiative in southern Africa?

DW Krüger sums up the country's dilemma well: 'The outbreak of the general European war came at a most inopportune time for South Africa,' he wrote. 'It came too soon after the unification experiment, because the people were not yet united … It came too soon after the political break in the ranks of Afrikanerdom, and it even came too soon after the South African War … South Africa faced the world crisis not as a united nation, but as one divided against itself.'[5] On 10 August, however, after intense discussion among members of a divided cabinet, South Africa informed the British government that its request would be met. But parliamentary approval had first to be obtained, and only volunteers would be used in any invasion of South West Africa.

Many Afrikaners, it must be said, would much rather have taken up arms against the British than the Germans. Memories of the Anglo-Boer War were still raw, and it was not easy to forgive 'the English' for the suffering they had caused. Some, like Koos de la Rey, saw the war in Europe as an ideal opportunity for the Union finally to cut its ties with Britain and become an independent republic under Afrikaner rule. Others were friendly with members of the German colonial army in South West Africa, or with their former countrymen now living across the long and porous border between the two territories.

It was Prime Minister Botha's invidious task to balance the conflicting demands of English-speaking South Africans, strongly in favour of supporting Britain, against those of his fellow Afrikaners, who were divided at this time into roughly three camps: those in the middle who supported reconciliation; pro-republicans who did not; and a minority of 'bittereinders' prepared, if necessary, to take up arms in defence of German South West Africa. Botha probably reasoned that even if some of his fellow Afrikaners doubted him, they would be much easier to bring into line than the more demanding and vocal 'English'.

British historians such as Ronald Hyam claim that Botha and Smuts took their country into the war against Germany from 'a hard headed and calculating belief that it was in South Africa's best interest to get hold of South West Africa for itself'. The possibility of post-war annexation of the German territory would certainly have occurred to both men, but it was hardly sufficient reason to put their drive for (white) reconciliation at such severe risk.[6]

The influential trio

At this critical moment in Afrikaner history, and in the life story of Louis Botha, let us pause briefly to consider the state of his relationship with the three most significant Afrikaner figures – besides Smuts and Hertzog – of the post-Boer War era, namely, Steyn, De Wet and De la Rey. The trio were at the very heart of the internecine conflict that lay ahead.

According to Marthinus Steyn's biographer, Johannes Meintjes, the key to the ex-president's behaviour since his return from Europe in 1905 was that, for him, the Anglo-Boer War would never be over until true independence had been achieved. 'He was,' says Meintjes, 'the last bittereinder'; unlike Botha, he was not prepared to forgive and forget.[7] Yet, as the enmity between the two Boer leaders unfolded over time, it was the uncompromising Steyn and not Botha who emerged as untainted in the eyes of the Afrikaner people. This was unfair, asserts Meintjes, 'for Botha was a man of vision sixty years ahead of his time, and beset by difficulties which would have tried a man who was both a genius and a saint'.[8]

Karel Schoeman goes so far as to say that, from a moral and psychological standpoint, Steyn's return from Europe in 1905 was, for the Boers, perhaps the most important development in the entire post-war period up to the formation of Union, including the founding of their two political parties, Het Volk and Orangia Unie and the granting of self-government to the two republics.[9] Such was the former president's reputation among his people.

Even though Steyn's view of the struggle for independence was so different from Botha's, the older man was always revered by Botha, says Engelenburg, 'both personally and for his political achievements, not as a matter of calculation but as the outcome of spontaneous admiration'. With his 'susceptible' nature, Botha held a lasting affection for the ex-president, who did not, unfortunately, reciprocate it.[10] Steyn now looked with distaste upon Botha as 'an Afrikaner who had lost his identity'.[11]

Botha was pleased to have Steyn back from Europe, but it was not long before the Free Stater's resentment of the Transvaal government's gift to the King of the Cullinan diamond, that colony's education legislation and Botha's 'objectionable intimacy' with Jameson began to gnaw away at him. Steyn's bitterness grew as poor health thwarted any ambition he might have had of becoming South Africa's first premier.

An indication of his antipathy to Botha emerged in 1908, in the run-up to the National Convention. Steyn had busied himself raising funds for the erection of a monument to the women and children who had died in British concentration camps during the Anglo-Boer War. Botha feared, however, that the memorial appeal would reopen the Boer-Afrikaners' unhealed wounds and impair his drive for reconciliation. He tried to pre-empt Steyn by writing to suggest instead that a memorial be built to the Voortrekkers under Piet Retief and Piet Uys, who had been massacred by the Zulu king, Dingane, back in 1838 and for whom no fitting monument had ever been erected.

Steyn was taken aback by Botha's letter. 'Dear friend,' he replied, 'it is unnecessary for me to assure you that such an undertaking would in normal circumstances have my most dedicated interest and support … At present, however, I have some objections. The first is purely practical. Is it the right time, as we are at present busy on a National Monument for the women and children? If we should undertake both tasks at the same time, both would suffer … My second objection is more serious and to my mind almost insurmountable. No matter how the death of Retief and his followers is viewed, one simply cannot ignore the fact that the basic cause of the tragic events was the oppression our people had to endure under British supremacy, which forced them to abandon their homes for the wilderness.'[12]

This exchange put an end to the pair's correspondence over the *Vrouemonument* (Women's Memorial), but Botha's fears about the appeal campaign were justified: the monument was opened with due ceremony in Bloemfontein on 16 December 1913, and aroused among Boer-Afrikaners the very emotions he had been dreading.[13]

At odds over Hertzog

After Union, as we have seen, Botha and Steyn had engaged in another, much lengthier correspondence over Hertzog and the rift in the SAP. Letters and telegrams flew between them as Steyn pleaded for Hertzog's reinclusion in the cabinet and Botha politely resisted. In April 1913, Steyn wrote Botha a long letter proposing that both he and Hertzog should agree to step down and serve under another prime minister. Botha replied by return, saying that his resignation would achieve nothing, and that he had not taken a single step without careful consultation with his colleagues. 'What really grieves me, President,' wrote Botha, 'is that from the start you have been prejudiced against me, without allowing me to voice my side of the case.'[14]

Knowing that he was writing to a desperately ill man, Botha struggled to keep his indignation under control: 'Much I have suffered in these last months, yet that the day should have come on which I have to say to you, whom I consider the greatest Afrikaner and also my dear friend, "Your way is not mine" causes me grief such as I had never dreamed could happen to me in my political life, and it is the greatest sorrow I have known since the day we gave up the independence of our land.'[15] 'It pains me to see that you have a personal grievance against me,' replied Steyn, 'by saying that I have been prejudiced against you from the start … I don't know what you mean.'[16] After these tense exchanges, the relationship between two proud characters would never be the same.

Distrustful De Wet

When it came to taking sides, Christiaan de Wet – like Steyn – had chosen to support Hertzog rather than Botha. De Wet's distrust of Botha had grown during the final months of the Anglo-Boer War and turned to active dislike at Vereeniging, when he and his Free Staters had no option but to agree to settlement terms acceptable to the Transvalers. He was particularly wounded by a remark Botha had made when Free State delegates argued that the war should not be ended but carried over into the Cape Colony. Botha had retorted, 'I may be permitted to have my own opinion on the subject. Chief Commandant De Wet was unable to invade the colony even in the best days when he had fresh horses and a large force. How, then, are we to manage now? Winter is coming and our forces are spent.'[17]

Botha had not intended to disparage De Wet, but the touchy Free Stater immediately took offence. He had twice attempted to infiltrate the colony with his commandos, and twice failed, and being reminded of his failure – where Smuts had succeeded – was more than he could bear. Like Steyn, De Wet did not find it easy to forgive and forget.

At the end of the war, he had set aside his dislike of Botha to join him and De la Rey as members of the Glorious Trio, when they visited Europe to raise funds for Boer rehabilitation. He and Botha seem to have rubbed along well enough, though De Wet kept largely to himself and concentrated on writing his well-received war memoirs. When the Orange River Colony was granted self-government in 1907, he was appointed as minister of agriculture, and was one of the Free State's delegates to the National Convention, where he strongly supported Steyn and Hertzog's efforts to have Dutch accepted as one of the Union's two official languages.

After Union, De Wet left politics and went to live on his farm, Allandale, near Memel in the Vrede district of the Free State. His only public office was as a member of the Union Defence Council, but when an anti-Botha movement – the Hertzog Demonstration Committee – was founded in Pretoria in December 1912 to protest at Hertzog's exclusion from the cabinet, De Wet hastened to be part of it. His famous 'dungheap' speech, mentioned in the previous chapter, put him back in the political limelight. In order to demonstrate his contempt for the Botha government (and the minister of defence, Smuts), he resigned from the Defence Council.

Yet De Wet was hesitant to break with the SAP. In a speech in the Transvaal, he declared, 'Botha is dear to me, but my People are dearer still.'[18] But not long after, he joined Hertzog in walking out of the SAP and helping to found the National Party. Although taking no further part in formal politics, he nonetheless took to the hustings in dorp after dorp in the Transvaal and Free State in support of the NP's slogan, 'South Africa First'.

The faithful De la Rey

After accompanying Botha and De Wet to Europe as a member of the Glorious Trio, the much-loved and deeply loyal Koos de la Rey under-took another trip – this time to Ceylon, via India – to persuade some die-hard Boer prisoners of war to return home and pledge allegiance to the British Crown. He supported the founding of Het Volk and in 1907 was elected to the first parliament of the self-governing Transvaal. A faithful devotee of Botha, he attended the National Convention as a Transvaal representative, and after Union became a nominated SAP sena-tor in the South African parliament. When the Union Defence Council was established, he joined his old comrade and friend, Christiaan de Wet, as a member.

Though De Wet was now a supporter of Hertzog, De la Rey remained loyal to Botha, who had an abiding love and respect for the older man. During the industrial unrest on the Witwatersrand in 1914, he and Smuts called up their former comrade to take command of Active Citizen Force troops and put down the uprising, which he duly did. Always more of a military man than a politician, however, the elderly De la Rey failed to grasp fully the reasons for the clash of loyalties within Afrikaner ranks. He had always believed that Botha, the man he revered, was intent on leading the country towards inde-pendence as a republic, and when the Great War broke out sensed that a chance had come to throw off the British yoke.[19]

Botha made what De la Rey's biographer, Meintjes, describes as the 'griev-ous mistake' of not disabusing the old warrior, whom he did not want to hurt, of this notion: 'As much as Botha felt committed to standing by his commitment to Britain, De la Rey felt committed to the independence of his people.'[20] Oom Koos was neither anti-British nor pro-German, but now that war had broken out between the two countries, the time was ripe for his people to claim their freedom, he fondly believed.[21]

The old 'Lion of the West' had never been able to reconcile himself to the loss of Boer independence. According to Engelenburg, the outbreak of the Great War – and the exciting opportunity it provided – affected De la Rey's mind to such an extent that he could no longer think logically. It was well known that by this time his son-in-law had ceased to regard him as accountable for his actions and found it necessary 'to have him looked after'.[22] As we shall see in the next chapter, when the news eventually reached him of his old friend's disquiet, Botha had to call in the aid of Smuts, Schalk Burger and others to help calm the distraught old man and dissuade him from any action he might regret later.

Rumours abound

The decision by the cabinet to invade German South West Africa had to be made without parliamentary approval, because Britain had insisted on an immediate answer and it would have taken some weeks to convene a parliamentary sitting. Until then, the government had to run the risk of losing the parliamentary vote, and Botha's ministers agreed that if the vote went against them, they would resign. But Botha made the error of not taking the country into his confidence: was the Union merely to be defended, or were the Germans to be attacked?[23] In the country at large, rumour ran wild: Afrikaners in the Transvaal and Free State, especially, were convulsed by reports that the government was planning to force them into military service to fight against Germany.

In cities and towns, the public were able to observe the movement of troops, but the government unwisely kept the newspapers and everyone else in the dark about its intentions. De la Rey himself was so disturbed by the reports of conscription that he sent out a call to his followers in the western Transvaal to meet at Lichtenburg on 15 August. The time had come, he believed, to saddle up and go into action once again in the interests of the Boer-Afrikaner people.

CHAPTER 22

REBELLION

A disloyal general

The first sign of resistance to the Union government's decision to enter the Great War on Britain's side came from none other than the head of the UDF's Active Citizen Force, Commandant-General Christiaan F Beyers. The UDF, at the time, had two arms, the Permanent Force under Brigadier General HT Lukin and the much larger Active Citizen Force, under Beyers. Neither commander ranked above the other and both reported independently to the minister of defence. Beyers had been appointed to the post in 1912 by Smuts, who had reservations about his loyalty but considered it politically necessary to appoint a number of former Boer officers to senior staff positions in the new defence force. Beyers disliked the way the Union Defence Act was being used to realise the ideal of 'national statehood' by integrating Englishmen and Afrikaners under arms.[1]

Seven years younger than Botha, Beyers was a lawyer who had distinguished himself as a fighting general in the Anglo-Boer War. After the Peace of Vereeniging, he had become a respected Speaker of the Transvaal parliament and, post-Union, an SAP member of the national parliament, where he was Botha's unsuccessful nominee for the speakership. A heavily built, talented sportsman and musician, Beyers was not universally popular: many people were put off by his religious obsessions and his vanity.[2] In politics, he was known to be a Hertzog man, hostile to the notion of conciliation and to fighting on the side of Britain.

Beyers was suspected of being a secret German sympathiser. In his book *Botha Treks*, the Australian-born police officer Major HF Trew records an incident at an official garden party in Pretoria shortly before war was declared. The

British commander-in-chief in South Africa, General JW Murray, inquired of Beyers, who had just returned from an official visit to various European countries, including Germany, 'Who will win this war?' Flinging his arms in the air, Beyers declared emphatically, 'The German armies will sweep across the world. There is nothing that can stop them.' Trew looked at Beyers with astonishment, for 'he spoke with a sort of holy conviction', and wondered if the general could be trusted.[3] Rumour had already reached South Africa that Beyers had been in contact with the Kaiser. Meintjes speculates that the Germans may have promised Beyers that if they won the war – an outcome they confidently expected – South Africa would be proclaimed an Afrikaner republic.[4]

After war was declared on 4 August, Beyers kept his head down for four weeks, giving no hint of his true intentions. While he did so, Botha and Smuts turned their attention to their old friend De la Rey, who had called upon his followers to arm themselves and assemble at Treurfontein in the Lichtenburg district on 15 August. On 12 August, Botha called De la Rey to his house in Pretoria, and, after a meeting at which Smuts, Schalk Burger and Botha's former military secretary, Advocate NJ de Wet, helped placate the old man, he played on De la Rey's devout religious feelings throughout the night, pleading earnestly with him not to incite his men to rebel. Finally, Botha said: 'Oom Koos, it may be the will of God that this nation shall be free and independent. But nothing will ever convince me that it is the will of God that this shall be brought about through treachery and dishonour.'[5]

Since 1899, however, De la Rey – well known for his interest in the super-natural – had fallen deeply under the influence of the Boer seer, Niklaas (Siener) van Rensburg, who had prophesied several of the Boers' victories in the Anglo-Boer War, and now told the credulous old warrior that he had been chosen by God to lead his people to freedom. In two minds how to proceed, De la Rey immediately consulted Beyers, who was against active participation in the war against Germany yet baulked at taking up arms against the state he still served.[6] Returning to Treurfontein, De la Rey advised his followers to come together, unarmed, on 15 August. At the gathering, which took place in an orderly fashion, he told an audience of 800 that Great Britain was involved in a war whose outcome was uncertain. He counselled those present to remain calm and disperse quietly, which they did after passing a unanimous vote of confidence in the Botha government's intentions to act in the best interests of the people.[7]

On 16 August, the day after Treurfontein, Botha called a meeting of Transvaal and Free State commandants at which he declined to allow South West Africa to be discussed because parliament had not yet voted on the matter. Several officers, including Beyers and former generals Jan Kemp and SG (Manie) Maritz, spoke out strongly against going to war on Britain's side – for political rather than military reasons. Surprised by the strength of resistance to his plans, Botha invited some of the dissenting officers to his home, where his powers of persuasion were such that most of them came round to his point of view. According to Meintjes, 'By the time they left, Botha's most bitter opponents could only talk of shooting Germans, such was his extraordinary power over men.'[8]

Political opposition to the government's plans crystallised on 26 August, during the first congress of Hertzog's National Party, in Pretoria, at which an invasion of South West Africa was unanimously condemned. Though known to be a 'Botha man', De la Rey was present at the congress and made a moving appeal for Afrikaner unity. 'General Botha and General Hertzog are both great men and both of them are my friends. In these troubled times, it is imperative that we all stand together. Let us not divide; let there be no rifts; let us maintain unity,' he declared.[9] Outside the hall, he was heard to remark: 'I refuse to fight under a German flag; nor will I fight under an English flag. Only under my own flag.'[10]

War debate

On 9 September, Viscount Sydney Buxton, who had succeeded Herbert Gladstone as governor-general a few days earlier, opened the special session of parliament convened to debate the war. At the SAP caucus meeting, Botha set out the reasons for South Africa's entry into the conflict. Although many party members were in favour of supporting Britain, they were less enthusiastic about taking action against kith and kin in German South West Africa. In the House of Assembly, Hertzog acknowledged that South Africa was constitutionally bound to aid Britain in wartime, but this did not extend to attacking a good neighbour without provocation. His argument failed to persuade the House, however, which voted by 92 votes to 12 in favour of the government's proposal, described by Botha as 'the way of faith, duty and honour' in contrast to Hertzog's 'way of disloyalty and dishonour'.[11] The Senate voted by 24 votes to 5 in favour of invading South West Africa.

One senator who could not bring himself to vote against Botha, but who would not support the invasion either, was De la Rey, who had a conscientious objection to any attack on South West Africa. On the afternoon of the vote on 13 September, he walked out of parliament and took the train back to Pretoria, intent on organising a public protest in the Transvaal. At the station to see him off was Louis Botha. De la Rey put his arms around the bulky frame of the prime minister and kissed him on the lips, then boarded the train, turned and kissed Botha again.[12] Through a mist of tears, an emotional Botha watched as the old man's train left Cape Town.[13]

Also aboard the train was the chief justice of South Africa, Sir James Rose Innes, who wrote afterwards that De la Rey had been 'excited and anxious' on the subject of South West Africa: 'He harped throughout our conversation on the same string. No word of objection on principle, nor hint of any active opposition, certainly not the speech of a man who was planning to overthrow the Government for taking aggressive action.'[14]

If De la Rey was still undecided as to what to do, General Beyers, Major Jan Kemp and Lieutenant Colonel Manie Maritz were more clear-minded. They intended to mobilise the Citizen Force troops under their command in training camps at Potchefstroom and in the Cape northwest and Free State. Many of the young men were disaffected and unemployed Afrikaners, who were to be marched to Pretoria, where they would seize the Transvaal capital and raise the old republican flag.

As joint UDF commander, Beyers was privy to Smuts's plans to muster three columns of Citizen Force volunteers for the invasion of South West Africa but, being a lawyer, knew he had to tread carefully. Plotting resistance to the UDF while in uniform was an act of treason. The only way out was to resign, and so, on Saturday 12 September, he began to draft a letter giving his reasons for stepping down. On Monday 14 September, parliament adjourned, and that same night the first UDF troopships departed for the coast of South West Africa.

Tuesday 15 September found the Cape Peninsula bathed in sunshine. Louis

Botha was in good spirits, playing a round of golf at Wynberg with Buxton, the recently arrived governor-general. Halfway through the game, he was given a message that General Smuts had motored out to see him. About 20 minutes later, records Buxton, Botha returned looking serious. 'Beyers has resigned quite unexpectedly,' he said, 'and as far as we can judge the position is a grave one. Smuts and myself must go to Pretoria tonight, and you must follow as soon as can be arranged.' The prime minister and Smuts then left for Cape Town, where a special train had been laid on to take them to Pretoria. Shortly before the train's departure that night, they were given the shattering news that Oom Koos de la Rey had been killed in a shooting incident in Johannesburg.

A tragic accident

After tendering his letter of resignation at noon on 15 September (and releasing it simultaneously for publication), Beyers had sent his grey Daimler motorcar to bring De la Rey from Johannesburg to Pretoria, and from there the two men left for Potchefstroom to address a meeting called for that evening. Botha and Smuts were aware of the gathering and had put the organisers under police surveillance. Driving to Potchefstroom via Johannesburg, Beyers' car ran into several police checkpoints, where officers were hoping to intercept members of the dangerous Foster gang, who had been terrorising the citizens of Johannesburg.

When his car was flagged down at the first roadblock, Beyers immediately thought his plot had been discovered, and ordered his driver, one AJ Wagner, to drive on. At the second and third checks, he again ignored orders to stop, but at the fourth a policeman fired a single shot at the wheels of the fleeing vehicle. The bullet ricocheted off the road and hit De la Rey in the heart. Murmuring '*dit is raak*' (I've been hit), the old Boer hero collapsed and died in the arms of Beyers, who was numbed with shock and grief at his demise.[15]

The Transvaal lawyer Ewald Esselen swore in an affidavit that he had seen De la Rey shortly before he started out on his motorcar ride with Beyers and was told by De la Rey that he was now prepared to support the prime minister and even, if necessary, serve with the UDF forces in South West Africa – another indication, perhaps, of the old man's confused state of mind.[16]

The news of De la Rey's death by shooting burst upon a saddened and disbelieving South Africa. The old man had been the most famous and universally respected of the Boer generals, known far and wide for his tender nature. His tragic death put an immediate but temporary end to any thoughts of insurgency. Beyers and Kemp, who had also resigned earlier in the day, dropped whatever plans they had up their sleeves and disbanded the training camp at Potchefstroom. An uneasy calm enveloped the country.

An emotional funeral

Among the thousands of mourners who gathered to pay tribute to the fallen De la Rey at his funeral at Lichtenburg on 20 September were Botha, Smuts, Beyers and De Wet, all of whom addressed the assembled audience. The air was thick with tension and emotion – and wild rumour. It was widely believed that De la Rey had not met his end by accident, but on the orders of the government so as to prevent an incipient Afrikaner uprising. According to Meintjes, one young firebrand even begged Kemp for his revolver so that he could shoot Botha and Smuts at the graveside.[17]

A grief-stricken Botha, recorded Buxton, 'pronounced a heart-felt eulogy of General De la Rey which did much to calm the feelings of those present and bring about a sense of the solemnity of the occasion'.[18] Speaking immediately after Botha, the Janus-faced Beyers vehemently denied that the pair had an uprising in mind: 'It is openly being said that General De la Rey and I were on our way to start a rebellion. In the name of the hero lying here, I reject the allegation. Nothing was further from my thoughts than rebellion.'[19] While that might have been said of De la Rey, a peace-loving man who would never have supported civil war, it could hardly have been true of Beyers himself.

Before leaving Lichtenburg, Botha assured his listeners that the campaign in South West Africa would be carried out by volunteers only, and announced that he would be taking over as head of the Active Citizen Force in Beyers' stead. His words made little impression, however: the next day, more than a thousand protesters gathered around the bullet-holed car, now standing in the market square draped in the flags of the old republics. To avoid misunderstanding, Beyers ordered the flags to be removed. At the emotion-filled meeting, the crowd passed a resolution requesting the government to abandon any aggressive military operations and to recall the UDF troops from South West Africa. A provisional committee, to which Beyers, Kemp and De Wet were elected, was charged with arranging further protest meetings.[20] Engelenburg suggests that while Beyers may have been primarily intent on preventing an invasion of South West Africa, Kemp and De Wet were really intent on overthrowing the government and restoring the independence of the Boer republics.[21]

Rising to the occasion

At this critical time, says WK Hancock, 'Botha rose to his full stature as a political and military leader. Throughout the anxious months ahead he was always clear-headed, resolute and masterful.'[22] While De Wet busied himself by fomenting opposition in the Free State, Botha set about marshalling volunteers for action in South West Africa, calling yet another meeting of Transvaal commandants to apprise them of his recruitment plans. Of the 35 officers present, only 15 were required for active service, but when Botha called for their support, to a man they all volunteered. Those who could not be given a command offered to take part in the campaign as privates. It was apparent that the new Active Citizen Force commander had not been abandoned by all Boer-Afrikaners.[23]

De la Rey's violent death, however, gave rise to anger and threats of insurrection throughout Nationalist Afrikanerdom. De Wet and other hotheads openly accused the government of being responsible for De la Rey's tragic demise, and the Transvaal and Free State seethed with rumours about the government's call-up plans. It only needed a spark to ignite an explosion, says DW Krüger, and that spark was duly supplied in the far-off northern Cape by Manie Maritz, a *veggeneraal* (fighting general) and *bittereinder* during the Anglo-Boer War. In spite of (or perhaps on account of) his fanatically anti-British and pro-German leanings, Maritz had been commissioned in the UDF by his friend Beyers, notwithstanding the reservations of defence minister Smuts.

CHAPTER 23

HEARTACHE

The unkindest cut

No episode in Louis Botha's life caused him more anguish than the Boer-Afrikaner rebellion of late 1914. His last five years on earth were made miserable by the enmity of men who had once been his loyal followers and friends. The burden of sorrow he bore uninterruptedly during and after the rebellion debilitated his health and led within a short time to his premature and untimely death.

Notwithstanding the growing militancy in Afrikanerdom aroused by De la Rey's death, at the end of September 1914 Botha must have thought he had matters under control. Armed protest – saddling up and riding with rifles to a meeting, but without any intention to shoot – was a traditional way for the Boers to let off steam, and he found it hard to believe that men like Beyers, De Wet and Kemp would take up arms against their own people. He was soon to be disillusioned, however.

At a meeting in Pretoria of UDF military commanders, including General Beyers, a preliminary plan for the invasion of German South West Africa was mapped out in mid-August 1914. The first of three South African columns, led by Colonel Percy Beves, would invade the colony from the sea via Lüderitzbucht; another column, under Brigadier General Henry Lukin, would cross the southern border of South West Africa at Raman's Drift; while a third, under Lieutenant Colonel Maritz, who was commanding Citizen Force training camps in Upington and Kakamas in the far northern Cape, would operate alongside Lukin in the Schuit Drift/Nakob area.[1]

Maritz, however, had no intention of fighting on behalf of the British and decided the time had come to take matters into his own hands. Before and

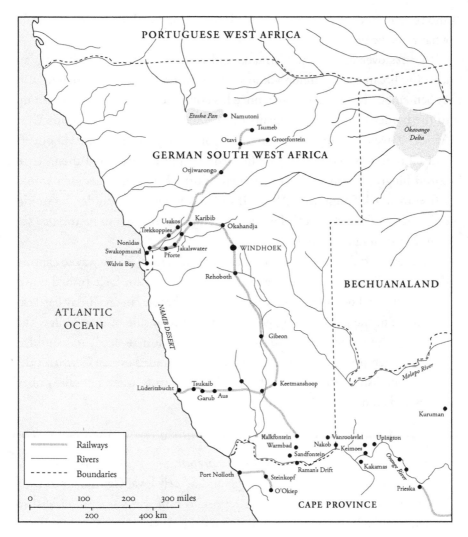

German South West Africa, 1914–1915

since Vereeniging, he had seethed with hatred for the British and now refused point-blank to go to war on their side. Like some of his die-hard colleagues, he was convinced that Germany would win the approaching European war, which would bring an end to Britain's connection with South Africa. For more than a year, he had been conniving with the German colonial authorities to obtain the arms and supplies he needed to mount an internal insurrection and reclaim Boer independence. The Germans played along, never quite sure what to make of him.

Maritz's overtures to the Germans and rumours that he was plotting an uprising became so commonly known that Smuts decided to test him. On 23 September, he ordered Maritz, once his comrade in arms, to move men up to the border to support the incursion of Lukin's 'A' Force into South West Africa. (Given the urgency, Smuts did not distinguish between volunteers and Citizen Force conscripts.) At first Maritz prevaricated, and then, in an astonishingly insolent telegram, warned Smuts that he and his men would refuse to attack South West Africa. If ordered to cross the border, he would rather resign from the UDF. Instructed by Smuts to come to Pretoria to see him, Maritz refused to do so.[2]

The very next day, 26 September, part of Lukin's force, on its way to capture the town of Warmbad, ran into a much stronger German force rushed down from Keetmanshoop to guard the Orange River border. In an all-day battle at Sandfontein, the first watering hole on the German side of the Orange, the UDF detachment was forced to surrender, having lost 16 dead, 40 wounded and 205 taken prisoner against 14 dead and 25 wounded on the German side. The demoralising setback was attributed largely to Maritz's refusal to obey orders and come to Lukin's aid.[3]

Smuts takes action

On 27 September, Smuts sent the tough and fiercely loyal General Coen Brits to Upington and ordered Maritz to report to him. Brits was so faithful to Botha, who had once saved his life during the Anglo-Boer War, that when asked to mobilise his unit, he famously agreed but wanted to know who he was to fight against – the Germans or the British.[4] He was also an officer who wore his rank lightly. As a brigadier general in South West Africa, he ran out of liquor before the end of the campaign and learnt that the only man with a full bottle left was a private in his command. Told that he could not drink with a mere private, Brits immediately promoted the man to second lieutenant, and demoted him again as soon the bottle was finished.[5]

By 9 October, Maritz had moved most of his command to Van Rooisvlei, a farm 35 kilometres to the west of Upington, closer to the border with South

West Africa. At a parade of his men, he gave them one minute to decide whether or not to join him in going over to the German side, saying to the young and impressionable audience, 'We don't want to be ruled by the Jews and financiers of England.'[6] Some 800 troops opted to join him, but 50 men, including the elder brother of Deneys Reitz, refused to do so and were put under arrest and marched across the border to ill-treatment in captivity.

Promoting himself to general on 12 October, the delusional Maritz raised the old republican Vierkleur and pronounced himself to be at war with Britain. Smuts responded immediately by declaring martial law throughout the Union, thereby putting an end to the policy of 'volunteers only'. Maritz then sent the government an ultimatum in which he threatened to take over the Cape province unless he could hold talks with generals De Wet, Hertzog, Beyers, Kemp and Muller. None of these men had any prior knowledge of Maritz's plans and were dismayed at the mention of their names, as it implied prior collusion. Hertzog was particularly annoyed. Although he refused to denounce the rebels, he had been careful not to call for the overthrow of the Botha government by any means other than constitutional.[7]

Maritz's distant mutiny might not have gained much traction were it not for its powerful effect on De Wet, Kemp and, to a lesser extent, Beyers. It was the spark that set fire to the simmering rebellion. To the government, already alarmed by newspaper reports of German incursions into the Union in the neighbourhood of Nakob, it appeared that the mounting unrest was part of a long-planned Boer-German conspiracy. Smuts's declaration of martial law asserted there was 'grave reason to think that the Government of German South-West has communicated with and corrupted other citizens of the Union under the false and treacherous pretext of establishing a republic in South Africa'.[8]

Convinced by now that the Boer-Afrikaner protests were German-inspired rather than spontaneous, Botha and Smuts began calling up commandos to suppress the growing rebellion. They argued that the uprising gave them no option but to cancel the government's earlier 'volunteers only' pledge. Moreover, if men refused to fight for their country, in order to keep the peace they could be interned for the duration of the war.[9] But abandoning the 'volunteers only' policy only increased the confusion among those called up, who were unsure whether they were being conscripted for domestic or cross-border service. The excitable De Wet chose to interpret martial law to mean the armed suppression of all republicans. What it really meant, however, was that Transvaal and Free State Afrikaners had finally to choose between the one side or the other.

By now, says Engelenburg, the Afrikaner people were becoming more and more agitated, and social turbulence was increasing.[10] There was even a plot to kidnap Botha, which led the commissioner of police, Colonel Truter, to assign a posse of bodyguards permanently to the protection of the prime minister.[11] From the Cape, the Dutch Reformed Church thought it necessary to issue a warning to its members not to commit any acts of treason, which were a sin in God's eyes.[12] De Wet took no notice, and began sweeping up audiences across the Free State and Transvaal. A small committee was elected to serve as the mouthpiece of those opposed to government policy. On 14 October, the committee met with Botha for four and a half hours, during which the prime minister firmly refused either to call a halt to the military campaign or to resign.[13]

At this point, Botha turned to the only man who might be able, he thought, to talk sense into De Wet and Beyers – ex-president Steyn. But Steyn was in poor health and disinclined to become involved. He did not agree with the SAP government's policy and, although disapproving of Maritz's mutiny and of rebellion, refused to make any public statement to that effect. In correspondence with Botha, he implied that it was the prime minister who had brought the situation upon his own head.[14]

Botha was unimpressed with Steyn's response. He believed it was the ex-president's duty to warn the Afrikaner people against treason, and to prevent 'the lasting stain … on our national honour and … the incalculably fatal consequences'.[15] Further correspondence on the matter between the two men went nowhere.

Hidden reasons?

There were other, undisclosed, reasons why Botha was keen to take Britain's side against Germany. Since the Anglo-Boer War, he had held a poor opinion of the erratic, unreliable Kaiser Wilhelm II, who had sent President Kruger a telegram of congratulation for having put down the Jameson Raid, and given moral support to the Boers in their fight against the British Empire. When Boer emissaries came to Germany during the war to seek financial help, however, he declined to see them. And when the exiled Kruger paid a courtesy call, the Kaiser did not even grant the much older man an audience. Instead, a flunkey came to Kruger's hotel to deliver a blunt and discourteous message that 'His Majesty' was unable to receive the president of the Transvaal and urged him to reconsider his plans to visit Berlin. It suddenly seemed, says Bossenbroek, 'as if the amicable telegrams the two heads of state had exchanged in earlier years were a figment of someone's imagination. There was no longer a place for Paul Kruger in Wilhelm II's scheme of things.'[16]

Not long afterwards, during the Glorious Trio's tour of Europe, the Kaiser again declined to receive the Boer visitors. Botha's resentment mounted when Wilhelm II claimed that he himself had been the inspiration behind the British tactics in South Africa, including the blockhouses and concentration camps. In Botha's mind there had grown an antipathy for Germany that he had never felt for Britain.

Furthermore, 'Africa for the Afrikanders' had long been a Boer slogan, and when it came to the Kaiser's African empire, territorial expansion was never far from Botha's or Smuts's minds. Their vision of a confederated southern Africa encompassed South West Africa, the British protectorates of Bechuanaland, Basutoland, Swaziland and Nyasaland (today Malawi), the two Rhodesias, and perhaps even the southern half of Portuguese East Africa. If South Africa were to aid Britain by driving the Germans out of South West Africa – they would have reasoned – the Union might justifiably lay claim to this sizeable part of southern Africa once the war was over.[17]

Botha also believed, as did Smuts, that the Kaiser's imperial designs and constant sabre-rattling were a threat to international peace. In *My Early Life*, Churchill – not always the most reliable of witnesses – records how, after Botha had returned from Bad Kissingen in 1913, he warned him most earnestly of the dangerous mood prevailing in Germany. 'Mind you are ready,' Botha said to Churchill. 'Do not trust those people. I know they are very dangerous. They mean you mischief. I hear things you would not hear. Mind you have all your ships ready. I can feel there is danger in the air.

'And what is more,' Botha added, 'when the day comes I am going to be ready too. When they attack you, I am going to attack German South West

Africa and clear them out once and for all. I will be there to do my duty when the time comes. But you, with the Navy, mind you are not caught by surprise.'[18]

Calls to arms

On 13 October 1914, the day after martial law was declared in South Africa, a meeting of Transvaal and Free State rebels took place at Kopjes, an agricultural settlement in the Free State pioneered by Christiaan de Wet. Maritz's revolt in the northern Cape had ignited an uprising in both provinces. Among the Transvaal commandos about to leave Lichtenburg for the border, there was tension between loyalists and rebels. At the last minute, Field Cornet Claasen refused to entrain for the front. Taking with him 300 men, as well as UDF-supplied horses and arms, he rode off towards nearby Treurfontein. Across other regions of the Transvaal and Free State as well, open mutiny was in the air.[19]

At a further meeting at Kopjes on 22 October, it was decided that De Wet would call his supporters to arms in the Free State, while Beyers and Kemp would do likewise in De la Rey's old stamping ground, the western Transvaal. At De Wet's command, says DW Krüger, thousands of men answered the call. Many of them had been too young to fight in the Anglo-Boer War and thrilled at the prospect of riding on commando with the world-renowned general. In the Lichtenburg district, Kemp rounded up 1500 men on his own, while Beyers, 'still disheartened, preferred wandering around the veld to fighting his own people'.[20]

At a cabinet meeting on 26 October, Botha announced to his colleagues that he would have no truck with treason but would go into action himself against Beyers.[21] On the same day, the nation was shocked by an official announcement that a rebellion had broken out in the northern reaches of South Africa. The success or failure of the uprising, as well as the planned invasion of German South West Africa, hinged on Botha, who now took personal command of UDF forces.[22] As the rebellion was confined to Afrikaners, he decided that it had to be put down by Afrikaners only: town-based English-speaking regiments were to be kept out of the fight. Making Pretoria the base from which he could quickly move thousands of men by rail and motorised transport, Botha set off immediately in pursuit of Beyers, known to have taken refuge on a farm in the Rustenburg area. Bidding farewell to Annie, Botha said: 'I have said goodbye to you in many difficult circumstances, but never on such a painful occasion as this. God give me strength to do my duty.'[23]

Hoping to help the UDF put down the rebellion, British colonial secretary Lewis Harcourt offered to divert an Australian naval convoy carrying several hundred troops bound for Colombo to South Africa, but the Union government, according to Buxton, was loath to accept any such assistance. In the first place, Botha preferred to put down the rebellion with his own troops, and, secondly, the Australians 'have a remarkably bad odour in South Africa, for their conduct during the Boer War. They were the only troops who gave a bad impression,' Buxton told Harcourt, who dropped his proposal forthwith.[24]

First shots fired

The rebellion was badly planned, poorly coordinated, and not properly led, and posed no real threat to the much larger government forces, well led by Botha himself. Many of the insurgent rank and file were drawn from the poorer classes, who saw rebellion as a means of recovering their land. At Commissie Drift, outside Rustenburg, Beyers' men were put to flight by government troops and as many as 90 were taken captive. Beyers and 50 others fled to the farm Rooiwal, 35 kilometres away. There, the first shots of the rebellion were fired.

After rapidly regaining control of the entire district, Botha took the bulk of his force back to Pretoria by train. Now on the run, Beyers joined Kemp at Treurfontein, where several rebels were killed in a skirmish with loyalists, and 240 taken prisoner. The only loss on the government side was a Colonel Nolte, who was shot – inexcusably – by rebels while trying to negotiate under a flag of truce.

With arms and ammunition in short supply, Kemp now called for volunteers to accompany him westwards to the border to bring back rifles and ammunition acquired from the Germans by Maritz. His almost month-long trek through the driest and most arid part of the country, although ultimately unsuccessful, was to become one of the epic feats of the rebellion.

With Kemp gone, Beyers hurried with the rump of his force down to the Free State to link up with De Wet. Despite being given safe conduct to discuss a way out of the conflict with ex-president Steyn, Beyers failed to make any headway and hostilities resumed. On 16 November, his force was scattered in a skirmish with government troops at Bultfontein, and several hundred more of his men were captured.

Having been chased for three weeks through the Free State, Beyers and a handful of rebels headed back to the Transvaal, but were tracked down to a farm just south of the swollen and dangerous Vaal River. All of the insurgents surrendered, except for Beyers and a companion, who tried to escape by swimming across the river while under fire. Both were swept away by the swirling waters. When Beyers' body was discovered a few days later, there was not a mark on his body, and his shoulder belt was full of cartridges. Not a single shot had been fired from his rifle.[25]

The rebellion peters out

After Beyers' death, the rebellion all but petered out in the Transvaal. There was a brief attempt by a small force under General Muller, head of the Land Bank, to attack Pretoria, but it was easily repulsed. More serious opposition came from a UDF officer turned rebel, Captain Jopie Fourie, who hatched a wild plan to capture Pretoria on 16 December, the symbolic Day of the Covenant. He was captured at the farm Nooitgedacht, northwest of Pretoria, in a skirmish in which 12 UDF soldiers were killed and 24 wounded.[26]

Fourie, who had not resigned his commission, was reckoned to have caused more deaths of loyalist troops than any other rebel. At a court martial on 19 December, he was given the death sentence himself for treason. Despite pleas for mercy from Afrikaner churchmen, including the rising Nationalist leader DF Malan, Smuts decided to make an example of Fourie to deter other rebels. Early on Sunday morning, 20 December 1914, Jopie Fourie met his end at the hands of a firing squad. As the only rebel to be executed, his place in the Nationalist-Afrikaner pantheon of martyrs was assured. Smuts said afterwards that refusing clemency to Fourie was the greatest political mistake he ever made.[27] Among diehard Nationalists, Smuts – and Botha – were never to be forgiven.

CHAPTER 24

MOPPING UP

Mushroom Valley

In the week before Beyers' death in the Vaal River, Botha put together a group of crack commandos drawn from the Transvaal and other parts of the country. Two of these commandos, led by the trusted generals Lukin and Brits, respectively, were recalled from duty on the South West Africa border. Taking personal charge of operations in the northeastern Free State, Botha sent troops after the rampaging De Wet, who had successfully recruited a rebel force of some 4000 men. On 8 November, a skirmish took place outside Winburg in which three members of a 170-strong volunteer force from the town and nine rebels lost their lives. One of the rebels killed was Danie de Wet, the general's own son.[1]

The next day, a grieving De Wet took revenge on Winburg, ransacking properties and looting shops. He personally assaulted the mayor and locked up the magistrate, one Colin Fraser, who said he felt the general to be 'temporarily insane'.[2] On hearing of De Wet's whereabouts, Botha and his men embarked on an overnight march to Winburg and reoccupied the town without opposition early on the morning of 11 November. Botha then had a stroke of fortune, described by Couzens as 'one of those small incidents that sometimes change the course of history'.[3]

He happened to be in the post office, trying to reach Smuts by telephone, when the phone rang. The call came from a farmhouse in the district, 64 kilometres away, where De Wet had taken members of the Schimper family hostage and locked them up in a small room in which the telephone was housed. The rebel general had not noticed the phone nor bothered to cut the line to the house. Speaking in a whisper, the caller said that De Wet planned to overnight there and move on the next day. 'Please tell General Botha ...' The location of the farm was Mushroom Valley.

Botha went into action immediately. Calling up Lukin and Brits, he instructed them to close off any retreat from the valley via the Korannaberg in the south and told Colonel Brand to do likewise in the west. His own commando under Colonel Myburgh would embark on a night march, a tactic used to great effect in the latter stages of the Anglo-Boer War. At 2.30 am, Botha's men set off on horseback, in pitch darkness and freezing cold, to Mushroom Valley, where they surprised the unsuspecting De Wet and his sleeping men at dawn.

As the sun came up, Botha – who had arrived in the dark in his green Vauxhall touring car – gave the order to open fire. Grabbing only their rifles, the rebels raced away on their horses – straight into the arms of the commandos encircling the valley. After two hours of fierce fighting, the battle of Mushroom Valley was over. Although the elusive De Wet managed once again to get away, he lost 22 men dead and 600 taken prisoner besides having to abandon his transport wagons and most of his arms and ammunition.[4]

Turning point

The rout of De Wet and his followers proved the turning point of the rebellion in the Free State.[5] Before Mushroom Valley, support for him had been growing; now it began to fade away as Botha loyalists began mopping up the last pockets of resistance around the province. On 16 November, De Wet lost more of his men in a clash with government troops at Virginia Station, after which he and a fast-dwindling force of 25 men crossed the railway line north of Vryburg into the Kalahari, making for a rendezvous with Kemp and Maritz.

Hard on the fleeing De Wet's heels was the determined Coen Brits, who switched from cars to horses as he picked off deserters from the rebel general's tiring band. On 2 December, Colonel Jordaan of Brits's force ran down and arrested the weary and dispirited De Wet party in the dry bed of the Molopo River on the farm Waterbury, in Bechuanaland. Upon surrendering, the defiant Free Stater was relieved to find he had been captured by fellow Afrikaners, and not the English troops whom he had defied throughout the

Anglo-Boer War. Yet it was an ignominious end to his distinguished military career. 'When I heard how the obstinate old guerrilla leader had been run to earth by mechanical contrivances,' wrote Deneys Reitz in *Trekking On*, 'I was almost sorry, for it spelt the end of our picturesque South African commando system. With these new engines of war, it would no longer be possible for mounted men to play hide and seek across the veld, and the good old days were gone forever.'[6]

In the eastern Free State, meanwhile, rebel units had stormed the towns of Harrismith, Reitz and Bethlehem. Reitz had been in insurgent hands since 24 October, when it was occupied by a force led by the MP for Frankfort, Niklaas Serfontein. On 2 December, Botha deployed his forces in the area on a wide front and Reitz was evacuated the next day without a 'semblance of resistance' from any quarter.[7] With the writing now on the wall, the rebel commanders Serfontein, Wessels and Van Coller and 1200 men surrendered unconditionally to Botha on 8 December, at Tiger River. The short-lived rebellion in the Free State was at an end.

A troubled Botha derived no satisfaction from the success of his operations in the province. As his bodyguard, Moore Ritchie, recalled: 'There was a sadness ... a profound pathos about it. No wonder if it seemed to me that General Botha looked downcast ... during the rebellion. Life, surely, was not dealing too fairly by him.'[8] Later, Botha was to say: 'For myself personally, the last three months have provided the most sad experiences of all my life ... The war – our South African War – is but a thing of yesterday. You will understand my feelings, and the feelings of loyal commandos when, among rebel dead and wounded, we found from time to time men who had fought in our ranks during the dark days of that campaign.'[9]

Maritz soldiers on

In the far northwestern Cape, Maritz and Kemp were still fighting on. On 28 November, Kemp's exhausted commando, now down from 800 to around 500 men, arrived to join Maritz at Nakob after a month-long 1300-kilometre trek through the waterless Kalahari, harried all the way by loyalist troops. In the meantime, Botha had taken himself by train to Upington to assess the situation at first hand and make plans to counter the two rebel generals.

After time for recovery and re-equipment by the Germans, Kemp's men joined Maritz in a series of skirmishes with UDF forces, now under the command of Colonel Jaap van Deventer. After a successful attack on a UDF base at Nous, Maritz and Kemp withdrew again across the border. Unlike Maritz, however, Kemp was not keen to fight for Germany. Having learnt of the death of Beyers and the capture of De Wet, he realised the rebellion was effectively over. With further resistance being pointless, he approached Van Deventer about terms of settlement.

While Van Deventer awaited a response from defence headquarters in Pretoria, Kemp and Maritz unwisely decided to launch an attack on the UDF's 2 000-strong garrison at Upington. After six hours of fighting, 70 rebels were captured and the rest 'retired' into the desert. At this point Kemp approached Van Deventer again, only to be told that the government's terms were unconditional surrender. Now ill with blackwater fever, Kemp offered to encourage his followers to lay down their arms. On 2–3 February, he and 1 230 rebels handed themselves over at Upington and were taken prisoner.[10] But Maritz and some 50 of his followers refused to surrender and went back over the border into German territory. The self-styled 'general' himself fled to Angola and then to Portugal, Spain and Germany. Returning to South Africa in 1924, he was put on trial and given a prison sentence, but before long Hertzog's newly elected NP government set him free.

The cost of rebellion

The UDF's *Official History* records that the number of rebels who took up arms against the government was 7 128 in the Free State, 2 998 in the Transvaal and 1 251 in Cape, a total of just under 11 500. Ranged against them was a UDF force of some 30 000. About 6 000 rebels were captured or surrendered in the field.[11] However, as the *Official History* notes regretfully, 'the number of rebels was out of all proportion to the damage which they caused, the bitterness which was engendered by their conduct, and the actual cost to the State of the suppression of their revolt.' A total of 132 government troops lost their lives and 242 were wounded, against a rebel casualty list of 190 dead and 300–350 wounded.[12]

Botha had seriously underestimated the extent of Afrikaner dissatisfaction at his SAP government's decision to invade South West Africa. On the other hand, as Buxton records, by taking to the field himself on three occasions – against Beyers and De Wet and at Upington – he boosted the confidence of the many Boer-Afrikaners still loyal to him and discouraged would-be rebels from joining up.[13] Furthermore, he kept his word to the British, saved the Union from disintegration and, through his tactics of surrounding, dispersing and capturing rebels rather than forcing them to fight, kept casualties during the five-month rebellion relatively light.[14]

Yet, despite enjoying the support of a large majority of Afrikaners in provinces other than the Free State, he also made political enemies who would never forgive him, and whose hostility knew no bounds. This section of Afrikanerdom found a new set of martyrs in De la Rey, Beyers and Jopie Fourie, whose deaths engendered a potent form of nationalist fervour, the effects of which were to be felt for decades after the rebellion was over.

Meting out justice

When the hostilities came to an end, there were many rebel leaders and some 5 000 men who had not taken advantage of offers of amnesty and were still languishing in prison. The difficult question was how to deal with them. Some of the insurgents believed they had done no wrong and were fighting for a just cause, as the Boers of old had done. On the other side were government loyalists who had lost property and possessions in the raiding and looting and felt entitled to compensation. And what was the appropriate punishment for the leaders of the rebellion, who were guilty of treason?

'While we must do our duty in seeing that never again shall there be a recurrence of this criminal folly,' Botha declared in a statement after the revolt was over, 'let us be on our guard against all vengeful policies and language and cultivate a spirit of tolerance, forbearance and merciful oblivion of the errors and misdeeds of those misguided people, many of whom took up arms against the State without criminal intent or a clear perception of the consequences of their action. While just and fair punishment should be meted out, let us also remember that now more than ever it is for the people of South Africa to practise a wise policy of forgive and forget.'[15]

HF Trew reports overhearing the prime minister in conversation with a colleague: 'It's easy for you to talk,' said Botha. 'The responsibility is not yours. I do not wish to leave a wealth of bitterness behind, to keep my people divided for ever.'[16]

For his customary moderation, the prime minister had to put up with criticism from both sides. Those against the rebellion accused him of being too lenient, laying too much emphasis on 'forgive and forget'. On the rebel side, many could not understand why they had to be punished at all. Explaining the need for leniency, Botha repeated over and over again that it was not the time for exultation or recrimination. 'Let us spare one another's feelings,' he said. 'Remember we have to live together in this land long after the war is ended.'[17]

Five hundred rebels were released immediately the fighting was over, and most of the rest were given their freedom early in 1915 under a Martial Law Indemnity Act that disqualified them from entering politics or being employed in the public service for ten years. They were also prohibited from possessing arms and ammunition. Some 280 rebel leaders were brought before a special court and charged with high treason, about 170 of whom were sentenced to terms of imprisonment, while the rest were fined and bound over to be of good behaviour.[18] De Wet was given a sentence of six years' imprisonment and a fine of £2000, while Kemp received seven years and a fine of £1000.

Uneasy at the thought of De Wet, a national hero and now an old man, suffering in prison, Botha ordered his release on parole after a few months. All other prisoners – leaders as well as rank and file – were out of jail within the next two years, their fines paid by a new Helpmekaar Fund, created to help Afrikaners in trouble or need.

Hertzog benefits

The politician who benefited most from the rebellion was, inevitably, JBM Hertzog, who had remained silent throughout the upheaval and now made his voice heard again. His Free Staters were more firmly behind him than ever, but so were many previously apolitical Afrikaners and their families in the Transvaal and the Cape, who now became supporters of his National Party. It was the policies of Botha and Smuts – Hertzog claimed again and again – that were the cause of the rebellion. The results of this tactic became apparent in the general election of October 1915.

In his memoirs, Buxton wrote that he doubted whether Botha, profoundly disturbed and distressed though he was at the schism in Afrikanerdom, ever fully realised the depth of the division in South African Party ranks, or recognised the extent of the antagonism to his policy of conciliation. Nor did he appreciate how much his own personal influence and popularity had waned as a result of the rebellion: in his mind, the mistrust of so many rural 'back-velders' was simply 'incomprehensible'.[19] Yet, as Buxton further records, the prime minister was still convinced he had been right to pursue the path of duty and honour, and would have done the same again in similar circumstances.[20]

Into South West Africa once more

In January 1915, with the rebellion over and an uneasy peace prevailing at home, Botha was able to re-focus his attention on the invasion of German South West Africa, on hold since the previous September. For several months the troops at Lüderitz had been kicking their heels aimlessly in the hot and desolate town, ankle deep in sand, waiting until the UDF's coordinated, three-pronged advance into the colony could be resumed. They were overjoyed at the news that General Botha had begun to mobilise a large mounted force and was ready to take the offensive once again.

CHAPTER 25

INTO GERMAN SOUTH WEST AFRICA

Huge and barren

The UDF's initial plan for the invasion of South West Africa had provided for an expeditionary force of some 4 000 men, divided into three separate columns, to converge on the huge, arid and sparsely populated German colony (see map on p 205). When the Afrikaner rebellion broke out in October 1914, 'A' Force, the standing army corps under Lukin's overall command, was on its way to Warmbad across the border via Raman's Drift, only to be recalled after the disaster at Sandfontein. With the help of the Royal Navy, 'C' Force, a mix of volunteers and conscripts under the command of Beves, had already landed at Lüderitzbucht, from where it had begun moving along the railway line into the interior. A third column, 'B' Force, under Maritz, would approach from bases at Upington and Kakamas and join up with Lukin.[1] Directed from Pretoria, the three forces were to advance across a 1 000-kilometre front and converge at the German military supply depot of Keetmanshoop, before setting off along the railway line to Windhoek to dismantle the powerful radio transmitter there.

Defending the huge colony against invasion was a small but well-trained German army, some 7 000 strong, under the command of Colonel Joachim von Heydebreck. It consisted of 140 officers and 2 000 men of the *Schutztruppen* (protection troops), 2 500 reservists, a camel corps, a small air wing, 1 500 policemen, some 200 rebel Afrikaners who had chosen to fight on the German side, and four batteries of field artillery.[2] Besides having a unified command structure and better military organisation than the South Africans, Von Heydebreck had the advantage of a long railway network running up the spine of the colony, and excellent communications links. His plan was to deploy troops at four key locations – Windhoek, Keetmanshoop and the ports of Lüderitz and Swakopmund – that could be reached by rail. Using his superior knowledge of the barren terrain, the German commander could move men quickly by train around the colony to deny the invaders access to key water points and good grazing for their horses. But Von Heydebreck's military capabilities, according to Collyer, were often questioned, and he was not popular with his troops, who preferred his deputy, Major Viktor Franke.[3]

While the Boer-Afrikaner rebellion raged at home, most of the 'C' Force troops in Lüderitz were kept occupied building a garrison, erecting blockhouse defences and constructing a reservoir. As the Germans retreated from the port, pulling up the railway line as they went, the infantry followed them into the interior, re-laying the rail link through the Namib Desert towards the heavily fortified base of Aus. The South African war correspondent WS Rayner, reluctantly granted permission to accompany the troops to Lüderitz, described their working conditions as 'one prolonged wallow in the desiccated dregs of an abominable hell'.[4]

'As often as not, sandstorms raged while they worked – sandstorms of inordinate length and unaccustomed violence – that enveloped them as completely as any London "pea-souper" could have done, when men see each other through a glass darkly. Goggles and veils offered them some protection from these fusillades of grit, but there were often moments when goggles and veils were the greater of two evils. I have seen toiling men rip the veils from their faces because it was necessary for them to breathe freely and at once, and they have then taken to great, big, life-giving gulps of air, sand notwithstanding. I have seen them blindly snatch off their goggles, searching hopelessly about them the while for rag that was dry wherewith to wipe away the condensing moisture that clouded the glass and pained their eyes.'[5]

On 3 October 1914, General Sir Duncan McKenzie, arrived in Lüderitz with additional troops from Natal, to take over command of 'C' Force from Beves. His now 6 600-strong unit comprised two infantry and two mounted brigades and four artillery batteries. Ordered to 'sit tight' until the rebellion was over, McKenzie did just that, but sent a vanguard of 600 mounted men and two field guns on to Tsukaib, a railway stop halfway along the line to Aus.[6] By the end of the five-month rebellion in the Union, Tsukaib had temporarily become South Africa's forward position in South West Africa.

The new plan

With the Afrikaner rebellion nearing its end by Christmas 1914, Botha and Smuts were able to turn their attention again to the campaign in South West Africa. A new plan was drawn up by Smuts to replace the old one. With his innate sense of theatricality – in the field, he preferred to be seen mounted on a large white horse – Botha decided that he should head the invading army himself in order to ensure a unity of command between the political and military spheres. He sensed – correctly – that only he, not Smuts nor anyone else, could unite the UDF's diverse assortment of volunteers and regulars, Rhodesians, Royal Navy auxiliaries, English-speaking troops and mounted burghers, the oldest of whom had fought the British at Majuba.[7] Some commando members from the platteland had never seen the ocean before and could not understand why their horses refused to drink seawater.[8]

The British were deeply concerned at the possibility of Botha becoming a war casualty. The colonial secretary, Lewis Harcourt, sent a private and personal message to Governor-General Buxton to say 'now more than ever General Botha's life is of such supreme importance to the Empire that I sincerely trust that he will not expose himself to any unnecessary danger. If he found it possible not to take personal command of the expedition to German South West Africa, I should be much relieved, but if he finds it imperative to do this, I hope he will run no unnecessary risks. His value as Prime Minister is infinitely greater than even his presence in the field.'[9] Buxton replied: 'Botha values your personal regard for his safety and will run no unnecessary risks. It is proposed to organise a bodyguard which will be an added protection.'[10]

In early January 1915, three more South African troop contingents began to converge on the German colony. Botha took personal command of the largest, the Northern Force, based at Walvis Bay. A new Eastern Force, led by Colonel CAL Berrangé, was on the move from Kuruman to invade South West Africa via Bechuanaland. In the centre, as General McKenzie's Central Force advanced further up the railway line towards Keetmanshoop via Aus, a Southern Force under General JL van Deventer was on its way across the border via Upington and Port Nolloth.[11] Abandoning any pretence at language and provincial equality, Botha had made sure that he had only tried and trusted commanders at his side – men such as Coen Brits, Manie Botha and MW Myburgh. He anticipated, correctly, that the UDF's real battle would not be against the Germans, but rather against geography and the elements – the long distances between towns, the waterless desert, the suffocating sandstorms and the blazing heat.[12]

The prime minister arrived at Lüderitz on 8 February 1915, en route to Swakopmund, and was given a rousing reception when he travelled by open rail-truck to Tsukaib, 72 kilometres away, to inspect troops and confer with McKenzie. Aware of the monotony and thanklessness of the tasks imposed upon his men, he had a salute and smile for all of them. In a short address in Afrikaans, translated by his secretary, Major Bok, he remarked on the fine condition of both soldiers and animals. As Rayner records, the cheering from the largely English-speaking contingent guarding the railway line 'started at Tsukaib ... and died down 40 miles away when the train was approaching the Lüderitzbucht parade ground'.[13]

Seated in a wicker chair on the open truck alongside Botha was the general manager of Reuters news agency, Roderick Jones, who wrote afterwards of the excellent view he was given of the terrain: 'But what a country. North and south, sand to the very horizon and beyond; east, sand also to the ridges that fringe the great interior plateau; a parched and ... a blinding desolation as far as the eye can reach, with sand dunes and lava kopjes here and there to break up the demoniacal monotony of the plains.'[14] HF Trew, the head of Botha's bodyguard, described the Namib 'as one of the most awful scenes of desolation to be found on the face of the globe ... For miles and miles it stretches, a great empty expanse of grey plain, with a thin sandy surface crust covered with small pebbles.'[15]

Logistics the key

Botha's strategy, according to the UDF *Official History*, was to secure a 'jumping off place beyond the desert' from which to attack and destroy the enemy's fighting strength before it could become a guerrilla campaign that might be impossible to put down in such inhospitable territory.[16] As Nasson records, the UDF's numerical and qualitative superiority over the enemy did not necessarily guarantee an easy passage: the colony's huge area (800 000 square kilometres) and waterless terrain made it a formidable objective. Logistics were a crucial factor: 'About half of the South African fighting force comprised mounted infantry which bobbed on a sea of remounts, mules, teams of oxen, carts, wagons, artillery, and twelve million rifle rounds.'[17] Nasson continues: 'The pace of advance beyond ports and railheads depended mainly on animal transport and meeting appetites for water, food and forage. What lay ahead was a shuffling campaign of consumption.'[18]

Logistical difficulties ensured that the UDF's invasion of South West Africa was a stop-start affair from beginning to end. Operational advances were determined by the availability of water, grazing and transport, with food and other supplies having to be carried on wagons drawn by teams of mules through heavy sand. To keep the troops moving forward at a steady pace, draught animals and motor lorries had to be brought up from Cape Town, almost 1300 kilometres away by sea.

On 11 February, Botha arrived in Swakopmund from Lüderitz, after a brief stopover at Walvis Bay. With him was his teenaged son, Jantje. When a friend asked him why he had brought the youngster along on the campaign, Botha replied: 'Look here, I am asking thousands of fathers and mothers in South Africa to send their sons to me. How could I face them afterwards and say, I thought my second son too young, so I left him behind in safety.'[19] To make sure that Swakopmund was unoccupied when his troops arrived, he had sent an advance party up ahead under Colonel Percy Skinner, an officer seconded by the British. Skinner's men had entered the unoccupied town in early January to prepare for the arrival of Botha and his men a month later.[20]

Still under nervous strain from the after-effects of the rebellion, the prime minister was not in the best of health during his first few days in Swakopmund. The town's brackish water made him and many others ill and, unusually for Botha, he had to take to his bed to recover. To revive him, his doctor prescribed a diet of fresh milk and eggs, which were of course unobtainable. So Annie Botha was sent for, and she left Cape Town immediately by naval cruiser, bringing cows and chickens with her.

Annie not only nursed her husband back to health but helped out at the military hospital as well, where she was shocked at the condition of the sick and wounded, and by the incompetence of the male nursing staff. She did what she could to improve conditions until sent home by her husband, who felt it was not right to have his wife with him while his men were parted from their families.[21]

Nonidas

Before moving out of Swakopmund, the Northern Force had to eject a detachment of German troops guarding an observation post on a nearby farm at Nonidas. Having successfully done so, Skinner and his men gulped down large quantities of the water from the farm, only to find that it had been poisoned. Botha formally advised Colonel Franke, who had succeeded Von Heydebreck, that poisoning wells was contrary to the provisions of the Hague Convention, but the German retorted that it was permissible as long as an advisory notice was positioned at the well. The notice at Nonidas had apparently been swept away by the wind.

Besides the poisoned wells, choking dust, flies and heat, another serious menace to the troops' well-being were landmines, liberally strewn about in the vicinity of railway tracks. These deadly devices were legitimate weapons of war, according to Franke. The South Africans, on the other hand, regarded them as a 'very unfair and unsportsmanlike' way of fighting, and had to bring in herds of goats to use as mine detectors.[22] In his account of the war, Lieutenant Commander Whittall, a Royal Navy officer serving with the UDF, described the Germans' use of mines as 'promiscuous'. 'It is beyond question,' he recorded, 'that the Germans overstepped the usages of civilised war in this as in many other directions.'[23]

Held up at Riet

On 18 March, the Northern Force's advance on Karibib from Swakopmund resumed. Botha accompanied his troops on night marches and camped with them under the stars as they made their way up the Swakop River in the direction of the German defensive line in the Riet-Pforte area. One night, as the prime minister lay on the river sand surrounded by his bodyguard, he reflected ruefully: 'As I sat in Kitchener's saloon carriage at Vereeniging, after signing the treaty which ended the Boer War, I said to myself, thank God, Louis Botha, you will have to ride your horse to no more wars, and look, now my duty calls me back once more to the thing I hate.'[24]

After an all-day battle for the heavily defended natural fortresses of Riet, Pforte and Jakkalswater, Botha's men succeeded in driving the enemy out of the area, but once again had to abandon hot pursuit because of the scarcity of water and lack of fodder for the exhausted horses. Next day, a mounted UDF brigade found documents at another hastily evacuated German camp at Modderfontein confirming that German forces were in the south for observation purposes only.[25]

The UDF's successful operations around Riet, records Collyer, had a decisive effect on the course of the war. Thereafter, the German commander yielded long tracts of the most difficult territory without making any attempt to defend them. 'The Germans never stood again,' wrote Collyer, 'until the last and greatest enveloping movements of their adversary compelled them to do so and surrender.'[26] Botha's bodyguard Moore Ritchie, in his war memoir, wrote that the actions along the 34-kilometre Pforte-Riet-Jakkalswater front were 'practically the deciding factors of the campaign'.[27]

Back to Swakopmund

A lack of water and fodder for the horses forced Botha to withdraw his mounted brigades to Swakopmund to recover. Any further advance depended on Riet's becoming a secure base for the stockpiling of supplies.[28] The Riet-Pforte area was deeply disliked by UDF troops, however, with one man labelling it 'a hole worse that any hole ever seen'.[29] O'Shaughnessy described the surrounds, with pardonable exaggeration, as being in '... a country which for its utter desolation is surely without parallel in any portion of the world; interminable miles – *sans* vegetation of any kind – of dreary sandy wastes out of which arise, in a variety of heights and a confusion of order, unscaleable granite rocks of massive proportion, intermingled with smaller series of serrated, barren ridges. Not a drop of water, not a sign of life – a truly forsaken wilderness.'[30]

For almost a month, the Northern Force marked time at Riet, living off the oxen of their field batteries until more rations were forthcoming. Then the infantry march towards Karibib resumed, for mile after mile through a desert bereft of water.[31] Keith Morris quotes this description by Botha of the horrors of dehydration:

> When I tell you that sometimes we trekked a distance of fifty miles without water, and that at the end of the trek the men had to scrape a dry river bed to find water, you will realise all the hardships they suffered. When

we brought the horses to the water their tongues were so dry that it was impossible for them to drink, and it was necessary to force water down their throats before they would drink. But I was told before I went that we must take all risks and responsibilities and push through, in hopes that we should find taps on the other side. I can never impress on you my thankfulness when, after a trek of one hundred and forty miles, we found water and also grass, and when I called the men together to give them water they said, 'You can give us any orders you like, because we have got what we want.'[32]

While his troops stayed put at Riet, Botha went back to Lüderitzbucht to confer with McKenzie, whose men had undertaken another waterless trek from Tsukaib to capture the railway halt at Garub, and were in no condition to advance immediately on Aus. Papers captured from the enemy provided further confirmation that the Germans had withdrawn most of their forces in the south of the colony to counter the UDF's northern thrust from Swakopmund and Walvis Bay.

In the south, Van Deventer was making steady progress towards Keetmanshoop, while from the east, Berrangé and his men were marching through the Kalahari from Kuruman. Botha's objective now was Karibib, where the Germans had concentrated a large force to prevent the fall of the nearby capital, Windhoek. Determined to maintain the pressure on the retreating Germans, he called up Smuts from Cape Town to take personal command of the Central Force and amalgamate it with the Southern Force in order to give 'one undivided direction' to the operation.[33]

CHAPTER 26

A Tactical Triumph

All-out offensive

Botha's strategy in the unfolding of the South West Africa campaign showed he had lost none of his tactical genius. His deployment of three forces in the south had been, in essence, a tactical feint to distract and divide the enemy while his large Northern Force advanced on its target of Windhoek, at the heart of the colony.[1] With captured documents revealing that most of Franke's Schutztruppen were intent on massing in the northern sector, Botha decided to amalgamate McKenzie's Central Force, Van Deventer's Southern Force and Berrangé's Eastern Force into a unified Southern Army, under the trusted Smuts. He now had more than sufficient strength for an all-out offensive against the German defenders.

The Southern Army's combined strength was some 14 000 mounted troops, while the Northern Force numbered 20 000 men, of whom 13 000 were mounted. The two force's operations were supported by over 33 000 black, coloured and Indian volunteer auxiliaries, who carried out duties as drivers, munitions carriers, railway and road workers and general labourers.[2] Botha also had 600 motorised vehicles at his disposal, but preferred to rely on actual horse power because of the softness and depth of the desert sands.[3]

While the Northern Force made ready for the advance from Riet, supplies had to be brought up on the railway line, which ended at Trekkoppies station, halfway between Swakopmund and Usakos on the way to Karibib. At Trekkoppies, Colonel Skinner's troops were the victims of a surprise attack by a much larger German force of mounted infantry and artillery, and had to be rescued by recently arrived Royal Navy armoured cars, under Lieutenant Commander Whittall, who developed a high regard for Botha 'and the astonishing South African infantry in the desert marches of the South-West African campaign'.[4]

Shortly after his arrival in the German colony, Whittall had been invited to tea by his commander-in-chief. 'I had heard a great deal about his wonderful influence among his own people,' Whittall wrote later. 'I knew also that Louis Botha was held in real affection by members of his staff, both personal and general, but it was not until I met him that I was able to understand the reason of his extraordinary power over men. And even then, though I could understand and appreciate it to the full, I could not pretend to define what it is that produces or accounts for its influence ... No one can meet and talk to Botha for five minutes without coming under the spell of his magnetic personality. He compels you at once to the conviction that this is indeed a leader of men.'[5]

Johannes Meintjes, whose father was an unwilling conscript in Botha's army rather than a volunteer, records that some of the burgher troops were most unhappy at having been commandeered to serve outside South Africa's borders. Many could see no reason for the campaign in South West Africa and were anxious to get back to their farms as soon as possible. English-speakers, on the other hand, were more positively inclined, and in much less of a hurry. But both factions had equal faith in their commander-in-chief, trusting his judgement better than their own. Many an argument was settled by the simple formula, 'Louis Botha says so.'[6]

To Karibib

On 28 April, the Northern Force began its advance on Karibib. Four mounted brigades led the way along the dry bed of the Swakop River, followed by infantry who moved up along the railway line. Riding at great speed, the mounted troops outflanked the retreating enemy, and after a dash of 64 kilometres across waterless country, Coen Brits entered Karibib on 5 May, only to find that its defenders had departed. The next day Botha himself and the tired infantry arrived in the town and took time off to rest and recover.

In the south, the UDF advance progressed steadily. By 14 April, Smuts's Southern Army had reached Keetmanshoop, where – with excellent timing – its three columns converged and set about chasing the retreating Germans northwards. A major skirmish took place at Gibeon on 25–26 April, during which the German rearguard sustained heavy losses at the hands of a mounted force under General McKenzie. The South Africans failed to sever the rail link, however, enabling the main body of Germans to escape in a northerly direction, where Botha's men awaited them. The engagement at Gibeon virtually cleared the southern region of German forces; it also prevented the outbreak of guerrilla warfare in the area, and ensured that there would be no German threat to the flank of Botha's northern thrust. After three weeks of 'blazing action', Smuts – having nothing more to do – was able to return to his political and administrative duties in South Africa.[7]

The Basters

The German defeat at Gibeon brought forth a reaction from the Baster communities in the Rehoboth Reserve that the Germans had not bargained for.[8] Large numbers of Baster carts, wagons and animals had been commandeered by Franke's retreating forces and many male inhabitants of the Reserve conscripted into the colonial army. In April, a deputation of Basters slipped away across the desert for an audience with Botha in Swakopmund, at which – as migrants from South Africa – they offered to assist the UDF in fighting the Germans. Botha politely declined the offer, saying this was a conflict in which 'the coloured people should not be involved',[9] blithely overlooking the large number of auxiliaries of colour in his own army.

Relations between the Basters and the Germans had turned nasty, with the latter shooting members of the community who tried to flee the Reserve, and the former retaliating by attacking German police officers and snatching arms, ammunition and livestock. In the last week of April, German troops wreaked revenge on the fleeing refugees, 'killing women and children and animals, and torching wagons'.[10] Hostilities subsided as the Germans retreated, but from UDF's viewpoint the internal rebellion was timeous, as it helped divert attention from Botha's inland thrust, as well as the steady advance of the Southern Army.[11]

On 5 May, when South African forces rode into Karibib, although food was in short supply in the town, Botha forbade his hungry troops from looting. As Whittall records: 'To say that a virtual famine existed does not exceed the truth. Everyone was on the shortest of short rations. Even the hospitals were living from hand to mouth.'[12] According to Collyer, the local newspaper commented that the South Africans 'behaved properly and courteously, and in such a way as becomes civilised soldiers'.[13] The town became Botha's new headquarters.

On to Windhoek

The road to Windhoek now lay open. Intercepted communications between the mayors of Karibib and Windhoek revealed that the Germans had abandoned the capital, which would fall to the South Africans without resistance. On the afternoon of 11 May, Botha and members of his staff set out by car along the sandy 190-kilometre road to Windhoek. They overnighted in the veld and early the next morning pressed on through rivers of such deep sand that Botha himself had to get out and push his vehicle.[14] At 11 am on 12 May, a nervous mayor of Windhoek formally handed over his capital to Botha, who declared martial law and ordered the Union Jack to be flown above the Rathaus. His valet wired Annie the next day: 'Me and the General took Windhoek yesterday. The General keeps well.' The town's huge radio mast, the second largest in the world, had been left intact but was without its working parts, the Germans clearly believing the occupation of Windhoek to be only temporary. After the war in Europe had been won, they reckoned, they would have further need of the facility.

The capture of Windhoek only 16 days after leaving Swakopmund was, in the judgement of Couzens, among others, 'an exceptional feat, an outstanding victory', all the more so because it had been achieved without a spectacular battle or much actual fighting and with a minimum of bloodshed.[15] For Botha, it had been another tactical triumph, brought about by his forces' speed of manoeuvre and their astonishing endurance. More importantly, he and the UDF had fulfilled to the letter the mandate they had been given by the imperial government.

Operations in the German colony were no means over, however. The towns of Otavi, Tsumeb and Grootfontein, to which Franke's force of some 4 000 troops had retreated, lay another 320 kilometres away.[16] It was now essential for the UDF to defeat what remained of the enemy forces quickly and decisively, for the bushy terrain in the north of the colony was conducive to a prolonged guerrilla war. Botha was conscious, too, of the rancorous opposition to his campaign from the Hertzogites and pro-German elements back home.

Once again, the South Africans were held up for some time by logistical difficulties. Having to rebuild sections of the railway line from Usakos to Okahandja meant that rations could not be brought up the line to the north, and were once again in short supply. And just as the Northern Force was about to advance, the colony's German governor, Theodor Seitz, asked for a truce of 48 hours so that he could confer with Botha. On 20 May, the two men met under an acacia tree midway between Karibib and Omaruru.

Seitz, a short, aggressive individual who did most of the talking, proposed that hostilities should ease, and that each side should keep control of the territory it occupied, with a neutral zone in between. At the end of the European war, a treaty would determine the future of the colony. Botha listened attentively and then said politely that his terms were unconditional surrender. This was rejected out of hand by Seitz, who believed that Franke's forces would be able to hold out successfully in the north. Both men went back to their respective lines, Botha to prepare for the advance and Seitz for further retreat.[17]

Considering settlement

Seitz's settlement proposals were formally referred to the governor-general, Buxton, and the Union cabinet for consideration, but were rejected as unacceptable. Characteristically, in a telegram to Smuts, a copy of which was sent to Buxton, Botha stated that, while his terms were the handing over of the territory, he would not insist on the Germans' unconditional surrender, 'as I felt we should not do anything to hurt their pride unnecessarily, and you know how bitter such demands on us (before Vereeniging) made us feel'.[18]

On 15 June, Botha reported to Buxton that the delay in pursuing the Germans after the occupation of Windhoek was taking much longer than expected: 'But this could not be avoided because our horses were in a very poor condition after the strenuous trek last month, and must be rested and fed. When we start again we have to march more than two hundred miles through thick bush country, all the way under conditions favourable to the enemy; want of water continues to be a great problem … and we shall be to a great extent dependent upon wells, which can quite easily be destroyed or rendered useless by the enemy.'[19]

Cornering the enemy

Three days later, the UDF's northward offensive from Karibib resumed. Using his favourite Zulu impi-style battle formation to avoid unnecessary casualties, Botha sent Brits and Myburgh and their mounted brigades off to the left and right on wide flanking sweeps to occupy the hilly ground behind the German outposts of Tsumeb and Grootfontein. His own unit would advance from the centre on Franke's troops, who had dug in 16 kilometres north of Otavi. Its progress was aided by the arrival of the first-ever reconnaissance aircraft to be deployed by the UDF, operating from a hastily built landing strip at Karibib.

Once again, the Germans were outmanoeuvred by the speed and mobility of the UDF's mounted forces. At Tsumeb, it was estimated the South Africans would arrive on the next Tuesday at the earliest, but Myburgh's mounted infantrymen turned up two days early, on Sunday. Huge stores of munitions were captured, 600 UDF prisoners set free, and an equivalent number of Germans taken prisoner. On the left flank, Brits's brigade took the town of Namutoni, on the edge of the Etosha Pan, encountering only token resistance.

Trapped by these pincer movements, Seitz called for another meeting to discuss surrender. Speaking to Brits and Myburgh on a telephone provided by the Germans (and no doubt tapped by someone who could understand English and Afrikaans), Botha took the precaution of conversing in Zulu – a language in which all three men were fluent.[20] After consulting Buxton, Smuts and the South African cabinet, he handed Seitz final terms of surrender on 6 July, insisting on receiving a reply by 2 am on the 9th.

A generous peace

South Africa's terms were extremely generous: regular German officers would be released on parole and allowed to retain their arms but not to possess ammunition; other ranks would be interned; and reservists would be permitted to return to their farms with both rifles and ammunition for self-protection

Botha (centre) negotiates with German colonial officials for the surrender of Windhoek.

HISTORICAL IMAGES ARCHIVE/ALAMY STOCK PHOTO

against the 'natives'. However, all machine guns, artillery pieces and means of transport had to be surrendered. After pleading for, and being refused, an extension of time, the Germans signalled their acceptance of the terms shortly after the deadline expired. At 10 am on 9 July the surrender took effect. Another huge territory had been added to the British Empire.[21]

South Africa's leniency towards the defeated Germans was criticised by, among others, *The Times* in London: 'For an enemy who has fought the campaign with every foul device that a malign ingenuity could invent, had poisoned wells, and had treated prisoners with infamous and deliberate brutality, those terms were … generous to a fault.'[22] But Botha, a firm believer in the virtue of magnanimity, was unrepentant – and humble in victory. Addressing his men in a farewell speech, he said: 'When you consider the hardships we met, the lack of water, the poisoned wells, and how wonderfully we were spared, you must realise and believe in God's hand protecting us and it was due to His intervention that we are safe today.'[23]

Casualty rates in the conflict, by comparison with those in Europe, were astonishingly low: In capturing a territory the size of Germany and Britain combined, South Africa lost 88 men killed in action, and 25 who died of their

Santry, 16 May 1915

'Well Played!', a cartoon by Irishman Denis Santry, who worked in South Africa for many years, uses the rising interest in rugby in the Union to celebrate the UDF's successful action in German South West Africa. Botha, as the Union Captain, comments, 'Well, if that doesn't finish the game, it gives us a wonderfully good land.'

injuries. A further 263 men were wounded but recovered over time. Illness and accidents resulted in 153 other deaths, more than were caused by enemy action, and 606 UDF soldiers were taken prisoner.

On the German side, the losses were 103 killed, 195 wounded and 890 captured. The *Cambridge History of the British Empire* described the campaign as 'one of the neatest and most successful' of the Great War ... At small cost and with great credit to itself, the Union had rendered an immense service to the Empire.'[24]

Leaving Beves, now a brigadier general, behind as military governor of British South West Africa and Colonel Mentz in command of Windhoek, Botha returned to a hero's welcome in South Africa. Huge crowds assembled to acclaim him in Cape Town and Johannesburg, and admirers gathered at every station along the railway line to Pretoria to cheer him home. Telegrams congratulating the UDF on its victory – the first Allied success in the Great War – poured into the prime minister's office in Pretoria. Kitchener was one of the first to congratulate Botha on his 'masterly conduct' of the campaign. King George V, Prime Minister Asquith, the colonial secretary, Bonar Law, and Dominion prime ministers were among the many who paid warm trib-ute to 'General Botha' for strengthening the bonds of Empire.[25]

Smuts's biographer, Sir Keith Hancock, describes the letters written by Botha to Smuts during the campaign in South West Africa as 'a precious series'. 'They reveal most vividly the simplicity and subtlety, the prudence and the daring, the patience and the gusto of a great leader of men. While he was attending most meticulously to the innumerable details of administrative preparation, Botha all the time was ushering his forces forward to hustle the enemy and "give them a good fright".'[26]

By the end of the campaign, Botha, at the age of 52, was in better physical condition than he had been for years. Riding, exertion and life in the open air had done wonders for his health. Buxton wrote to a friend that he had heard that Botha was 'in the pink of condition' and 'looked ten years younger in consequence of all the exercise he was having'.[27]

Fitter though he may have been, in the aftermath of victory the prime minister's sensitive soul was deeply troubled. For it was the British – and English-speaking South Africans – who were celebrating the UDF's triumph, not his own people. Many Afrikaners had come to doubt the man they once revered, sceptical of his claim to 'have taken the difficult course … the road of honour, truth and justice'.[28] Was Louis Botha still one of them, or had he betrayed his roots, more and more of his fervent, once-faithful supporters wondered.

CHAPTER 27

TROUBLED TIMES

A bitter campaign

The tensions that surfaced from time to time between English-speaking and Afrikaner sections of the UDF in South West Africa were writ large in South Africa itself. Despite Smuts's proud claim that the conquest of the German colony was 'the first achievement of a united South African nation, in which both races have combined all their best and most virile characteristics',[1] Hertzog's Nationalists did not see it that way. Their relentless vilification of Botha and Smuts resulted in the October 1915 election campaign's being one of the bitterest and most divisive ever held in white South Africa.[2]

For the Botha government, the 1915 election was never going to be easy. As Sarah Gertrude Millin observed, 'Within a few years, the South African Party, which had so triumphantly marched into office after Union, had offended Britons, Boers, natives, Indians and democrats in South Africa. And now the NP of Hertzog, among whites, was suddenly the "patriotic party".'[3]

The UDF's triumph in South West Africa served only to fuel the anger and resentment of that section of Afrikanerdom that had opposed the operation and supported the rebellion. By now, the NP – led by Hertzog with the moral support of the ailing President Steyn – had grown in numbers far beyond the Free State. Shortly after Smuts's return from South West Africa, a German U-boat sank the British passenger liner *Lusitania* off the coast of Ireland, with horrendous loss of life. The incident led to wild anti-German protests across urban South Africa and the burning of buildings and properties. In Johannesburg alone, three German-owned bioscope theatres, the German Club and eight hairdressing salons were burnt down.[4] The government's hesitance in taking firm action against the rioters, whose support they might need in the election, further weakened its position among Afrikaners.

To his dismay, Botha realised that, far from coming together, the two white races were drawing further apart. Accompanying the growth in support for the National Party (NP) was a resurgence of Afrikaner cultural and language sentiment in churches, universities and schools. Emotions were aroused to fever pitch by a propaganda campaign that accused Botha and Smuts of responsibility for the deaths of De la Rey, Beyers and Jopie Fourie. 'Judases', 'traitors', 'murderers' were some of the epithets flung at them by hecklers at political meetings. Former Cape premier John X Merriman declared that never, in his 46 years in politics, had he known such feeling between English and Dutch, 'so bitter, so absolutely impossible … What is going to be the end of all this?' he wondered.[5]

Writing to Smuts while Botha was still away on campaign, a deeply worried Merriman said that 'the only bond of union is a professed hatred of Botha and yourself, which … is based not on your mistakes and errors, but on your good deeds … But you must have courage and take the job in hand, organise! organise! … The one-stream policy will carry the day if you explain it … [Hertzog's] cause is based on personal jealousy, race hatred [between Afrikaners and English-speakers] and narrow-minded exclusiveness, and is bound to fail if we grapple it properly.'[6]

The red-hot issue in the October 1915 election was whether or not South Africa should continue to support Britain in the war against Germany. The SAP and Unionists were in favour, with the Nationalists and half of the Labour Party against. Though dispirited by the numbers of Afrikaners turning against him, Botha criss-crossed the country, arguing that reconciliation between white South Africans, under the protective umbrella of the Empire, was the best way forward for the Union.

Pyrrhic victory

In the all-white general election, Botha's SAP won 54 seats, 20 fewer than before; Smartt's Unionists took 40 seats, Hertzog's Nationalists 26 seats (up from eight), and Labour and Independents six and four seats, respectively. SAP supporters thought their party had performed reasonably well, given the

acrimony on the hustings, but their leader was not fooled. Three of his ministers had lost their seats and support from Afrikaners had fallen by 40 per cent.
The Hertzogites had polled over 78 000 votes, many of them in rural constituencies. In order to pass critical legislation, the SAP would now have to
rely on the support of the Unionists – the pro-British party containing many
unreconstructed jingoes. The prospect left Botha disturbed and depressed,
and he began again to harbour thoughts of resignation.

After discussions with colleagues, and especially with Governor-General
Buxton – whose counsel he had come to value – he was persuaded that it
would be wrong to resign. He had just won an election fought mainly over
his leadership and policies, and taking Britain's side in the war still enjoyed
majority support among all voters besides the Nationalists. According to
Buxton, Botha mistakenly thought the dissolution of parliament had brought
an end to his government, and was much relieved to find that he would be
able to remain in office until he chose to resign. Ever conscious of being
called a coward, he told Buxton that, although deeply disappointed at the
election result, he had decided it was his duty 'under the circumstances' to
carry on in office. 'We shall get over our difficulties. We shall get over them
slowly but surely,' he declared.[7]

East Africa

Around the time of the 1915 election, as a sequel to the successful operation
in South West Africa, the UDF was asked to come to the aid of imperial forces
attempting to eject the Germans from their prized possession of Tanganyika
in East Africa. Botha and Smuts were keen to provide troops for an exercise
that, if successful, would thwart the Kaiser's expansionist aims in Africa and
perhaps ensure that, after the war, East Africa would fall within the Union's
sphere of influence. Up to that point, the British-led East African campaign
had been hampered by ineffective leadership (and a secretary of state for war
in Britain reluctant to sanction offensive action elsewhere than in Europe[8]),
so the experienced Smuts was invited to take command of imperial forces in
the territory.

After turning down the invitation in November 1915 – possibly because
the nature of the battle and the terrain were so different from anything he

'At manoeuvres – Generals Smuts and Botha.' Another caricature by DC Boonzaier,
the leading cartoonist of his time, who was no admirer of Botha or Smuts and attacked
both men relentlessly in the cartoons he drew for various pro-Nationalist publications
(from Rand Faces, *1915).* BRENTHURST LIBRARY

had encountered before, but certainly because of the unsettled political
climate at home – Smuts accepted at the second time of asking 'with many
a pang and many a grave misgiving'.[9] He arrived at Mombasa in early 1916
to take command of a polyglot army of Indians, East Africans and South
Africans, Rhodesians and British troops. By March, there were as many
as 19 000 UDF servicemen in East Africa, including a mounted 'burgher
force' under Jaap van Deventer.[10]

The year before, when Botha had gone to South West Africa, Smuts had
stayed behind in Pretoria to run the government. Now the roles were reversed:
Smuts was in the field, while Botha remained as commandant-general and
defence minister *pro tem*, thereby doubling his official duties. He wrote to
Smuts saying, 'My heart and soul are with you, and I shall do everything in my
power to help you, be assured of that. Just tell me what can be done … Your

going has everyone's approval and I can only wish you God's best blessing.'[11] It was the first time Botha did not have Smuts at his side in government, and he felt the latter's absence as much as he missed the services of his devoted private secretary, Dr WE Bok, who had recently become the secretary for justice.

Parliamentary difficulties

It was Unionist supporters, however, rather than the reinvigorated Nationalists who were the first to cause problems for Botha after the election. The issue arousing their ire was the pay differential between the 6 000 UDF volunteers sent to Britain in 1915 and those in the field in German East Africa. Troops in Europe were paid at the British rate of one shilling per day, while the men in East Africa received three shillings. In parliament, the Unionists demanded equal pay of three shillings for all troops in uniform outside the country. On the other side, the Nationalists weighed in with objections to the Union's exchequer making extra payment to men fighting – in their eyes – not for South Africa but for Britain and the Empire. Many in Botha's own party agreed with the NP that it was up to the British to make good the shortfall.

No longer having an outright parliamentary majority and not wishing to further inflame Afrikaner/English tensions, Botha trod warily. He warned the Unionists that if he were pushed on the matter, he would side with his own people. As he explained to Buxton, how to avoid making a choice was giving him sleepless nights: 'I am neither pro-English, nor pro-Dutch ... I have stood out against such a policy for ten years ... such a position I could not and would not tolerate.'[12]

During the debate in parliament, the prime minister declared himself personally in favour of equal pay, but it was not merely a matter of pounds, shillings and pence. Many members of his own party were strongly against South Africa funding any extra payment to troops in Europe and – hard though he had tried – he was unable to gain their assent. 'The most unfortunate position that we could create today,' he declared, 'would be ... to divide the Boers and British in this House. This would be more fatal to our living together in this country than anything else. If it takes place, it is my sacred duty to resign immediately ... To divide the people on this matter at the present time is wrong and is in conflict with the true and real interests of

South Africa. We must continue to give our help to Europe until the Empire emerges from its trouble.'[13]

'It was a damnable thing,' Botha told Buxton after the debate, 'to have to speak against a motion [proposing equal pay] in the justice of which I believed. I feel very uncomfortable. It was a bad job, but I had to consider my party. It would have been the greatest mistake in my life if I had not done as I did.'[14] The divisive pay issue resurfaced in October, when the cabinet resolved to inform the imperial government that while South Africa hoped to send troops from East Africa to reinforce the numbers in Europe, it could not afford to pay three shillings per day. The matter was eventually resolved by parliament's agreeing to pay the British government £1 million for 'general war purposes', funds that were used to pay UDF troops in Europe at the higher rate.

A troubled year

The year 1916 was not a good one for Botha. It began with an exchange of letters with De Wet, who had been released from prison on condition he signed an undertaking not to take part in politics or public meetings and to remain on his farm until the war was over. So many of his followers rallied to see the old Boer hero, however, that an alarmed Botha felt it necessary to write formally to him expressing the government's concern at his actions. De Wet replied that he had not expected 'the concourse of people who had come of their own accord'. His exhortation that his supporters 'must prepare themselves for great things' was being done in the hope that God would end the war soon; no one, he claimed, could blame him for praying for the restoration of Boer freedom without force.[15]

These excuses failed to convince Botha, resentful of the rebels' continuing defiance of his authority and patient attempts at reconciliation. He wrote by return to De Wet, reminding him of an agreement whose terms were quite simple: 'Your sense of honour must show you the direction in which you must go to carry out your solemn promises.'[16] From then on De Wet kept silent, anxious to demonstrate to Botha that he was also a man of his word.

Shortly before parliament reconvened, the prime minister had to rush home in distress to Rusthof, where a wildebeest had killed two of his farm workers. By now, he had grown weary, both physically and in spirit.[17] He missed the presence of Smuts at his side and was increasingly disillusioned at the prospects for reconciliation. Nonetheless, in the House, he held doggedly to his middle-of-the-road position between two extremes. Yet he remained careful to keep his distance from the Unionists for fear of alienating his own anti-jingo supporters, and did whatever he could to identify himself more closely with Afrikaner sentiments.

'A terrible country'

The weary Botha was troubled, too, by the rising cost of the UDF's involvement in the war in East Africa, and by the Nationalists' frenzied propaganda against it. On arrival in Kenya, Smuts had immediately gone on the offensive against the wily and elusive German commander, General Paul von Lettow-Vorbeck. Operational circumstances were even more formidable than they had been in South West Africa. The huge territory was part bushveld and, in summer, part swamp, with malaria a constant hazard. UDF troops fell ill by the thousand and had to be repatriated, while tens of thousands of horses and mules succumbed to the mosquito and tsetse fly. Though Smuts was able to win back much German-held territory, he could never quite pin down Von Lettow-Vorbeck, who resorted to the kind of mobile warfare that Smuts himself had employed in the Anglo-Boer War.[18]

In mid-year, Botha paid a visit to UDF forces in East Africa and witnessed for himself the severity of conditions on the ground. He had never fought alongside Smuts before and may secretly have had reservations about the latter's aggressive tactics, but was wise enough not to say so. Instead he wrote to Smuts to commiserate with his problems: 'I am proud of your work, old chap, and on leaving, I can only say that all my weight is at your disposal, and be assured, Jannie, that we pray for your success and safe return.'[19]

Describing what he had found to his friend Buxton, he said the enemy was the least of the problems the Union forces had to contend with in East Africa. The thick bush, impenetrable jungle, high grass, wild beasts, overflowing rivers and swampy conditions in the rainy season made it 'a terrible country to negotiate'. Transport and supply difficulties and food and water shortages meant that UDF troops had to subsist on the scantiest of rations. The good temper and grit with which they bore these discomforts filled Botha with pride and admiration.[20]

He was also pleased with the achievements of the 1st South African Infantry Brigade, which had gone into action in Egypt before being sent to France. During the Battle of the Somme in mid-1916, 2 815 South African soldiers lost their lives, most of them at Delville Wood, 'the most glorious feat of arms'[21] in the country's military history. Paying tribute in the House of Assembly to those who died at Delville Wood and in subsequent battles, Botha said: 'Those men who have stood there and have fallen there have done honour to our name, they have upheld our reputation, they have shown that South Africa produces some of whom the world may justly be proud.'[22]

Shortly before the Battle of the Somme, Botha learnt with shock of the death, at sea, of Lord Kitchener. Announcing the news in the House, he was moved to speak some words of sympathy in English – 'in a broken whisper', says Buxton.[23] Memorial services for Kitchener were held in various parts of South Africa. Before one of them, the governor-general was touched to receive the following telegram from Lichtenburg: 'Widow De la Rey wishes you kindly convey to Secretary of State her deepest sympathy at the calamity which befell Lord Kitchener and his staff; an honourable man and great friend to her late husband.'[24]

Like Botha, old Mrs De la Rey believed in thinking well of former enemies.

CHAPTER 28

IN POOR HEALTH

Melancholia

Two events towards the end of 1916 gave Botha the opportunity to identify himself more closely with Afrikaner sentiment. The first was the death of the revered ex-president Marthinus Steyn after many years of painful physical suffering. While in the midst of a speech to a women's organisation in Bloemfontein, the elderly Steyn collapsed and died on the scene. On 3 December 1916, a huge crowd gathered in the city for his state funeral.

Although he had wished to be buried in a simple grave on his farm, Steyn was given the honour of being laid to rest at the shrine of Afrikanerdom, Bloemfontein's Vrouemonument. Botha and Hertzog were both present to pay him tribute, and for a brief moment forgot their differences.[1] In his heartfelt eulogy, Botha said he was incapable of finding words to express his sorrow at the passing of one of Afrikanerdom's iconic figures. Sadly surveying an audience that had largely lost faith in him, the prime minister said the people of the Free State had been richly blessed under Steyn's leadership: 'The old President had died as he had lived, among his own people and working for their well-being ... For me personally, it is the loss of a dear friend. It seems but yesterday that we were both young and bosom friends ...'[2]

Botha's melancholia was so much deeper because he realised that with Steyn's death another vital link with the past had been broken; there was now scant chance of Afrikaner reunification. The mourners present, records Meintjes, noticed a physical change in the prime minister: he was portlier and his shoulders sagged, and his eyes 'which used to be so bright were sad and reflective. There was a hunted look about Louis Botha, and he was ageing though still a man in his prime.'[3]

Less than two weeks after Steyn's funeral, Botha spoke to another great audience of Afrikaners, at the Dingane's Day commemoration at Paardekraal. The occasion was well organised and well attended, but it was noticeable that the prime minister's political opponents had stayed away, pretending to be indignant that he was 'roping in Paardekraal for his own purposes'.[4]

Near the end of a tribulation-filled year, Annie Botha took seriously ill, a cause of much anxiety to her husband, who had come to lean heavily on his wife for moral support. Then, in early 1917, as Annie's condition improved, his own health began to deteriorate. In February, the British government invited him to attend the Imperial War Conference in London. With himself and Annie both unwell and rumours of another Afrikaner rebellion in the air, he felt unable to leave South Africa and proposed to the cabinet that Smuts, who was hoping for some rest after the rigours of the East African campaign, should represent the Union in his stead.

Smuts in London

Smuts's arrival in London was a public relations coup for the Union. Coming at a time when the morale of the British public was at its lowest ebb, the South African defence minister was hailed as one of the Allies' few successful generals, and treated to a hero's welcome. Before long, he had become a well-respected member of the Imperial War Cabinet, entrusted by the British prime minister, David Lloyd George, with a number of delicate military and diplomatic assignments, which were to earn him the sobriquet 'Handyman of the Empire'. Botha, needless to say, was delighted.

At home, the Nationalists were stepping up their attacks on his government. Encouraged by US President Woodrow Wilson's advocacy of the right of self-determination for small nations, the Hertzogites began to talk openly about the possibility of South Africa becoming an Afrikaner republic. Their leader's often intemperate utterances inside and outside parliament aroused much bitter criticism among English-speakers, who accused Hertzog of being a traitor and often shunned him socially. When Botha reproached the NP leader for being a republican in name only, Hertzog replied that he was a republican not merely in theory but also in practice. It was his belief that South Africa should secede from the British Empire.[5]

Despite the steady defections of Afrikaners from his own ranks, Botha continued to resist the temptation to seek a coalition with the Unionist Party. He told Buxton that it was essential to 'keep responsibility on the shoulders of as many Dutch-speaking people as possible', as any attempt to fuse the SAP with the Unionists would be misunderstood by members of his own party and might easily lead to secession.[6] He held fast to this view, even when the Nationalists made political capital out of an imperial scheme to buy the whole of South Africa's wool clip in 1917.

Wool sales

Towards the end of May, the British government offered to purchase the Union's entire wool clip at a price 55 per cent above the ruling price in 1914, terms already accepted by Australia and New Zealand. In response, South Africa informed the British that the Union could not sell its entire clip since some of it had already been promised to other customers. The government issued a leaflet, however, recommending the sale of wool to the imperial authorities, and about a third of the clip was sold within the recommended scheme.[7]

No sooner had the sale been concluded than the world price for good wool suddenly rose to much more than the amount offered by the imperial government. Those sheep farmers within the scheme, mostly supporters of the SAP, were disappointed and angry that their fellow farmers who had stayed out of the scheme were able to earn much higher prices for their wool. They felt they were being made to suffer for their loyalty to the government, and the issue escalated rapidly into a test of political allegiance. Botha was so worried he came to see Buxton more than once to tell the governor-general that he might find himself unable to carry on in office. The matter was finally resolved by the imperial government's agreeing, on Buxton's advice, that, in view of the special circumstances, it would release those farmers who had voluntarily come into the scheme and now desired to sell their wool elsewhere.[8]

The South African Native Labour Contingent

In early 1917, in response to repeated British requests for the recruitment of labourers to help at ports and railways behind the fighting lines on the

Western Front, Botha sent his brother-in-law, General J Cheere Emett, to Europe with 10 000 black members of what was designated the South African Native Labour Contingent (SANLC). Recruitment of the labour force had not been easy because of African fears of ships (and U-boats) and rumours that signing up was a ruse to entice rural men from their land.[9] Most black men – understandably – could not see why they should risk their lives in a white man's war, and those who joined up were mainly poor, uneducated and unemployed.

In white political circles, there was strong opposition to the recruitment of black South Africans for service in Europe, where they might be 'socially and morally contaminated' by being exposed to uninhibited contact with other races. The SANLC, which was under white command, had to be strictly segregated from other labour contingents.[10] Both the National and Unionist parties were opposed to the scheme, as were some members of the SAP. Yet, since Britain was bearing the financial costs of the SANLC, Botha was able to avoid a parliamentary vote and press on with a domestic recruiting campaign.

Of the first SANLC convoy that sailed for France, two ships arrived safely, but a third, the SS *Mendi*, sank off the Isle of Wight on 21 February after colliding with another vessel in thick fog. Over 600 men lost their lives in a tragedy that took several years to be appropriately commemorated. In the House of Assembly, however, MPs joined the prime minister in rising in silent, respectful tribute to their lost compatriots – an unprecedented tribute, wrote the *Cape Times*, to the 'natives in their bereavement'.[11]

The British wished to recruit at least 40 000 non-combatants from South Africa, but only 20 000 were eventually secured. Privately, Botha expressed his dissatisfaction to Buxton that the 'natives', by their reluctance to join up, did not recognise more fully what the imperial and Union governments had done for them.[12] But to those who had gone to France he paid a warm tribute in parliament on 10 March:

> If we have ever lived in times when the Native people of South Africa have shown great and true loyalty, it is in times like the present … I have all my life dealt with the Natives, but at no other times have they displayed greater loyalty than they have done in the difficult, dark days through which we are now passing. These people said, 'This war is raging

and we want to help' and in so doing they have shown their loyalty to their flag, their King and country, and what they have done will redound to their lasting credit.[13]

On 10 July 1917, King George V inspected and addressed the SANLC at Abbeville in France (Botha and Smuts also took the opportunity, when in France, to visit SANLC troops). In his speech, he praised the contingent's efforts and assured its members that they were part of 'my great armies fighting for the liberty and freedom of my subjects of all races and creeds throughout the Empire'.[14] Those words were to be flung back at the British government after the war when an SANLC delegation made a vain effort to persuade Whitehall to put pressure on the Union to ease the political and economic disabilities of black South Africans.

When the war was over, the SANLC returned to South Africa and its members were demobilised. To their bitter disappointment and resentment, despite their sacrifices in Europe, they were not awarded the British War Medal, given to all those who fought on the British side, and many of the promises made to them during recruitment were simply brushed aside. To make matters worse, fellow Africans from the Protectorates serving in the same units were given awards, as were those who had supported Union forces in South West Africa and East Africa.[15] The government made no effort to recognise the role of the SANLC in the European conflict because it realised, as did many black political leaders, that to acknowledge that whites had needed the help of blacks during the war would have strengthened the latter's political claims after the war. The Nationalist politician Oswald Pirow gave voice to the fears of many whites when he warned that black soldiers returning from Europe would demand the vote.[16] Sol Plaatje described the official attitude towards the returnees with his customary candour: 'Lest their behaviour merit recognition, their deeds and acts must, on account of their colour, not be recorded.'[17]

The decision not to award medals to the SANLC, says the military historian Ian Gleeson, was one of the most unworthy taken by the South African authorities of that time.[18] The injustices and slights that were meted out to the SANLC rankled for years. One aggrieved veteran wrote that the government had promised all sorts of good things to those who helped it in the war against Germany: 'Some of us were so foolish as to give belief to what they said ... We were a help in overcoming the Germans. But when we came back we still had to have passes and we even had to make payment of the poll tax for the time we were away.'[19] Plaatje noted caustically that 'natives' had been deliberately engaged 'in a capacity in which their participation would demand no recognition'.[20]

The SANLC exercise, from beginning to end, had not been the UDF's finest hour.

Thoughts of stepping down

By the middle of 1917, Botha's health had deteriorated further: he was suffering from carbuncles, an enlarged liver, swollen legs and was having difficulty getting to sleep.[21] A worried Annie suggested, for the first time, that he should give thought to resignation, as she feared that he might otherwise break down. Writing to the colonial secretary in London, Buxton expressed his own concern: 'I am somewhat anxious,' he noted, 'about his [Botha's] health. The pressure on him has been enormous and exceptionally trying; and the wonder is that he has not knocked up badly before.'[22] The governor-general thought it his duty to alert Smuts also to his concerns about the prime minister's poor health.[23]

In July, FS Malan took over the premiership temporarily while Botha retired to the waters at Warmbaths to get some rest. He stayed for only two weeks, however, because the number of visitors deprived him of any respite or relaxation. Buxton dropped in to see him on the way to Bechuanaland and thought Botha looked in much better health and colour, though a sore leg was preventing him from getting much-needed outdoor exercise. On Buxton's return a few weeks later, the prime minister came up from Standerton to see him. 'I noted that he looked seriously unwell and was worried and depressed about himself and things generally ... He hinted that he might not be able to go on as, unless he improved, he did not think he would be able to face another Session,' Buxton wrote.[24]

Besides the bad news from Europe about the Allies' fortunes, another worry on Botha's mind was a defamation action he had brought against an old wartime comrade and now Nationalist senator, one ADW (Danie) Wolmarans.

Louis Botha and some of his family in 1918. From left: Annie Botha, Jantje Botha (standing), Philip Botha, Louis Botha, Helen Botha and Louis Botha (Jnr), then a captain in the UDF.

CLASSIC IMAGE/ALAMY STOCK PHOTO

At a meeting in Pretoria in 1916, Wolmarans had slandered Botha by claiming that the prime minister had fraudulently altered a map of the South West Africa border, had boasted of the killing of rebel Afrikaners, and had once been a supporter – in the old ZAR Volksraad – of a man of dubious loyalty. In a counter-claim, Wolmarans alleged further that Botha had cast doubt publicly upon his physical courage. To Botha's relief, after two days of argument in court, the matter was settled by both parties' withdrawing their claims and the defendant's agreeing to pay the plaintiff's costs. The legal proceedings were a telling example of the intemperate language and intensity of feeling within the Boer-Afrikaner 'establishment'.[25]

Ill and depressed

Though buoyed up by a successful SAP conference, Botha found the 1918 parliamentary session heavy going, and by August was still feeling decidedly unwell. Annie wrote to Buxton to express her concern: 'During his tour through his constituency, we had wretchedly cold weather and downpours all the time. Most of his meetings were open-air ones, and as the people of the districts came up through cold and storm, he felt he could not disappoint them, and the result was a very bad throat, and a severe cold on the liver. I was very unhappy about him – he was so depressed and his heart quite out of order. But we have kept him out of his office, and he is taking a thorough rest.'[26] Her concern was heightened because of the onset of the deadly influenza pandemic, known as the 'Spanish flu', that had begun to sweep the world.

A few weeks later, Botha came to Buxton to confess that he was greatly depressed about his health. He thought his heart was weakening, and he often felt faint and had to lie down. Buxton was concerned enough to write to Botha's physician in the Cape, Dr Hugh Smith, to say that he thought the prime minister's illness was as much mental as physical.[27]

Botha's despondency had deepened because of an inner sense that he only had one more year to live: his father had died at more or less the same age, as had his elder brother. In each case, the symptoms they displayed had been similar to his own. 'He is therefore firmly convinced that he is destined for the same fate and at the same age. This militates, of course, against his recovery, and also makes him less careful about following out doctor's instructions,' Buxton wrote.[28]

A restful stay of some weeks with the Graaff family at their beautiful estate, De Grendel, outside Cape Town, helped Botha to feel better and restored his spirits. While making preparations for a recuperative sea voyage aboard the flagship of Admiral Edward Fitzherbert, commander of the Royal Navy's Cape of Good Hope Station, he was given the welcome news of the collapse of the Central Powers in Europe and an end – at long last – to the Great War.

Soon afterwards, an invitation arrived from the imperial government for South Africa's prime minister to proceed immediately to England, and then to Europe, to take part in the peace negotiations. Botha accepted the invitation with alacrity. In his absence, FS Malan would stand in again as the Union's prime minister.[29]

CHAPTER 29

PEACEMAKING

A pleasant voyage

Botha was not really well enough to travel to Europe, but was excited at the prospect of attending the peace conference in Paris and thought it his duty as prime minister to go. His medical advisers relented, believing a three-week sea journey might do him good. In late November, he and Annie – accompanied by a party of aides and friends – sailed to Britain from Table Bay.

Also on board was Lady (Mildred) Buxton, wife of the governor-general, who recorded her impressions of Botha during the voyage. The prime minister, she minuted, was a very big man in size, height and girth and looked like what he was – 'a born leader of men, the head of any table at which he sat. His eyes were extraordinarily bright and full of life, and nothing escaped them.' Watching Botha at close quarters while he played bridge, she noted his absorption in the game and mental alertness: 'His face was very mobile and full of expression and his quick response to any appeal or emotion was reflected at once, whether it were annoyance, or pleasure, gratification or worry – he was transparent in his betrayal of what he felt.'[1]

On the occasions she had watched the prime minister from the visitors' gallery in the House of Assembly, Lady Buxton had been struck by Botha's openness of expression and inability to disguise his true feelings: 'If a beloved supporter and friend were speaking, the General used to look radiant with pleasure and delight. But if he considered that he was being unfairly attacked or misrepresented, his face darkened and his annoyance and acute sense that the other side wasn't playing the game was very obvious. If the Nationalists were making bitter speeches and raising hot and angry feeling ... the General used to look profoundly unhappy, as if he could not bear the consciousness of division between his own people. He was perhaps too sensitive and felt things too deeply for any enjoyment of public life.'[2]

Sir David Jones of Reuters was another to have noted Botha's lack of guile. 'Moved to satisfaction or annoyance, pleasure or anger, General Botha betrays his feelings without any pretence at concealment. He is possessed of an almost feminine sensitiveness, combined with the most robust virility and his tact is proverbial … Unconsciously he conforms to the advice of Marcus Aurelius to receive the gifts of fortune without arrogance, and resign them without a pang,' Jones wrote.[3]

Having time on his hands aboard ship, Botha managed to take an unusual amount of exercise, walking every day for one and a half hours with Sir David Graaff, playing quoits and taking twice-daily swims in seawater. 'He looks really very well,' Lady Buxton recorded, 'and is in very good spirits.'[4] This was confirmed by Smuts, who wrote to his wife, Isie, after the Bothas arrived in England on Dingane's Day, 16 December 1918. 'I was really glad,' said Smuts, 'to see old Louis looking so much better. He is not at all so fat and looks strong. I hope he will not tire himself too much and lose ground again during his stay here.'[5]

Botha was overjoyed at being with Smuts again after a separation of almost two years. He had felt the latter's absence from the Union – and unavailability for consultation and decision-making – keenly, often being heard to sigh, '*Ag, as Jannie maar hier was.*' (Ah, if only Jannie were here.)[6] Despite their different spheres of responsibility, the two men still found themselves in agreement on almost every matter – and in particular on the need for Germany to be treated with magnanimity now that the war was over.

Deneys Reitz, awaiting demobilisation from the British Army, visited Botha and Smuts in London several times but did not share the latter's optimism about the prime minister's health. 'General Botha looked ill and worn,' he recorded in *Trekking On*, 'for the long strain had told upon him, and the knowledge that so many of his own race misunderstood his actions and looked upon him as an enemy, was breaking his heart. Of his position in South Africa, he spoke sadly. He said narrow men were still conducting a relentless racial [between white and white] campaign that was dividing the people, and a united nation was far off.' Reitz went on to say that Botha was 'the most honourable and lovable man I ever knew'.[7]

To Paris

On 11 January 1919, two months after the Armistice, Botha and Smuts left for Paris as members of the official British delegation, led by Prime Minister David Lloyd George. A week later, the first formal meeting of some 70 representatives of the victorious Allied powers took place. According to Engelenburg, one of Botha's temporary secretaries in Paris, South Africa was regarded as having an independent status among the 'Allied and Associated Powers', within the framework of the League of Nations,[8] whose covenant had been drafted by Smuts. Besides Marshal Foch of France, Botha and Smuts were the only delegates in Paris who had actually faced the enemy in the field.[9]

In his *Memoirs of the Peace Conference*, Lloyd George recorded that there were three men present in Paris 'whose names will ever be associated with the history of South Africa – General Botha, General Smuts and Lord Milner – who in 1919 stood for a peace out of which every punitive element should be purged'.[10] He noted that Milner had not been in favour of conciliation at Vereeniging, but had now joined his former antagonists 'in resistance to that spirit of relentlessness which would humiliate the vanquished foe and keep them [sic] down in the dust into which they had been cast by their complete overthrow'.[11]

Of these three noteworthy men, Lloyd George declared, 'Botha was the most striking personality in terms of his physical appearance, in strength of character and in his general impressiveness. He was one of those men whose presence you feel in a room even when they are silent. He attracted attention without making any effort to do so.'[12]

The two prime ministers' high regard for each other was mutual. Writing to Buxton from Paris, Botha said of the British prime minister, 'The more I see of David Lloyd George, the more admiration I get for his ability, personality and strength of character. To my mind he is the outstanding figure at the Peace Conference.'[13]

South West Africa

High on the South Africans' agenda in Paris was the future status of South West Africa. Botha and Smuts were hopeful that the Union might be allowed to annex the territory outright, but this ran contrary to US President

Woodrow Wilson's intentions: the new League of Nations, he decided, had to be given ultimate responsibility for Germany's former colonies under a 'mandate' system he had not clearly thought through himself and was devised, ironically, by Smuts. Sympathetic though he was to the appeals of the South African delegates (both of whom he liked), the American president declined to give them their way, taking for granted that the inhabitants of South West Africa would freely choose one day to unite with the Union.[14] On 7 May, the former German South West Africa was allocated to South Africa as a 'C' mandate, on terms that fell only slightly short of full annexation.

In the view of the Empire delegation, Botha's most valuable contribution at Versailles was smoothing over ruffled feelings (and calming down an angry Wilson) when talks over the mandate system were about to stall. Observing that one had to give way in small things in order to achieve a greater good, he announced that South Africa was prepared to forego outright annexation of South West Africa in favour of a mandate, in order to ensure that the remaining peace discussions did not falter. He, for one, appreciated the ideals of President Wilson: 'They were the ideals of the people of the world and they would succeed if all appreciated them in the same spirit and supported them in the manner they were intended.'[15] The president, for one, was extremely grateful for Botha's intervention.[16]

Reparations

The mood in Paris was vengeful. The British wanted to see Germany severely punished but not destroyed; the French, who had borne the brunt of the war, were determined not to let Germany rise again, while at home the Americans were retreating into isolationism. Article 231 of the peace treaty, the so-called war guilt clause, forced the Germans into admitting that the war had been all their fault. 'This isn't a peace,' declared Marshal Foch presciently, 'it's a ceasefire for twenty years.'[17]

Botha and Smuts were far from satisfied with the political and economic reparations the victorious Allies intended to impose upon Germany. In a cable to Buxton from Paris, Botha complained that some of the peace terms were impracticable of execution, and others were in the nature of 'pinpricks and therefore unnecessary'. 'No one can accuse us of being pro-German, but our idea has been to defeat the Germans and then give them a Peace which will result in lasting peace and ... save the world from a similar catastrophe to that which has just passed,' he wrote to Buxton.[18] (Domestic political considerations would also have weighed heavily on his mind. An election was due in 1920, and he knew that he and Smuts would have to defend the terms of the treaty to a partly pro-German electorate.)

South Africa's prime minister also interceded in the debate over whether or not to arraign the German emperor and his senior officers before an international court. 'Hang the Kaiser' and 'Squeeze the Germans until the pips squeak' were popular cries in Britain at this time. In his remarks, Botha explained that, after the Anglo-Boer War, the return of peace had been greatly enhanced by a policy of not prosecuting rebels. As long as war criminals were to be 'smelt out', he declared, Europe would know no peace.[19]

A British participant in the discussions, George Barnes MP, wrote in his reminiscences that Botha's intercession over the treatment of Germany had lingered in his mind. 'Botha was a great man,' thought Barnes. 'Never made long speeches but his presence in any gathering could be felt. What little he had to say was always to the point; and always on the side of a long and generous view of things.'[20] Twenty years earlier, Engelenburg reflected, the Kaiser had turned Botha and his colleagues away when they came to seek help. Now one of the three supplicants on that occasion was pleading for clemency to be shown him in Paris.[21]

Botha was opposed also to a triumphal entry by the victors into Berlin. 'My soul has felt the harrow,' he declared. 'I know what it means.'[22] Robert Lansing, the US secretary of state, wrote the following about South Africa's leader: 'Botha was essentially logical and unemotional in whatever he said or did. The enthusiasm of the visionary made no headway with him. Reason and facts were what appealed to him. He looked forward to the final judgement of men, and not to the temporary popularity which a policy might gain under the stress of existing conditions, or the passing emotions of an aroused public opinion. He possessed that foresight which sees the end at the beginning and prevents the adoption of a course which may be disastrous, or unwise, or of doubtful expediency.'[23]

Botha and Milner

From a South African perspective, a remarkable aspect of the Paris talks was the cordiality that sprang up between Botha and his former *bête noire*, Lord Milner, now Britain's colonial secretary. Smuts had long ago made his peace with the once-hated Milner, serving alongside him in Britain's war cabinet. In the Hall of Mirrors at the Palace of Versailles, Botha found himself seated next to Milner, who happened to share his [Botha's] views about war reparations from Germany.

During the rowdy exchanges at the plenary session, the German-born and -educated Milner was having difficulty in putting across the argument that Germany should be treated forgivingly, when Botha rose to his feet. Speaking slowly in Afrikaans, which Milner was able to understand, he added his voice to the colonial secretary's appeal for clemency. He did not know of anyone there besides himself and his colleague Smuts, said Botha, who had gone through the experience of a war in which all had been lost – government, flag, country, all. 'You cannot, you must not destroy a nation; you cannot, you must not take vengeance on a whole people and punish them so as to make it impossible for them to recover or even to exist.'[24]

Touching Milner lightly on the shoulder, Botha continued: 'Seventeen years ago my friend and I made peace at Vereeniging. It was a bitter peace for us – bitter hard. We lost all for which we had fought for three long years and had made untold sacrifices. For us there seemed to be nothing left; but we turned our thoughts and efforts then to saving our people; and they – the victors helped us. It was a hard peace for us to accept … but it was a generous peace that the British people made with us. And that is why we stand with them today side by side in the cause that has brought us all together. Remember, I say to you, there was no spirit or act of vengeance in that peace; we were helped to rise again and were placed on equal terms, and today I feel that our people have proved themselves worthy of that trust and that opportunity.'[25]

Lloyd George wrote that it was 'difficult to convey the power of General Botha's deliverance by a mere summary of the words and the attractive and compelling personality of this remarkable man. The President [Wilson] told me immediately afterwards that it was the most impressive speech to which he had ever listened.'[26]

Towards the end of January, Botha was asked to become chairman of the Peace Commission appointed by the Great Powers, but had to decline because of a bad bout of influenza. In late April, the offer was renewed by Lloyd George and this time Botha accepted. He chaired eight meetings of the commission, at which Poland, the Ukraine and Lithuania pressed their respective claims for settlement. Though in poor health again, Botha was determined to undertake a railway journey to Warsaw for an inspection *in loco*, but was prevented from doing so by his private secretary, supported by Engelenburg, who thought the undertaking too onerous for someone in his condition. Their decision was reinforced by Annie Botha.[27]

Hertzog arrives

A minor diversion for Botha and Smuts in Paris was the arrival, after a lengthy boat journey from Cape Town via New York, of General Hertzog and a delegation of Nationalist Afrikaners, among whom were DF Malan, Klasie Havenga, EG Jansen, Hjalmar Reitz and others. The Hertzogites had decided to take the idealistic Wilson at his word when he said that every people should have the right to choose their own sovereignty, and had come to plead for the restoration of republican government in South Africa. In the words of DW Krüger, 'There in Paris, surrounded by snarling delegates from all parts of the world quarrelling over the spoils of war, were present three generals of the South African war, two of them trying to consolidate the Union within the Empire and the third to get out of it.'[28]

Lloyd George was disinclined to see the visitors and it took the personal intervention of Botha for Hertzog's delegation to be granted a meeting with the reluctant British prime minister. The Nationalist delegation was politely told that Botha, as the elected prime minister of the Union, was the only one who could speak on South Africa's behalf in Paris, not Hertzog, who represented only one political party. In a written response to the delegation's claim that there was uncertainty in South Africa over the meaning of self-government, Lloyd George reaffirmed, in writing, the status that South Africa enjoyed in the world: 'It is surely no mean one. As one of the Dominions of the British Commonwealth, the South African people control their destiny in the fullest sense. In regard to the common Imperial concerns, they participate in the deliberations which determine Imperial policy on a basis of complete equality.'²⁹ In his account of the discussions, Hjalmar Reitz recorded that, although Herzog had spoken 'earnestly, clearly and convincingly', he [Reitz] had the feeling all along 'that General Smuts was behind the door and nothing that was said would be any use'.³⁰

From Cape Town, Buxton reported to colonial secretary Milner on the reception given to the NP's 'argosy' to Versailles: 'The general impression here in regard to Hertzog's speech to Lloyd George, and the latter's reply, was I think expressed by a leading Nationalist to [acting prime minister] Malan, "Hertzog has made a damned fool of himself", and it would be very much better if he left the explanation of their position to Dr [DF] Malan … The Nationalists are trying to discount Lloyd George's reply, the firmness of which is much appreciated here by saying it was clearly dictated by Botha and Smuts … the voice of Jacob, the hand of Esau,' wrote Buxton.³¹

Smuts objects

Towards the end of the drawn-out deliberations in Paris, while back in London, Botha was startled by a message from Smuts that he had decided to leave the negotiations because he did not wish to put his signature to a flawed Versailles Treaty. As a member of the Imperial War Cabinet, he had declared for a peace treaty very different from the one proposed and believed that the new treaty was a breach of President Wilson's agreement of 5 November 2018. As the refusal of the co-architect (with Wilson) of the League of Nations to sign the Peace (to which the Germans had already agreed under duress) would have caused an international sensation, Botha returned post-haste to Paris to try to retrieve the situation.

'Surely you won't desert now?' he asked the determined Smuts.³² Together, the two men paid a visit to Lloyd George, to whom Smuts had already written several times suggesting revisions to the treaty saying, 'Prime Minister, do not for a moment imagine that I write in any other but a most friendly and sympathetic spirit, which I am sure you will not resent. Perhaps the main difference between us is that you are struggling in the water, while I shout advice from the shore.'³³ Lloyd George was not about to pay heed to Smuts's objections. Hiding any exasperation he felt, Lloyd George suggested that if

*The lines written by Botha on his agenda paper at
the signing of the Versailles Treaty.*

FROM FV ENGELENBURG, *GENERAL LOUIS BOTHA*, 1929

Smuts felt so strongly, his proper course was to 'sign first and then protest afterwards – if protest you must'.[34]

Botha had already decided it was his duty to put his name to the treaty on behalf of South Africa. Cabling Buxton, he said: 'Smuts refuses to sign Treaty and will publish statement giving grounds for action. While I substantially share his difficulties against Treaty, I have decided to sign because my position as prime minister is different from his, and my signature is necessary to make Union a member of the League of Nations and secure for her a new status in the world.'[35]

Taking the advice of Lloyd George, and heeding Botha's plea that for him to sign and Smuts to refuse to sign would make the one look noble and the other ignoble and suggest a division between them, Smuts reluctantly decided to append his name to the Treaty of Versailles. During the closing formalities in the Hall of Mirrors on 28 June 1919, Botha scribbled in Dutch on his agenda paper: 'God's justice will be imposed on every nation with righteousness under the new Sun, and we shall continue to pray that it will be applied to mankind in love, peace and Christian charity. Today, I recall the 31st May 1902.'[36]

'Vereeniging was haunting Versailles,' recorded Engelenburg.[37]

Botha put a signature to his scribble, as did Smuts, who reflected later: 'At that moment when jubilation filled all hearts, he [Botha] heard the undertone of the ages and felt only the deepest pity for the fate of humankind.' [38] Still determined to register a protest, Smuts sent a long letter to *The Times* in London, which appeared the day after the guns at Versailles had thundered in celebration of the Peace. 'This Treaty is not the Peace,' wrote Smuts; 'it is the last echo of the war. It closes the war and armistice stage. The real Peace must still come and it must be made by the Peoples.'[39]

Homeward bound

Four days after the Versailles ceremony, leaving Smuts behind in London, Botha sailed home from Southampton. In a speech before departing from England, he said: 'I return to Africa happy in the knowledge that my native land emerges from this terrible conflict with its status raised and its destiny assured. I carry away with me also the conviction that of all the people in the Alliance, the peoples of the British Empire have played a greater part than any … I go back to Africa more firmly convinced than ever that the mission of the British Empire now, and in the time to come, lies along the path of freedom and high ideals. Britain is the cornerstone upon which our civilisation must rest. It largely depends upon her action and upon her spirit whether the new-born League of Nations will be a success or not. The essence of the League of Nations lies in the ideal brotherhood, in making this World a better place to live in. In the League, the British Empire will continue its historic role and play the part of the big brother.'[40]

CHAPTER 30

AN IRREPARABLE LOSS

'I shall continue to serve'

The long sea voyage home failed to restore the prime minister to health. On the contrary: according to the *Rand Daily Mail*, between Plymouth and Madeira the ailing Botha suffered a heart attack from which he never recovered.[1] During most of the voyage he sat in a corner of the lower deck, lost in thought.[2] For Annie, as well as the faithful Engelenburg, the journey was one 'of anxiety and foreboding'. But as the ship drew closer to Cape Town, Botha's spirits lifted at the thought of being on home soil again, and at having won recognition for South Africa in Paris as an independent entity within the Empire and the League of Nations. His improved mood gave him the mental strength he knew he would require for the tiring programme of celebratory functions and speeches that lay ahead.[3]

On 14 July 1919, he landed in Table Bay, having been away from South Africa for eight months. Along with Smuts, who returned from Britain a week later, he plunged into an arduous round of appearances and functions, first in Cape Town, then in Pretoria and Johannesburg, and finally in Bloemfontein. At the Union Buildings in Pretoria, he told a crowd assembled from every corner of the Transvaal: 'Thank God, my health is better than it was when I left for the Conference; as long as my country has need of me, I shall continue to serve.'[4]

Less than a week later, he expressed his satisfaction to an audience of 700 at a banquet in Johannesburg 'at seeing those who were once chasing each other in South Africa, sitting around one and the same table' together. But Buxton's daughter, who encountered Botha at the time, wrote to her father to say, 'the General does not look at all well, and his face is quite grey'.[5] Observing the prime minister in the House of Assembly, the journalist Arthur Barlow recorded that Botha, whom he admired, 'looked like a man stricken with an incurable illness whose sun was setting'.[6]

At the SAP conference in Bloemfontein, the prime minister declared himself convinced that *hereniging* (reunion) of his party and the NP was essential; now that 'the war is a thing of the past, any racial policy would be fatal. Responsibility rests with the moderates,'[7] he said. The wish, unfortunately, was father to the thought. His opponents, feeling duty bound to save the face of the NP delegation to the Peace Conference, refused to acknowledge that South Africa's independence within the Empire had been established, and their party newspapers laughed Botha and Smuts to scorn.

Last days

As Natal waited impatiently for its turn to pay homage to Botha and Smuts, the prime minister called in at Rusthof on his way to Pietermaritzburg to look over his estate. He had embarked upon the journey with a slight cold, but a brief meeting with his farm workers in a biting wind brought on influenza, possibly the Spanish flu pandemic that swept the world in 1918–1919.[8] He was obliged to return to Pretoria, where his doctor ordered a complete rest. Smuts went on to Natal on his own.

Botha took to his bed on the afternoon of 25 August 1919 without there being any presentiment or suspicion on the part of himself, his family or his doctor that the end had come. A day and a half later, shortly after midnight on 26 August, he died peacefully in his sleep. Engelenburg, who was one of the first to comfort Annie, recorded that 'in the dead face I recognised the well-known, friendly expression, besides the will-power still delineated in his countenance. His bulky frame had shrunk to almost youthful slenderness.'[9] Botha was not yet 57 years old. (Engelenburg says that Botha died shortly *before* midnight on 26 August, but it must have been shortly *after* midnight as his headstone records the date of his death as 27 August.)

Smuts, who had left Durban hurriedly for Pretoria when he learned from the SAP secretary, Louis Esselen, that the prime minister was fading rapidly, was awoken with the sad news early on the morning of 27 August at Volksrust station, where a telegram was delivered to his train. It read: 'General Botha died at midnight of heart failure. Passed away peacefully.' Smuts took the telegram, groaned as he read it, and turned his face to the wall.[10]

Isie Smuts met her husband's train at Irene later that day and the couple drove immediately to Sunnyside to commiserate with Annie. The same night, a devastated and deeply grieving Smuts wrote to his English confidant AB Gillett: 'He was South Africa's greatest son and among men my best friend.'[11]

A wave of emotion, Buxton records, passed over South Africa at the news of Botha's sudden, unexpected and untimely death. A powerful, steadying influence had been removed and a commanding presence – 'a remarkable combination of courage, sympathy, constancy and leadership' – was no more '… A strong and well-tempered link between South Africa and the Empire had been severed.'[12]

Among the first to send a message of condolence to Smuts was Winston Churchill: 'Botha came to see me here before he sailed, and I did what I have so far done for no other visitor – escorted him downstairs and put him into his carriage myself. Almost immediately after (as it seemed) while the impression of his presence was strong with me I learned that he has gone. I know what a loss this will be to you, and believe me I felt a keen personal pang as if someone I had known all my life has passed away. He was one of the truly great men of the world, and thank God of the British Empire.'[13]

Churchill was later to write that the names of three most famous generals he had known in his life, none of whom had won great battles over a foreign foe, all began with 'B': General Booth, General Botha and General Baden-Powell.[14]

The obsequies

Botha was given a state but not a military funeral on 30 August in Pretoria. After a solemn church service, a brigade of former commandos, headed by General Coen Brits, led a lengthy procession of mourners ahead of the cortege, which was followed by Annie Botha and family and a host of dignitaries in their carriages. Church Street was lined for more than a kilometre by soldiers with arms reversed and behind them members of the public standing in silent tribute to their fallen leader. It was an occasion without pomp and ceremony, which prompted Vere Stent, editor of the *Pretoria News*, to complain to Arthur Barlow: 'These Calvinists have no idea of the greatness of things. Botha should have been buried with military pomp and ceremony; he was a statesman and a soldier. Look at this pitiful affair!'[15]

At the graveside in Pretoria's new Rebecca Street cemetery, Smuts delivered one of the most eloquent orations of his life: 'Today at this grave we are all united, one in our deep feeling of national loss, one in our grateful pride in this greatest son of the mother of us all, one in our appreciation of the man whom God gave us as our leader in the most difficult creative years of our history. His great work was the Union of South Africa; his untiring efforts through all difficulties were directed to the unity of the people of South Africa, to the promotion of a strong feeling of national brotherhood among all sections of our community, to the healing of old wounds and the laying to rest of old enmities …'[16]

'But now he has gone from us,' Smuts continued. 'Fate had willed it that he should be taken away from us at a comparatively early age, at the height of his brilliant powers as a statesman, and just after his return from the World Conference, where he had done so much to obtain for South Africa an equal position among the nations of the world. His voice will no longer be heard, early and late, pleading for cooperation. His noble and strong figure will no longer be a living inspiration to a whole.'[17]

'I have spoken of Louis Botha as a commander and statesman,' Smuts went on. 'But how can I speak of him in the greater quality of friend, of the friend beyond compare which he was? After an intimate friendship and unbroken cooperation extending over twenty-one years, during which we came as close together as it is ever given to men to come, I have the right to call him the largest, most beautiful, sweetest soul of all my land and days. Great in his life, he was happy in his death; for his friend was reserved the hard fate to bury him and to remain with the task which even for him was almost too much.'[18]

In their tributes to the fallen prime minister, South Africa's newspapers picked up on his passionate commitment to white unity. *The Star*'s editorial was typical of many: 'This is the first and last judgement to be passed on General Botha in storm or sunshine, peace or war. Whatever the cost, whatever the sacrifice, he never deviated by a hair's breadth from the path of duty and honour. From the beginning to the end of his public life he affirmed with passionate emphasis the principle of co-operation and of unity and his whole life's work is the record and embodiment of that faith. Of him it may be said, with truth, that deserving a monument, he needs none, since his monument is in the minds and memories of men.'[19]

The Nationalist mouthpiece, *Die Vaderland,* noted that Botha's death 'has for the first time during many years stirred the whole people in the recollection that, despite our political differences, every one of us in one or other period of his life, have had admiration for him.'[20] The Afrikaner historian DW Krüger made this assessment of the late prime minister: 'He had died before completing his task. In part, he himself was to blame because he showed weakness where strength was needed, and strength where weakness would have paid better dividends. He failed also because he underestimated the force of national feeling amongst Afrikanerdom. But in part he had to contend with forces he did not understand and would have broken even a stronger man. They broke him and it was left to his successor to build up a new defence.'[21]

New prime minister

Smuts himself had resisted pressure to remain in Britain after the end of the Great War to continue his work as an international statesman and peace-maker, and had returned home largely out of loyalty to Botha. 'It meant coming [back] to a land where too often my countrymen hated my ideas and despised my larger hopes …'[22] he wrote. Above and beyond the call of the veld, the lure of the mountains, flora and fauna of South Africa, and the interests of his family, Smuts felt that his place was to be at the side of Louis Botha. 'In the end,' he wrote to Isie, 'I came back because of Botha.'[23] And now his great friend and comrade had been taken from him.

Governor-General Buxton, who had stayed on for longer than his five-year term at Botha's special request, now called upon Smuts to form a new government. Reluctantly, Smuts accepted, aware of the 'colossal responsibility' that he had inherited, but also keenly aware of his own temperamental deficiencies. At his first party caucus meeting, he warned his colleagues that, unlike Botha, he had 'neither tact, nor patience'; they would have to take him for what he was worth.[24]

'I am now prime minister', he wrote to his friend, Margaret Gillett, on 6 September, 'but my heart is not in the thing and only an overwhelming disaster brought me here. Botha's loss to this country is quite irreparable. His was just the role which I temperamentally could not play, and you know how necessary that role is in the world. I shall do my best without being sanguine about success.'[25]

Hancock records that if Smuts had ever imagined he could step aside and leave Botha's mantle to fall upon someone else, he had only to reread the letter that Annie Botha wrote him after her husband's death. It had always been Louis's wish, she said, that Smuts would become prime minister:

> I just want to say once more, many, many thanks for all your loving utterances in honour of the man who loved you so greatly during his lifetime. You never had a truer or more faithful friend and brother; and he thought the world of you and always said that you were the greatest man in our country, the coming man of the age. I thought I would tell you this – although I know you must often have realised what his thoughts and opinions were of you. I cannot tell you all I wish for you – and I shall just end by saying again – God bless Jannie, Louis's faithful friend in storm and calm.[26]

There were doubtless many motives and forces, Hancock concludes, that led and drove Smuts to become prime minister – a mix of ambition, duty, the habit of hard work, realism, idealism, love of power, love of country. 'Yet to this list, one compelling motive needs to be added: his abiding loyalty to Louis Botha.'[27]

Unveiling his statue

Twenty-seven years later, it fell to Smuts, again prime minister of South Africa after a long interval, to unveil a statue at the Union Buildings of Louis Botha. The prime minister paid tribute to the veterans and comrades of bygone wars who had come to warm their hearts around Botha's memory and to recall the inspiration he was to them when they were young. There was a greatness of soul in Botha, Smuts recalled, that endeared him to his fellows and secured for him their loyalty and devotion, and inspired thousands who never knew him in person. 'I do not minimise his intellectual qualities,' said Smuts, 'his massive intelligence, his intuitive insight, his sure and faultless judgement. But in a remarkable degree he had those qualities of sympathy and under-standing, of kindness and compassion, which made him perhaps the most sensitive and lovable among the great men I have known …'[28]

'You could not meet him without being deeply struck by him at first sight,' Smuts concluded. 'I had opportunity to see the deep impression he made not only on simple men of the veld (who are often very shrewd judges of men), but also on those very distinguished statesmen whom he met at the end of the Great War in London and in Paris, men of wide experience who were able to recognise a great man when they saw him. Many of them have recorded their impression of him and placed him very high among the world leaders of their time. He was indeed a prince among men, and they felt it … Such was Louis Botha. Of the great South Africans I have known, I put Paul Kruger and Louis Botha in a class by themselves, though as types, as personalities they were poles apart … A country so small as ours that can produce such great men cannot itself be lacking in greatness.'[29]

Other verdicts

In 1900, the American author and journalist Howard Hillegas, who covered the Anglo-Boer War for the *New York World*, gave his assessment of Botha:

> There are few men who have a certain magnetic power which attracts and holds the admiration of others. Louis Botha was a man of this class. Strangers who saw him for the first time loved him. There was an inde-scribable something about him which caused men looking at him for the first time to pledge their friendship for all time. The light in his blue eyes seemed to mesmerise men, to draw them, willing or unwilling, to him. It was not the quality which gained friends for Kruger, nor that which made Joubert popular, but rather a mysterious, involuntary influence which he exerted over everybody with whom he came in contact. A man less hand-some, of less commanding appearance than Botha might have possessed such a power, and been considered less extraordinary than he, but it was

not wholly his personal appearance – for he was the handsomest man in the Boer army – which aroused the admiration of men. His voice, his eyes, his facial expression and his manner – all combined to strengthen the man's power over others. It may have been personal magnetism or a mysterious charm which he possessed – but it was the mark of a great man.[30]

In 1929, Lloyd George wrote of Botha: 'I never met a man who seemed to be more of an embodiment of wisdom in speech or action. He was truly a great man. He was a great warrior, and an even greater counsellor and conciliator. Throughout the Paris negotiations he stood for a settlement that would leave the roots of bitterness behind.'[31]

Some years later, the British author and biographer of Smuts, HC Armstrong, wrote: 'When Botha died, there went away a great man. Many men had greater capabilities and greater virtues, but there was about Botha a Majesty which all felt but which none could understand or explain by his looks, or by what he said, or even by what he did. It came of some Greatness in the man himself.'[32]

These judgements find support from Earl Buxton, who came to know Botha so well: '[He] was a steadfast friend, and a chivalrous enemy. Very loyal to his friends, he inspired deep, abiding and reciprocal loyalty and love ... Unaffected, modest and unassuming, he combined natural simplicity with inherited shrewdness; he was at once both wise and simple, with a refreshing fund of common sense ... He possessed in a marked degree personality and character, which are of the essence of greatness.'[33]

A Man Apart, it must be said.

Notes

PREFACE

1 Quoted in Harold Spender, *General Botha: The Man and the Career*, Constable, 1916, p 323.
2 FV Engelenburg, *General Louis Botha*, George G Harrap, 1929, p 16.
3 Ibid, p 28.
4 Earl Buxton, *General Botha*, John Murray, 1924, p 124.
5 Ibid, p 125. I am indebted to Charles van Onselen for the observation that perhaps the only other Afrikaner whose personal charisma could be compared to Botha's was the late Progressive Federal Party leader, Frederik van Zyl Slabbert.
6 Martin Meredith, *Diamonds, Gold and War: The Making of South Africa*, Jonathan Ball Publishers, 2007, p 497.
7 Buxton, *General Botha*, p 286.
8 Martin Plaut, *Promise and Despair: The First Struggle for a Non-Racial South Africa*, Jacana, 2016, p 123.
9 Buxton, *General Botha*, p 287.
10 Engelenburg, *General Louis Botha*, p 232.
11 AJP Taylor, *From the Boer War to the Cold War*, Hamish Hamilton, 1995, p 26.
12 Gordon S Wood, *The Purpose of the Past*, Penguin Press, 2008, p 11.
13 Henry Kissinger, quoted in Niall Ferguson, *Kissinger 1923–1968: The Idealist*, Penguin Books, 2016, p 299.

INTRODUCTION

1 Ronald Hyam, *Britain's Imperial Century, 1815–1914: A Study of Empire and Expansion*, second edition, Barnes & Noble, 1995, p 45.
2 Denis Judd and Keith Skinner, *The Boer War: A History*, IB Tauris, 2013, p 18.
3 Hermann Giliomee and Bernard Mbenga, *New History of South Africa*, Tafelberg, 2007, p 112.
4 Sarah Gertrude Millin, *Rhodes*, Chatto & Windus, 1934, p 75.
5 Judd and Skinner, *The Boer War*, p 21.
6 Meredith, *Diamonds, Gold and War*, p 8.
7 Trewhella Cameron and Burridge Spies (eds), *An Illustrated History of South Africa*, Southern Book Publishers/Human & Rousseau, 1988, p 176.
8 CJ Barnard, *Genl. Louis Botha op die Natalse Front 1899–1900*, AA Balkema, 1970, p 1.

CHAPTER 1 GROWING UP

1 Spender, *General Botha*, p 17.
2 Johannes Meintjes, *General Louis Botha: A Biography*, Cassell, 1970, p 5.
3 Ibid, p 36.
4 Ibid, p 4.
5 Ibid, p 9.
6 Ibid, p 7.
7 Giliomee and Mbenga, *New History of South Africa*, p 164.
8 TRH Davenport, *South Africa: A Modern*

History, fourth edition, Macmillan, 1992, p 177.

9 Bill Nasson, *The War for South Africa: The Anglo-Boer War 1899–1902*, Tafelberg, 2010, p 42.

10 Engelenburg, *General Louis Botha*, p 27.

11 Spender, *General Botha*, pp 33–35.

12 Engelenburg, *General Louis Botha*, p 21.

13 Meintjes, *General Louis Botha*, p 9.

CHAPTER 2 MAKING HIS MARK

1 Meintjes, *General Louis Botha*, p 10.

2 Ibid.

3 Ibid.

4 Ibid.

5 Spender, *General Botha*, p 42.

6 Meintjes, *General Louis Botha*, p 14.

7 Ibid.

8 Spender, *General Botha*, p 45.

9 Meintjes, *General Louis Botha*, pp 13–14.

10 Ibid, p 12.

11 Ibid.

12 Ibid, p 13.

13 Barnard, *Genl. Louis Botha op die Natalse Front 1899–1900*, p 170 and note 27 on p 161.

14 Spender, *General Botha*, p 54.

15 Engelenburg, *General Louis Botha*, pp 34–35.

16 Ibid, p 35.

17 Spender, *General Botha*, pp 48–49.

18 Ibid, p 49.

19 Engelenburg, *General Louis Botha*, p 36.

20 CT Gordon, *The Growth of Boer Opposition to Kruger (1890–1895)*, Oxford University Press, 1970, p 131.

21 As Charles van Onselen reveals in *The Cowboy Capitalist* (Jonathan Ball, 2017), Rhodes was not the only one with designs on the Transvaal gold mines. The American mining engineer, John Hays Hammond, had his own plans to advance American interests in the ZAR.

22 Roy Digby Thomas, *Two Generals: Buller and Botha in the Boer War*, Author House, 2012, loc 326 of ebook.

23 Engelenburg, *General Louis Botha*, p 26.

24 Barnard, *Genl. Louis Botha op die Natalse Front 1899–1900*, pp 4–5.

25 Ibid.

26 Ibid.

27 Ibid, p 6.

CHAPTER 3 WAR CLOUDS

1 Meintjes, *General Louis Botha*, p 18.

2 Gordon, *The Growth of Boer Opposition to Kruger (1890–1895)*, p 21.

3 Ibid, pp 278–279.

4 Ibid, p 24.

5 Meintjes, *General Louis Botha*, p 19.

6 Ibid.

7 Hermann Giliomee, *The Afrikaners: Biography of a People*, Tafelberg, 2003, p 237.

8 Ibid.

9 Engelenburg, *General Louis Botha*, p 39.

10 Gordon, *The Growth of Boer Opposition to Kruger (1890–1895)*, pp 126–127.

11 Ibid, p 127.

12 Engelenburg, *General Louis Botha*, p 40.

13 Barnard, *Genl. Louis Botha op die Natalse Front, 1899–1900*, p 7.

14 Ibid.

15 Meintjes, *General Louis Botha*, p 21.

16 Ibid.

17 CW de Kiewiet, *A History of South Africa: Social and Economic*, Oxford University Press, 1957, p 135.

18 Reader's Digest Association, *Illustrated History of South Africa: The Real Story*, Reader's Digest Association, 1989, p 340.

19 Hyam, *Britain's Imperial Century*, p 245.

20 Giliomee, *The Afrikaners*, p 247.

21 Meintjes, *General Louis Botha*, p 27.

22 Ibid.

23 Barnard, *Genl. Louis Botha op die Natalse Front, 1899–1900*, p 12.

24 Ibid, p 13.

25 Engelenburg, *General Louis Botha*, p 42.

26 Johannes Meintjes, *De la Rey: Lion of the West*, Hugh Keartland Publishers, p 81.

CHAPTER 4 THE WAR BEGINS

1 Peter Trew, *The Boer War Generals*, Jonathan Ball Publishers, 1999, p 139.

2 WK Hancock, *Smuts: The Sanguine Years*

1870–1919, Cambridge University Press, 1962, p 108.

3 Trew, *The Boer War Generals,* p 8.

4 Judd and Skinner, *The Boer War,* p 92.

5 Martin Bossenbroek, *The Boer War,* Jacana, 2016, p 145.

6 Barnard, *Genl. Louis Botha op die Natalse Front 1899–1900,* p 20.

7 Bossenbroek, *The Boer War,* p 146.

8 Ibid.

9 Barnard, *Genl. Louis Botha op die Natalse Front 1899–1900,* p 17.

10 Deneys Reitz, *Commando,* Faber & Faber, 1975, p 24.

11 Nicki von der Heyde, *Field Guide to the Battlefields of South Africa,* Struik Travel & Heritage, 2015, p 154.

12 Thomas Pakenham, *The Boer War,* illustrated edition, Jonathan Ball Publishers, 1993, p 94.

13 Trew, *The Boer War Generals,* p 141.

14 Meintjes, *General Louis Botha,* p 33.

15 Edgar Holt, *The Boer War,* Putnam, 1958, p 93.

16 Ibid.

17 Trew, *The Boer War Generals,* p 141.

18 Barnard, *Genl. Louis Botha op die Natalse Front 1899–1900,* p 24.

19 Von der Heyde, *Field Guide to the Battlefields of South Africa,* pp 121–123

20 Nasson, *The War for South Africa,* pp 105–106.

21 Michael Davitt, *The Boer Fight for Freedom: From the Beginning of Hostilities to the Peace of Pretoria,* Funk & Wagnall, 1902, pp 135–136.

22 Nasson, *The War for South Africa,* p 105.

23 Holt, *The Boer War,* p 96.

24 Pakenham, *The Boer War,* p 82.

25 Rayne Kruger, *Good-bye Dolly Gray: The Story of the Boer War,* Pan Books, 1959, p 88.

26 Barnard, *Genl. Louis Botha op die Natalse Front 1899–1900,* pp 28–32, and Von der Heyde, *Field Guide to the Battlefields of South Africa,* pp 112–114.

27 Holt, *The Boer War,* p 100.

28 Kruger, *Good-bye Dolly Gray,* p 93.

29 Barnard, *Genl. Louis Botha op die Natalse Front 1899–1900,* p 31.

30 Kruger, *Good-bye Dolly Gray,* p 95.

31 Holt, *The Boer War,* p 100.

CHAPTER 5 TAKING CHARGE

1 Bill Nasson, *The South African War 1899–1902,* Arnold, 1999, p 117.

2 Digby Thomas, *Two Generals,* p 27.

3 Ibid, p 21.

4 Winston S Churchill, *My Early Life,* Fontana, 1972, p 240.

5 Thomas Pakenham, *The Boer War,* Futura, 1988, p 170.

6 Candice Millard, *Hero of the Empire: The Making of Winston Churchill,* Allen Lane, 2016, pp 104–105.

7 Churchill, *My Early Life,* p 263.

8 Barnard, *Genl. Louis Botha op die Natalse Front 1899–1900,* pp 37–38.

9 Ibid, pp 38–39.

10 Ibid, p 39–40.

11 Trew, *The Boer War Generals,* p 22.

12 Barnard, *Genl. Louis Botha op die Natalse Front 1899–1900,* p 42.

13 Pakenham, *The Boer War,* p 174.

14 Barnard, *Genl. Louis Botha op die Natalse Front 1899–1900,* p 86.

15 Ibid, pp 86–87.

16 HC Hillegas, *With the Boer Forces,* Methuen, 1900, p 201.

17 Kruger, *Good-bye Dolly Gray,* p 119.

18 Pakenham, *The Boer War,* p 215.

19 Ibid.

CHAPTER 6 BULLER OUTWITTED

1 Barnard, *Genl. Louis Botha op die Natalse Front 1899–1900,* pp 54–56.

2 Holt, *The Boer War,* p 146.

3 Ibid, pp 146–147 et seq.

4 Ibid, p 148.

5 Pakenham, *The Boer War,* p 230.

6 Trew, *The Boer War Generals,* p 25.

7 Holt, *The Boer War,* p 151.

8 Barnard, *Genl. Louis Botha op die Natalse Front 1899–1900,* p 67.

9 John Buchan, *The History of the Royal Scots Fusiliers, 1678–1918,* Thomas Nelson & Sons, 1925, p 271.

10 Arthur Conan Doyle, *The Great Boer War,* Smith, Elder & Co, 1902, p 197.

11 Digby Thomas, *Two Generals*, p 95.

12 Pakenham, *The Boer War*, p 239.

13 CJ Barnard, 'General Louis Botha at the Battle of Colenso', *Military History Journal*, Vol 1, No 7 (December 1970), pp 1–6.

14 Trew, *The Boer War Generals*, p 26.

15 Von der Heyde, *Field Guide to the Battlefields of South Africa*, pp 106–107.

16 Ibid, p 108.

17 Meintjes, *General Louis Botha*, p 53.

18 Digby Thomas, *Two Generals*, p 103.

19 Judd and Skinner, *The Boer War*, p 132.

20 Winston Churchill, *London to Ladysmith via Pretoria*, WW Norton, 1990, p 131.

21 Kruger, *Good-bye Dolly Gray*, pp 186–198.

22 Reitz, *Commando*, p 47.

23 Trew, *The Boer War Generals*, p 149.

24 Churchill, *London to Ladysmith via Pretoria*, p 138.

25 Reitz, *Commando*, p 45.

26 Digby Thomas, *Two Generals*, p 111.

27 Kruger, *Good-bye Dolly Gray*, p 200.

CHAPTER 7 THE TIDE TURNS

1 Barnard, *Genl. Louis Botha op die Natalse Front 1899–1900*, p 110.

2 Ibid, p 112.

3 Holt, *The Boer War*, p 186.

4 Ibid.

5 Ibid, p 187.

6 Barnard, *Genl. Louis Botha op die Natalse Front 1899–1900*, p 118.

7 W Baring Pemberton, *Battles of the Boer War*, Pan Books, 1964, p 197.

8 Pakenham, *The Boer War*, p 307.

9 Kruger, *Good-bye Dolly Gray*, p 211.

10 Judd and Skinner, *The Boer War*, p 162.

11 Nasson, *The War for South Africa*, p 177.

12 Trew, *The Boer War Generals*, p 151.

13 Ibid, pp 150–151.

14 Ibid.

15 Reitz, *Commando*, p 90.

16 Churchill, *London to Ladysmith via Pretoria*, p 212.

17 Ibid.

18 Barnard, *Genl. Louis Botha op die Natalse Front 1899–1900*, p 147.

19 Trew, *The Boer War Generals*, p 152.

CHAPTER 8 ON THE BACK FOOT

1 Barnard, *Genl. Louis Botha op die Natalse Front 1899–1900*, p 148.

2 Ibid, p 149.

3 Ibid, p 150.

4 Ibid, p 152.

5 JEH Grobler, *The War Reporter: The Anglo-Boer War Through the Eyes of the Burghers*, Jonathan Ball Publishers, 2004, p 53.

6 Ibid.

7 Ibid.

8 Barnard, *Genl. Louis Botha op die Natalse Front 1899–1900*, p 153.

9 Grobler, *The War Reporter*, p 20.

10 Barnard, *Genl. Louis Botha op die Natalse Front 1899–1900*, p 156.

11 Hillegas, *With the Boer Forces*, pp 196–201.

12 Barnard, *Genl. Louis Botha op die Natalse Front 1899–1900*, p 155.

13 Meintjes, *General Louis Botha*, p 61.

14 Judd and Skinner, *The Boer War*, p 179.

15 Ibid, p 178.

16 Hillegas, *With the Boer Forces*, p 44.

17 Ibid, p 38.

18 Pakenham, *The Boer War*, p 421.

19 Meintjes, *General Louis Botha*, p 63.

CHAPTER 9 PRETORIA FALLS

1 Bossenbroek, *The Boer War*, p 238.

2 Ibid, p 245.

3 Hillegas, *With the Boer Forces*, p 38.

4 Meintjes, *General Louis Botha*, p 65.

5 Ibid.

6 Trew, *The Boer War Generals*, p 153.

7 Nasson, *The War for South Africa*, p 201.

8 Trew, *The Boer War Generals*, p 153.

9 Nasson, *The War for South Africa*, p 203.

10 Bossenbroek, *The Boer War*, p 252.

11 Ibid, p 256.

12 Meintjes, *General Louis Botha*, p 68.

13 Judd and Skinner, *The Boer War*, p 184.

14 Grobler, *The War Reporter*, p 79.

15 Ibid, p 85.
16 Trew, *The Boer War Generals*, p 154.
17 Ibid, p 155.
18 Von der Heyde, *Field Guide to the Battlefields of South Africa*, p 206.
19 Tim Couzens, *South African Battles*, Jonathan Ball Publishers, 2013, p 267.
20 Ibid.

CHAPTER 10 BURNING FARMS

1 See correspondence in National Army Museum, UK, Files 7101/23/189/1 and 7101,23.8310/155.62.
2 Holt, *The Boer War*, p 256.
3 Ibid, pp 256–257.
4 Kruger, *Good-bye Dolly Gray*, p 344.
5 Meintjes, *General Louis Botha*, p 75.
6 Digby Thomas, *Two Generals*, p 158.
7 Ibid, p 75.
8 Judd and Skinner, *The Boer War*, p 191.
9 Meintjes, *General Louis Botha*, p 76.
10 Nasson, *The War for South Africa*, p 212.
11 Ibid, p 210.
12 Digby Thomas, *Two Generals*, p 154.
13 Ibid, p 155.
14 Nasson, *The War for South Africa*, p 210.
15 Spender, *General Botha*, pp 93–95.
16 Pakenham, *The Boer War*, p 471.
17 Ibid.
18 Digby Thomas, *Two Generals*, p 156.
19 Pakenham, *The Boer War*, p 472.
20 Meintjes, *General Louis Botha*, p 77.
21 Holt, *The Boer War*, p 246.
22 Grobler, *The War Reporter*, p 101.
23 Judd and Skinner, *The Boer War*, p 187.
24 Christiaan de Wet, *Three Years War (October 1899 to June 1902)*, Galago, 1986, p 242.
25 Trew, *The Boer War Generals*, pp 159–160.
26 Digby Thomas, *Two Generals*, p 165.
27 Nasson, *The War for South Africa*, p 223.
28 Trew, *The Boer War Generals*, p 160.
29 Holt, *The Boer War*, p 261.

CHAPTER 11 THE WAR DRAGS ON

1 Digby Thomas, *Two Generals*, p 167.
2 Judd and Skinner, *The Boer War*, p 108.

3 Meintjes, *General Louis Botha*, p 85.
4 Spender, *General Botha*, p 113.
5 Meintjes, *General Louis Botha*, pp 85–86.
6 Kruger, *Good-bye Dolly Gray*, pp 431–432.
7 Meintjes, *General Louis Botha*, p 86.
8 Trew, *The Boer War Generals*, p 139.
9 Digby Thomas, *Two Generals*, p 158.
10 Ibid.
11 Meintjes, *General Louis Botha*, p 88.
12 Ibid, p 70.
13 Von der Heyde, *Field Guide to the Battlefields of South Africa*, p 208.
14 Trew, *The Boer War Generals*, p 164.
15 Von der Heyde, *Field Guide to the Battlefields of South Africa*, p 209.
16 Trew, *The Boer War Generals*, p 165.
17 Engelenburg, *General Louis Botha*, p 76.
18 Peter Warwick, quoted in Cameron and Spies (eds), *An Illustrated History of South Africa*, p 216.
19 Ibid.
20 Nasson, *The War for South Africa*, p 248.
21 Fransjohan Pretorius, *Life on Commando during the Anglo-Boer War 1899–1902*, Human & Rousseau, 1999, p 273.
22 Peter Warwick, quoted in Cameron and Spies (eds), *An Illustrated History of South Africa*, p 316.
23 Ibid, p 217.
24 Grobler, *The War Reporter*, p 107.

CHAPTER 12 PEACE AT LAST

1 Digby Thomas, *Two Generals*, p 158.
2 Grobler, *The War Reporter*, p 134.
3 Meintjes, *General Louis Botha*, p 94.
4 Ibid, p 95.
5 Judd and Skinner, *The Boer War*, p 215.
6 Holt, *The Boer War*, pp 286–287.
7 Bossenbroek, *The Boer War*, p 388.
8 Trew, *The Boer War Generals*, p 166.
9 Judd and Skinner, *The Boer War*, p 278.
10 Grobler, *The War Reporter*, p 141.
11 Meintjes, *General Louis Botha*, p 98.
12 Holt, *The Boer War*, p 288.
13 Ibid, p 289.
14 Reitz, *Commando*, p 320.

15 Bossenbroek, *The Boer War*, p 398.
16 Judd and Skinner, *The Boer War*, p 288.
17 A non-verbatim summary of Botha's words, in Meintjes, *General Louis Botha*, p 100.
18 Ibid.
19 JD Kestell and DE van Velden, *The Peace Negotiations between Boer and Briton in South Africa*, Richard Clay & Sons, 1912, pp 88–90.
20 Bossenbroek, *The Boer War*, p 400.
21 Holt, *The Boer War*, p 290.
22 Bossenbroek, *The Boer War*, p 400.
23 Judd and Skinner, *The Boer War*, p 295.
24 Ibid, p 236.
25 Kruger, *Good-bye Dolly Gray*, p 506.
26 Engelenburg, *General Louis Botha*, p 97.
27 Ibid, p 99.

CHAPTER 13 DEALING WITH MILNER
1 Spender, *General Botha*, p 149.
2 Digby Thomas, *Two Generals*, p 179.
3 Bossenbroek, *The Boer War*, p xv.
4 Holt, *The Boer War*, p 293.
5 Bossenbroek, *The Boer War*, p xvi.
6 Meintjes, *General Louis Botha*, p 111.
7 Neil Parsons, *Black and White Bioscope: Making Movies in Africa 1899 to 1925*. University of Chicago Press, 2018, p 6.
8 Ibid, p 10.
9 Ibid, p 4.
10 Ibid, pp 112–115.
11 Ibid, p 116.
12 Spender, *General Botha*, p 158.
13 Meintjes, *General Louis Botha*, p 116.
14 Ibid, p 118.
15 p 119.
16 Engelenburg, *General Louis Botha*, p 110.
17 Meintjes, *General Louis Botha*, p 120.
18 Ibid.
19 HC Armstrong, *Grey Steel: JC Smuts: A Study in Arrogance*, Arthur Barker, 1937, p 149.
20 Hancock, *Smuts: The Sanguine Years*, p 192.
21 Ibid.
22 Engelenburg, *General Louis Botha*, p 116.
23 Spender, *General Botha*, p 163.
24 Meintjes, *General Louis Botha*, p 122.

25 Karel Schoeman, *Imperiale Somer: Suid Afrika tussen Oorlog en Unie, 1902–1910*, Protea Boekhuis, 2015, p 148.
26 Engelenburg, *General Louis Botha*, p 117.

CHAPTER 14 INTO POLITICS AGAIN
1 Engelenburg, *General Louis Botha*, p 121.
2 Meintjes, *General Louis Botha*, p 123.
3 Hancock, *Smuts: The Sanguine Years*, p 194.
4 Ibid.
5 Ibid, p 128.
6 Ibid, p 183.
7 Meintjes, *General Louis Botha*, p 130.
8 Engelenburg, *General Louis Botha*, p 128.
9 Johannes Meintjes, *President Paul Kruger: A Biography*, Cassell, 1974, p 261.
10 Ibid, p 266.
11 Meintjes, *General Louis Botha*, p 133.
12 Armstrong, *Grey Steel*, p 158.
13 Meintjes, *General Louis Botha*, p 133.
14 Engelenburg, *General Louis Botha*, pp 131–132.
15 Meintjes, *General Louis Botha*, p 134.
16 Earl Buxton to Colonial Secretary Milner, 8 Sept 1919, Buxton Papers, British Library, File ADD 86948.
17 Meintjes, *General Louis Botha*, p 135.
18 Ibid, p 137.
19 Ibid, p 140.
20 Edward Crankshaw, *The Forsaken Idea: A Study of Viscount Milner*, Longmans Green & Co, 1952, p 113.

CHAPTER 15 COMING TO POWER
1 'Chinese South Africans', Wikipedia, 10 April 2018. Available at en.wikipedia.org/wiki/Chinese South Africans, accessed on 5 June 2018.
2 Sarah Gertrude Millin, *General Smuts, Volume 1*, Faber & Faber, 1936, p 207.
3 Reader's Digest Association, *Illustrated History of South Africa*, p 268.
4 Millin, *General Smuts*, p 211.
5 Hancock, *Smuts: The Sanguine Years*, p 215.
6 Millin, *General Smuts*, p 213.
7 Ibid, p 214.

8 Engelenburg, *General Louis Botha*, p 16.

9 Ronald Hyam and Ged Martin, *Reappraisals in British Imperial History*, Palgrave Macmillan, 1975, p 180.

10 Giliomee, *The Afrikaners*, p 270.

11 Davenport, *South Africa: A Modern History*, p 219.

12 Reader's Digest Association, *Illustrated History of South Africa*, p 270.

13 Meintjes, *General Louis Botha*, p 146.

14 Davenport, *South Africa: A Modern History*, p 219.

15 Engelenburg, *General Louis Botha*, p 144.

16 Noel Garson, quoted in Schoeman, *Imperiale Somer*, p 156.

17 Engelenburg, *General Louis Botha*, p 145.

18 Meintjes, *General Louis Botha*, p 147.

19 Engelenburg, *General Louis Botha*, p 148.

20 Ibid.

21 Meintjes, *General Louis Botha*, p 146.

22 Ibid, p 147.

23 Ibid, p 148.

24 John Wilson, *CB: A Life of Henry Campbell-Bannerman*, Constable, 1975, p 490.

CHAPTER 16 THE REFORMER

1 Engelenburg, *General Louis Botha*, p 149.

2 Churchill, *My Early Life*, p 261.

3 Buxton, *General Botha*, p 179.

4 Meintjes, *General Louis Botha*, p 150.

5 Spender, *General Botha*, p 184

6 David Lloyd George, *Memoirs of the Peace Conference, Volume I*, Yale University Press, 1939, p 167.

7 Meintjes, *General Louis Botha*, p 149.

8 Engelenburg, *General Louis Botha*, p 152.

9 Ian Colvin, *The Life of Jameson, Volume II*, Edward Arnold, 1923, p 255.

10 Meintjes, *General Louis Botha*, p 149.

11 Engelenburg, *General Louis Botha*, p 152.

12 Ibid.

13 Ibid, p 142.

14 Meintjes, *General Louis Botha*, p 151.

15 Spender, *General Botha*, p 187.

16 Ibid, p 186.

17 Engelenburg, *General Louis Botha*, p 162.

18 Meintjes, *General Louis Botha*, p 154.

19 Engelenburg, *General Louis Botha*, p 164.

20 Millin, *General Smuts*, p 228.

21 Engelenburg, *General Louis Botha*, p 332.

22 Quoted in Meintjes, *General Louis Botha*, p 44, by Millard in *Hero of the Empire*, p 232.

23 Spender, *General Botha*, p 190.

24 Charles van Onselen, *New Babylon, New Nineveh: Everyday Life on the Witwatersrand 1886–1914*, Jonathan Ball Publishers, 1982, p 29.

25 Ibid, p 192.

26 Spender, *General Botha*, p 193.

27 Ibid, 194.

CHAPTER 17 UNIFICATION

1 Johannes Meintjes, *President Steyn: A Biography*, Nasionale Boekhandel, 1969, p 215.

2 Hancock, *Smuts: The Sanguine Years*, p 248.

3 Ibid, p 246.

4 Engelenburg, *General Louis Botha*, p 167.

5 Ibid, p 168.

6 Spender, *General Botha*, p 203–204.

7 Engelenburg, *General Louis Botha*, p 170.

8 Hancock, *Smuts: The Sanguine Years*, p 262.

9 Rodney Davenport and Christopher Saunders, *South Africa: A Modern History*, fifth edition, Macmillan, 2000, p 258.

10 Leonard M Thompson, *The Unification of South Africa, 1902–1910*, Oxford University Press, 1960, p 179.

11 Ibid, p 253.

12 Engelenburg, *General Louis Botha*, p 174.

13 Ibid.

14 Ibid, p 175.

15 Ibid, p 173.

16 Meintjes, *President Steyn*, p 218.

17 Engelenburg, *General Louis Botha*, p 178.

18 The official make-up of South Africa's population, in the year after Union, stood at 4 019 000 Africans (67.3 per cent), 1 276 000 whites (21.3 per cent), 526 000 coloureds (8.9 per cent) and 152 100 Indians (2.5 per cent).

19 WT Stead (ed), *Review of Reviews*, August 1909.

20 Plaut, *Promise and Despair*, pp 122–123.

21 RW Johnson, *South Africa: The First Man, The Last Nation*, Jonathan Ball Publishers, 2004, p 112.
22 Frank Welsh, *A History of South Africa*, HarperCollins, 2000, p 373.
23 Leonard Thompson, *A History of South Africa*, Radix, 1990, p 152.
24 Letter from HH Asquith to General Botha, 27 August 1909, Asquith Papers, Bodleian Library, Oxford.
25 Meintjes, *General Louis Botha*, p 168.
26 Johnson, *South Africa: The First Man, The Last Nation*, p 112.

CHAPTER 18 PREMIER OF THE UNION

1 Phyllis Lewsen, *John X Merriman: Paradoxical South African Statesman*, Ad Donker, 1982, p 329.
2 Ibid.
3 Meintjes, *General Louis Botha*, p 167.
4 Engelenburg, *General Louis Botha*, p 186.
5 Ibid, p 193.
6 Thompson, *The Unification of South Africa*, p 452.
7 Meintjes, *General Louis Botha*, p 171.
8 Engelenburg, *General Louis Botha*, p 192.
9 Ibid, pp 202–203.
10 BK Long, quoted in Schoeman, *Imperiale Somer*, p 149.
11 James Barber, *South Africa in the Twentieth Century: A Political History – In Search of a Nation State*, Blackwell, 1999, p 60.
12 Engelenburg, *General Louis Botha*, p 222
13 Ibid. p 223.
14 AP Cartwright, *The First South African: The Life and Times of Sir Percy FitzPatrick*, Purnell, 1971, p 183.
15 Ibid, p 93.
16 Engelenburg, *General Louis Botha*, p 225.
17 Spender, *General Botha*, pp 233–224.
18 Schoeman, *Imperiale Somer*, p 432.
19 Engelenburg, *General Louis Botha*, p 225.

CHAPTER 19 SIGNS OF TROUBLE

1 Meintjes, *General Louis Botha*, p 179.

2 Spender, *General Botha*, p 225n.
3 Ibid, p 226.
4 Thompson, *The Unification of South Africa*, p 468.
5 Hancock, *Smuts: The Sanguine Years*, p 284.
6 Meintjes, *General Louis Botha*, p 181.
7 Spender, *General Botha*, p 229.
8 Hancock, *Smuts: The Sanguine Years*, p 352.
9 Ibid, p 353.
10 Meintjes, *General Louis Botha*, p 182.
11 Spender, *General Botha*, p 228.
12 Meintjes, *General Louis Botha*, p 182.
13 Ibid, p 183.
14 Spender, *General Botha*, p 231.
15 Ibid, pp 230–231.
16 Meintjes, *General Louis Botha*, p 183.
17 Engelenburg, *General Louis Botha*, p 244.
18 Spender, *General Botha*, p 232.
19 Colvin, *The Life of Jameson, Volume II*, p 300.
20 Ibid.
21 Ibid, p 302.
22 Hancock, *Smuts: The Sanguine Years*, p 354.
23 Ibid, p 355.
24 DW Krüger, *The Making of a Nation: A History of the Union of South Africa, 1910–1961*, Macmillan, 1969, p 65.
25 Hancock, *Smuts: The Sanguine Years*, p 356.
26 Ibid, p 357.
27 Krüger, *The Making of a Nation*, p 63.

CHAPTER 20 SCHISM

1 Krüger, *The Making of a Nation*, p 63.
2 Hancock, *Smuts: The Sanguine Years*, p 355.
3 Engelenburg, *General Louis Botha*, p 253.
4 Ibid, p 256.
5 Meintjes, *President Steyn*, p 215.
6 Ibid, p 228.
7 Engelenburg, *General Louis Botha*, p 258.
8 Ibid, p 259.
9 Meintjes, *President Steyn*, p 229.
10 Meintjes, *General Louis Botha*, p 195.
11 Spender, *General Botha*, p 248.
12 Krüger, *The Making of a Nation*, p 68.
13 Ibid.
14 Meredith, *Diamonds, Gold and War*, p 497.
15 Ibid.

16 Book review by Xolisa Phillip in *Business Day*, 8 May 2018, p 10.

17 CFJ Muller (ed), *500 Years: A History of South Africa*, Academica, 1981, p 396.

18 Engelenburg, *General Louis Botha*, p 270.

19 Krüger, *The Making of a Nation*, p 74.

20 Muller (ed), *500 Years*, p 398.

21 Hancock, *Smuts: The Sanguine Years*, p 345.

22 Lawrence James, *Empires in the Sun: The Struggle for Mastery in Africa*, Jonathan Ball Publishers, 2016, p 179.

23 Plaut, *Promise and Despair*, pp 103–104.

CHAPTER 21 GOING TO WAR

1 Churchill, *My Early Life*, p 261.

2 Ibid, p 262.

3 Ibid.

4 John Buchan, quoted in Ian van der Waag, *A Military History of Modern South Africa*, Jonathan Ball Publishers, 2015, p 90.

5 Krüger, *The Making of a Nation*, p 79.

6 Hyam and Martin, *Reappraisals in British Imperial History*, p 180.

7 Meintjes, *President Steyn*, p 206.

8 Ibid.

9 Schoeman, *Imperiale Somer*, p 131.

10 Engelenburg, *General Louis Botha*, p 210.

11 Meintjes, *President Steyn*, p 206.

12 Meintjes, *General Louis Botha*, pp 158–159.

13 Ibid, p 160.

14 Ibid, p 196.

15 Ibid, p 196.

16 Meintjes, *President Steyn*, p 229.

17 Engelenburg, *General Louis Botha*, p 264.

18 Eric Rosenthal, *General De Wet: A Biography*, Unie-Volkspers Bpk, 1946, p 141.

19 Meintjes, *General Louis Botha*, p 212.

20 Ibid.

21 Ibid.

22 Engelenburg, *General Louis Botha*, p 282.

23 Meintjes, *General Louis Botha*, p 209.

CHAPTER 22 REBELLION

1 Bill Nasson, *WW1 and the People of South Africa*, Tafelberg, 2014, p 78.

2 Meintjes, *General Louis Botha*, p 211.

3 HF Trew, *Botha Treks*, Blackie & Sons, 1936, p 1.

4 Meintjes, *General Louis Botha*, p 208.

5 Engelenburg, *General Louis Botha*, p 282.

6 Krüger, *The Making of a Nation*, p 82.

7 Ibid.

8 Meintjes, *General Louis Botha*, p 219.

9 Meintjes, *De la Rey*, p 355.

10 Ibid.

11 Krüger, *The Making of a Nation*, p 83.

12 Meintjes, *De la Rey*, p 362.

13 Meintjes, *General Louis Botha*, p 225.

14 Meintjes, *De la Rey*, p 363.

15 Ibid, p 380 et seq.

16 Buxton to Colonial Secretary, 24 September 1914, Buxton Papers, British Library, File AD 86949 H030 G.

17 Meintjes, *General Louis Botha*, p 227.

18 Buxton, *General Botha*, p 52.

19 Meintjes, *General Louis Botha*, p 228.

20 Ibid, p 229.

21 Engelenburg, *General Louis Botha*, p 294.

22 Hancock, *Smuts: The Sanguine Years*, p 385.

23 Engelenburg, *General Louis Botha*, p 295.

CHAPTER 23 HEARTACHE

1 Adam Cruise, *Louis Botha's War: The Campaign in German South-West Africa, 1914–1915*, Zebra Press, 2015, pp 32–33.

2 Meintjes, *General Louis Botha*, p 233.

3 Ibid, p 234.

4 Ibid.

5 Byron Farwell, *The Great War in Africa, 1914–1918*, Viking, 1987, p 89.

6 Tim Couzens, *The Great Silence: From Mushroom Valley to Delville Wood, South African Forces in World War One*, Art Publishers/*Sunday Times*, 2014, p 40.

7 Meintjes, *President Steyn*, p 234.

8 Meintjes, *General Louis Botha*, p 231.

9 Anne Samson, *World War I in Africa: The Forgotten Conflict Among the European Powers*, IB Tauris, 2013, p 87.

10 Engelenburg, *General Louis Botha*, p 295.

11 Meintjes, *General Louis Botha*, p 211.

12 Engelenburg, *General Louis Botha*, p 295.
13 Ibid, p 296.
14 Meintjes, *General Louis Botha*, pp 236–237.
15 Ibid.
16 Bossenbroek, *The Boer War*, p 305.
17 Cruise, *Louis Botha's War*, p 16.
18 Churchill, *My Early Life*, p 261.
19 Couzens, *The Great Silence*, p 46.
20 Krüger, *The Making of a Nation*, p 90.
21 Buxton to Colonial Secretary, 26 October 1914, Buxton Papers, British Library, File ADD 86951 4030 G.
22 Van der Waag, *A Military History of Modern South Africa*, p 99.
23 Couzens, *The Great Silence*, pp 46–47.
24 Buxton to Colonial Secretary, 2 November 1914, Buxton Papers, British Library, File ADD 86951 4030 G.
25 Meintjes, *General Louis Botha*, p 245.
26 Couzens, *The Great Silence*, p 58.
27 Krüger, *The Making of a Nation*, p 93.

CHAPTER 24 MOPPING UP

1 Couzens, *The Great Silence*, p 51.
2 Ibid.
3 Ibid, p 52.
4 Gerald L'Ange, *Urgent Imperial Service: South African Forces in German South West Africa*, Ashanti Publishing, 1991, p 68.
5 Couzens, *South African Battles*, p 362.
6 Deneys Reitz, *Trekking On*, Faber & Faber, 1933, p 87.
7 *Official History: The Union of South Africa in the Great War 1914–1918*, Naval & Military Press Ltd and the Imperial War Museum, 2015, p 23.
8 Moore Ritchie, *With Botha in the Field*, Longmans, Green & Co, p 215.
9 Meintjes, *General Louis Botha*, p 251.
10 *Official History*, p 24.
11 Buxton, *General Botha*, p 69.
12 *Official History*, p 25.
13 Buxton, *General Botha*, p 82.
14 Ibid, p 83.
15 Ibid, p 86.
16 Trew, *Botha Treks*, p 36.

17 Ibid, p 87.
18 Ibid, p 88.
19 Ibid, p 178
20 Ibid, pp 179–180.

CHAPTER 25 INTO GERMAN SOUTH WEST AFRICA

1 Evert Kleynhans, 'South African Invasion of German South West Africa (Union of South Africa)', *1914–1918 Online*, the International Encyclopedia of the First World War, 1 July 2015. Available at encyclopedia.1914-1918-online.net, accessed on 6 June 2018.
2 Ibid.
3 Ibid.
4 WS Rayner and WW O'Shaughnessy, *How Botha and Smuts Conquered German South West Africa*, Simpkin, Marshall, Hamilton, Kent & Co, 1916, p 61.
5 Ibid, p 61-62.
6 Couzens, *The Great Silence*, pp 73–74.
7 Farwell, *The Great War in Africa*, p 87.
8 Peter Joyce (ed), *South Africa's Yesterdays*, Reader's Digest Association, 1981, p 291.
9 Letter from Lewis Harcourt to Buxton, 6 October 1914, Buxton Papers, British Library, File ADD 86950 4030 G.
10 Ibid, 8 October 1914.
11 Kleynhans, 'South African Invasion of German South West Africa'.
12 Ibid.
13 Rayner and O'Shaughnessy, *How Botha and Smuts Conquered German South West Africa*, p 91.
14 Ibid, p 92.
15 WW O'Shaughnessy, quoted in Farwell, *The Great War in Africa*, p 95.
16 Couzens, *The Great Silence*, p 86.
17 Bill Nasson, *Springboks on the Somme: South Africa in the Great War 1914–1918*, Penguin, 2007, p 65.
18 Ibid, p 66.
19 Farwell, *The Great War in Africa*, p 91.
20 Cruise, *Louis Botha's War*, p 79.
21 Farwell, *The Great War in Africa*, p 93.
22 Ibid, p 94.

23 W Whittall, *With Botha and Smuts in Africa*, Cassell, 1917, p 40.

24 Trew, *Botha Treks*, p 99.

25 Brig-Gen JJ Collyer, *The Campaign in German South West Africa, 1914–1915*, reprint edition, Naval and Military Press, 2011, p 77.

26 Ibid.

27 Ritchie, *With Botha in the Field*, p 39.

28 Nasson, *Springboks on the Somme*, p 71.

29 Ibid.

30 L'Ange, *Urgent Imperial Service*, p 182.

31 Meintjes, *General Louis Botha*, p 262.

32 Keith Morris, *Louis Botha or Through the Great Thirst Land*, William Stevens, 1917, p 47.

33 JJ Collyer, quoted in Couzens, *The Great Silence*, p 101.

CHAPTER 26 A TACTICAL TRIUMPH

1 Cruise, *Louis Botha's War*, p 80.

2 Nasson, *Springboks on the Somme*, p 65.

3 Samson, *World War I in Africa*, p 83.

4 Whittall, *With Botha and Smuts in Africa*, p 26.

5 Ibid, p 25.

6 Ibid, p 24.

7 Hancock, *Smuts: The Sanguine Years*, p 399.

8 Nasson, *Springboks on the Somme*, p 73.

9 Ibid.

10 Ibid, p 74.

11 Cruise, *Louis Botha's War*, pp 134–135.

12 Whittall, *With Botha and Smuts in Africa*, p 85.

13 Collyer, *The Campaign in German South West Africa*, p 108.

14 Couzens, *The Great Silence*, p 102.

15 Ibid, p 103.

16 Ibid, p 105.

17 Cruise, *Louis Botha's War*, pp 159–160.

18 Buxton, *General Botha*, p 114.

19 Ibid, pp 114–115.

20 Meintjes, *General Louis Botha*, p 269.

21 Whittall, *With Botha and Smuts in Africa*, p 159.

22 Farwell, *The Great War in Africa*, p 102.

23 Ibid, p 103.

24 Ibid.

25 L'Ange, *Urgent Imperial Service*, pp 330–331.

26 Hancock, *Smuts: The Sanguine Years*, p 396.

27 Meintjes, *General Louis Botha*, p 267.

28 Ibid, p 271.

CHAPTER 27 TROUBLED TIMES

1 Hancock, *Smuts: The Sanguine Years*, p 400.

2 Meintjes, *General Louis Botha*, p 273.

3 Sarah Gertrude Millin, *The South Africans*, Constable & Co, 1937, p 151.

4 Parsons, *Black and White Bioscope*, p 42.

5 Meintjes, *General Botha*, p 273.

6 Hancock, *Smuts: The Sanguine Years*, p 403.

7 Buxton, *General Botha*, pp 239–240.

8 Samson, *World War I in Africa*, p 96.

9 Hancock, *Smuts: The Sanguine Years*, p 409.

10 Ibid, p 411n

11 Ibid, p 409.

12 Buxton, *General Botha*, p 250.

13 Ibid, p 251.

14 Ibid.

15 Meintjes, *General Botha*, p 282.

16 Ibid.

17 Krüger, *The Making of a Nation*, p 106.

18 Ibid, p 105.

19 Hancock, *Smuts: The Sanguine Years*, p 419.

20 Buxton, *General Botha*, p 300.

21 Ibid, p 306.

22 Meintjes, *General Botha*, p 287.

23 Buxton, *General Botha*, p 157.

24 Ibid, p 158n.

CHAPTER 28 IN POOR HEALTH

1 Krüger, *The Making of A Nation*, p 106.

2 Meintjes, *President Steyn*, p 255.

3 Meintjes, *General Louis Botha*, p 385.

4 Engelenburg, *General Louis Botha*, p 314.

5 Ibid, p 314.

6 Buxton, *General Botha*, pp 242–243.

7 Ibid, pp 256–257.

8 Ibid, pp 258–260.

9 Ibid, p 288.

10 David Olusoga, *The World's War: Forgotten Soldiers of Empire*, Head of Zeus, 2014, p 314.

11 *Cape Times*, 10 March 1917, quoted in Nasson, *WW1 and the People of South Africa*, p 186.

12 Buxton, *General Botha*, p 288.

13 JS Mohlamme, 'Soldiers Without Reward: Africans in South Africa's Wars', *Military History Journal*, Vol 10, No 1 (June 1995).

14 John Gribble and Graham Scott, *We Die Like Brothers: The Sinking of the SS Mendi*, Historic England, 2017, p 145.

15 Ian Gleeson, *The Unknown Force: Black, Indian and Coloured Soldiers Through Two World Wars*, Ashanti, 1994, pp 45–46.

16 Ibid, p 26.

17 Gribble and Scott, *We Die Like Brothers*, p 33.

18 Gleeson, *The Unknown Force*, p 45.

19 Albert Grundlingh, *Fighting Their Own War: South African Blacks and the First World War*, Ravan Press, 1987, p 128.

20 Gribble and Scott, *We Die Like Brothers*, p 27.

21 Buxton, *General Botha*, p 323.

22 Ibid.

23 Hancock, *Smuts: The Sanguine Years*, p 551.

24 Buxton, *General Botha*, p 324.

25 Meintjes, *General Louis Botha*, pp 288–289.

26 Buxton, *General Botha*, p 325.

27 Ibid, p 326.

28 Ibid.

29 Meintjes, *General Louis Botha*, p 290.

CHAPTER 29 PEACEMAKING

1 Buxton, *General Botha*, p 188.

2 Ibid, p 189.

3 *The Star*, 28 August, 1919.

4 Buxton, *General Botha*, p 191.

5 Hancock, *Smuts: The Sanguine Years*, p 553.

6 Meintjes, *General Louis Botha*, p 294.

7 Reitz, *Trekking On*, p 341.

8 Engelenburg, *General Louis Botha*, pp 318–319.

9 Ibid, p 326.

10 Lloyd George, *Memoirs of the Peace Conference, Volume 1*, p 166.

11 Ibid, p 167.

12 Ibid.

13 Botha to Buxton, 22 April 1919, Buxton Papers, British Library, File ADD 87011 4031C.

14 Meintjes, *General Louis Botha*, p 294.

15 Lloyd George, *Memoirs of the Peace Conference, Volume 1*, pp 360–362.

16 Ibid, p 362.

17 Rupert Colley, *World War One*, William Collins, 2013, p 60.

18 Meintjes, *General Louis Botha*, p 295.

19 Ibid.

20 Ibid, p 320.

21 Ibid, p 321.

22 Ibid.

23 Engelenburg, *General Louis Botha*, p 321.

24 FitzPatrick, *South African Memories*, pp 129–130.

25 Ibid.

26 David Lloyd George, *The Truth About the Peace Treaties, Volume 1*, Victor Gollancz, 1935, p 546.

27 Engelenburg, *General Louis Botha*, p 323.

28 Krüger, *The Making of a Nation*, p 108.

29 Meintjes, *General Louis Botha*, p 298.

30 CM van den Heever, *General JBM Hertzog*, APB Bookstore, 1946, p 188.

31 Buxton Papers, British Library, File ADD 87011 4031C.

32 Meintjes, *General Louis Botha*, p 298.

33 Hancock, *Smuts: The Sanguine Years*, p 544.

34 Buxton Papers, British Library, File ADD 87011 4031C.

35 Meintjes, *General Louis Botha*, p 298.

36 Engelenburg, *General Louis Botha*, p 326.

37 Ibid.

38 Meintjes, *General Louis Botha*, p 298.

39 WK Hancock and J van der Poel (eds), *Selections from the Smuts Papers, Volume IV*, Cambridge University Press, 1973, p 282.

40 Buxton, *General Botha*, p 186.

CHAPTER 30 AN IRREPARABLE LOSS

1 *Rand Daily Mail*, 1 September, 1919, p 5.

2 Engelenburg, *General Louis Botha*, p 327.

3 Ibid.

4 Ibid, p 328.

5 Buxton, *General Botha*, p 328.

6 Arthur Barlow, *Almost in Confidence*, Juta & Co, 1952, p 163.

7 Meintjes, *General Louis Botha*, pp 300–301.

8 Kirsty E Duncan, *One Scientist's Search for a Killer Virus*, University of Toronto Press, 2006, p 16.

9 Engelenburg, *General Louis Botha*, p 329.

10 Hancock, *Smuts: The Sanguine Years*, p 556.

11 Ibid, pp 556–557.

12 Buxton, *General Botha*, p 331.

13 Hancock, *Smuts: The Sanguine Years*, p 557.

14 Winston S Churchill, *Great Contemporaries*, Leo Cooper, 1990, p 233.

15 Barlow, *Almost in Confidence*, p 134.

16 Hancock and Van der Poel (eds), *Selections from the Smuts Papers, Volume I*, p 287.

17 Ibid, pp 287–288.

18 Ibid, p 288.

19 *The Star*, 28 August 1919.

20 *Die Vaderland*, quoted in *The Star*, 29 August 1919.

21 DW Krüger, *The Age of the Generals*, Dagbreek Book Store, 1958, p 109.

22 Meintjes, *General Louis Botha*, p 304.

23 Ibid, pp 304–305.

24 FS Crafford, *Jan Smuts: A Biography*, Howard Timmins, 1946, p 187.

25 Hancock, *Smuts: The Sanguine Years*, p 560.

26 Ibid, p 561.

27 Ibid.

28 Hancock and Van der Poel (eds), *Selections from the Smuts Papers, Volume I*, p 67.

29 Ibid.

30 Hillegas, *With the Boer Forces*, pp 200–201.

31 Lloyd George, *Memoirs of the Peace Conference, Volume I*, p 169.

32 Armstrong, *Grey Steel*, p 334.

33 Buxton, *General Botha*, pp 125–126.

SELECT BIBLIOGRAPHY

Articles

Barnard, CJ. 'General Louis Botha at the Battle of Colenso', *Military History Journal*, Vol 1, No 7 (December 1970).

Kleynhans, Evert. 'South African Invasion of German South West Africa (Union of South Africa)', *1914–1918 Online*, the International Encyclopedia of the First World War, 1 July 2015. Available at encyclopedia.1914–1918-online.net, accessed on 6 June 2018.

Mohlamme, JS. 'Soldiers Without Reward: Africans in South Africa's Wars', *Military History Journal*, Vol 10, No 1 (June 1995).

Paterson, Hamish. 'First Allied Victory: The South African Campaign in German South-West Africa 1914–1915', *Military History Journal*, Vol 13, No 2 (2004).

Samson, Anne. 'Louis Botha', *1914–1918 Online*, International Encyclopedia of the First World War, 23 April 2015. Available at encyclopedia.1914-1918-online.net, accessed on 15 June 2018.

Wessels, André, 'Afrikaner (Boer) Rebellion (Union of South Africa)', *1914-1918 Online*, International Encyclopedia of the First World War, 5 August 2015. Available at encyclopedia.1914-1918-online.net, accessed on 15 June 2018.

Books

Armstrong, HC. *Grey Steel: JC Smuts: A Study in Arrogance* (Arthur Barker, 1937).

Barber, James. *South Africa in the Twentieth Century: A Political History – In Search of a Nation State* (Blackwell, 1999).

Barlow, Arthur. *Almost in Confidence* (Juta & Co, 1952).

Barnard, CJ. *Genl. Louis Botha op die Natalse Front 1899–1900* (AA Balkema, 1970).

Bossenbroek, Martin. *The Boer War* (Jacana, 2016).

Buchan, John. *The History of the Royal Scots Fusiliers, 1678–1918*, (Thomas Nelson & Sons, 1925).

Buxton, Earl. *General Botha* (John Murray, 1929).

Cameron, Trewhella and Burridge Spies (eds). *An Illustrated History of South Africa* (Southern/Human & Rousseau, 1988).

Cartwright, AP. *The First South African: The Life and Times of Sir Percy FitzPatrick* (Purnell, 1971).

Churchill, Winston S. *My Early Life*, (Fontana, 1972).

Churchill, Winston S. *London to Ladysmith via Pretoria* (WW Norton, 1990).

Churchill, Winston, S. *Great Contemporaries* (Leo Cooper, 1990).

Colley, Rupert. *World War One* (William Collins, 2013).

Collyer, Brig-Gen JJ. *The Campaign in German South West Africa, 1914–1915*, reprint edition (Naval and Military Press, 2011).

Colvin, Ian. *The Life of Jameson, Volume II* (Edward Arnold, 1923).

Couzens, Tim. *South African Battles* (Jonathan Ball Publishers, 2013).

Couzens, Tim. *The Great Silence: From Mushroom Valley to Delville Wood, South African Forces in World War One* (Art Publishers/*Sunday Times*, 2014).

Crafford, FS. *Jan Smuts: A Biography* (Howard Timmins, 1946).

Crankshaw, Edward. *The Forsaken Idea: A Study of Viscount Milner* (Longmans Green & Co, 1952).

Cruise, Adam. *Louis Botha's War: The Campaign in German South-West Africa, 1914–1915* (Zebra Press, 2015).

Davenport, TRH. *South Africa: A Modern History*, fourth edition (Macmillan, 1992).

Davenport, Rodney and Christopher Saunders, *South Africa: A Modern History*, fifth edition (Macmillan, 2000).

Davitt, Michael. *The Boer Fight for Freedom: From the Beginning of Hostilities to the Peace of Pretoria* (Funk & Wagnall, 1902).

De Kiewiet, CW. *A History of South Africa: Social and Economic* (Oxford University Press, 1957).

De Wet, Christiaan. *Three Years War (October 1899 to June 1902)* (Galago, 1986).

Digby Thomas, Roy. *Two Generals: Buller and Botha in the Boer War*, ebook (Author House, 2012).

Doyle, Arthur Conan. *The Great Boer War* (Smith, Elder & Co, 1902).

Engelenburg, FV, *General Louis Botha* (George G Harrap, 1929).

Farwell, Byron. *The Great War in Africa, 1914–1918* (Viking, 1987).

FitzPatrick, Sir J Percy. *South African Memories* (Cassell, 1932).

Giliomee, Hermann. *The Afrikaners: Biography of a People* (Tafelberg, 2003).

Giliomee, Hermann and Bernard Mbenga. *New History of South Africa* (Tafelberg, 2007).

Gleeson, Ian. *The Unknown Force: Black, Indian and Coloured Soldiers Through Two World Wars* (Ashanti, 1994).

Gordon, CT. *The Growth of Boer Opposition to Kruger (1890–1895)* (Oxford University Press, 1970).

Grobler, JEH. *The War Reporter: The Anglo-Boer War Through the Eyes of the Burghers* (Jonathan Ball Publishers, 2004).

Gribble, John and Graham Scott. *We Die Like Brothers: The Sinking of the SS* Mendi (Historic England, 2017).

Grundlingh, Albert. *Fighting Their Own War: South African Blacks and the First World War* (Ravan Press, 1987).

Hancock, WK. *Smuts: The Sanguine Years 1870–1919* (Cambridge University Press, 1962).

Hancock, WK and J van der Poel (eds). *Selections from the Smuts Papers, Volume IV* (Cambridge University Press, 1973).

Hillegas, HC. *With the Boer Forces* (Methuen, 1900).

Holt, Edgar. *The Boer War* (Putnam, 1958).

Hyam, Ronald. *Britain's Imperial Century, 1815–1914: A Study of Empire and Expansion*, second edition (Barnes & Noble, 1995).

Hyam, Ronald and Ged Martin. *Reappraisals in British Imperial History* (Palgrave Macmillan, 1975).

James, Lawrence. *Empires in the Sun: The Struggle for Mastery in Africa* (Jonathan Ball Publishers, 2016).

Johnson, RW. *South Africa: The First Man, The Last Nation* (Jonathan Ball Publishers, 2004).

Joyce, Peter (ed). *South Africa's Yesterdays* (Reader's Digest Association, 1981).

Judd, Denis & Keith Skinner, *The Boer War: A History* (IB Tauris, 2013).

Kestell JD and DE van Velden. *The Peace Negotiations between Boer and Briton in South Africa* (Richard Clay & Sons, 1912).

Krüger, DW. *The Age of the Generals* (Dagbreek Book Store, 1958).

Krüger, DW. *The Making of a Nation: A History of the Union of South Africa, 1910–1961* (Macmillan, 1969).

Kruger, Rayne. *Good-bye Dolly Gray: The Story of the Boer War* (Pan Books, 1959).

L'Ange, Gerald. *Urgent Imperial Service: South African Forces in German South West Africa* (Ashanti Publishing, 1991).

Lewsen, Phyllis. *John X Merriman: Paradoxical South African Statesman* (Ad Donker, 1982).

Lloyd George, David. *The Truth About the Peace Treaties, Volume I* (Victor Gollancz, 1935).

Lloyd George, David. *Memoirs of the Peace Conference, Volume I* (Yale University Press, 1939).

Meintjes, Johannes. *De la Rey: Lion of the West* (Hugh Keartland Publishers, 1966).

Meintjes, Johannes. *President Steyn: A Biography* (Nasionale Boekhandel, 1969).

Meintjes, Johannes. *General Louis Botha: A Biography* (Cassell, 1970).

Meintjes, Johannes. *President Paul Kruger: A Biography* (Cassell, 1974).

Meredith, Martin. *Diamonds, Gold and War: The Making of South Africa* (Jonathan Ball Publishers, 2007).

Millard, Candice. *Hero of the Empire: The Making of Winston Churchill* (Allen Lane, 2016).

Millin, Sarah Gertrude. *Rhodes* (Chatto & Windus, 1934).

Millin, Sarah Gertrude. *General Smuts, Volume 1* (Faber & Faber, 1936).

Millin, Sarah Gertrude. *The South Africans* (Constable & Co, 1937).

Morris, Keith. *Louis Botha or Through the Great Thirst Land* (William Stevens, 1917).

Muller, CFJ (ed). *500 Years: A History of South Africa* (Academica, 1981).

Nasson, Bill. *The South African War 1899–1902* (Arnold, 1999).

Nasson, Bill, *Springboks on the Somme: South Africa in the Great War 1914–1918* (Penguin, 2007).

Nasson, Bill. *The War for South Africa: The Anglo-Boer War 1899–1902* (Tafelberg, 2010).

Nasson, Bill. *WW1 and the People of South Africa* (Tafelberg, 2014).

Official History: The Union of South Africa in the Great War 1914–1918 (Naval & Military Press

Ltd and the Imperial War Museum, 2015).

Olusoga, David. *The World's War: Forgotten Soldiers of Empire* (Head of Zeus, 2014).

Pakenham, Thomas. *The Boer War* (Futura, 1979).

Pakenham, Thomas. *The Boer War*, illustrated edition (Jonathan Ball Publishers, 1993).

Parsons, Neil. *Black and White Bioscope: Making Movies in Africa 1899 to 1925* (University of Chicago Press, 2018).

Pemberton, W Baring. *Battles of the Boer War* (Pan Books, 1964).

Plaut, Martin. *Promise and Despair: The First Struggle for a Non-Racial South Africa* (Jacana, 2016).

Pretorius, Fransjohan. *Life on Commando during the Anglo-Boer War 1899–1902* (Human & Rousseau, 1999).

Rayner, WS and WW O'Shaughnessy. *How Botha and Smuts Conquered German South West Africa* (Simpkin, Marshall, Hamilton, Kent & Co, 1916).

Reader's Digest Association. *Illustrated History of South Africa: The Real Story*, second edition (Reader's Digest Association, 1989).

Reitz, Deneys. *Trekking On* (Faber & Faber, 1933).

Reitz, Deneys. *Commando* (Faber & Faber, 1975).

Rosenthal, Eric. *General De Wet: A Biography* (Unie-Volkspers Bpk, 1946).

Ritchie, Moore. *With Botha in the Field* (Longmans, Green & Co, 1915).

Samson, Anne. *World War I in Africa: The Forgotten Conflict Among the European Powers* (IB Tauris, 2013).

Schoeman, Karel. *Imperiale Somer: Suid Afrika tussen Oorlog en Unie, 1902–1910* (Protea Boekhuis, 2015).

Spender, Harold. *General Botha: The Man and the Career* (Constable, 1916).

Thompson, Leonard M. *The Unification of South Africa, 1902–1910* (Oxford University Press, 1960).

Thompson, Leonard M. *A History of South Africa* (Radix, 1990).

Trew, HF. *Botha Treks* (Blackie & Sons, 1936).

Trew, Peter. *The Boer War Generals* (Jonathan Ball Publishers, 1999).

Van den Heever, CM. *General JBM Hertzog* (APB Bookstore, 1946).

Van der Waag, Ian. *A Military History of Modern South Africa* (Jonathan Ball Publishers, 2015).

Van Onselen, Charles. *New Babylon, New Nineveh: Everyday Life on the Witwatersrand 1886–1914* (Jonathan Ball Publishers, 1982).

Von der Heyde, Nicki. *Field Guide to the Battlefields of South Africa* (Struik Travel & Heritage, 2015).

Welsh, Frank. *A History of South Africa* (HarperCollins, 2000).

Whittall, W. *With Botha and Smuts in Africa* (Cassell, 1917).

Wilson, John. *CB: A Life of Henry Campbell-Bannerman* (Constable, 1975).

Manuscript Sources

British Library, London
    Buxton Papers
    Gladstone Papers
National Army Museum, Chelsea
    Kitchener correspondence with War Office
Bodleian Library, Oxford
    Selborne Papers
    Milner Papers
    Asquith Papers

Newspapers

The Rand Daily Mail
The Star
The Cape Times
Die Vaderland
De Volksstem

ACKNOWLEDGEMENTS AND THANKS

The eminent Marxist historian Christopher Hill observed that history has to be rewritten every generation, because although the past doesn't change, the present does. That seems also to be the view of Jonathan Ball Publishers, whose new managing director, Eugene Ashton, invited me to write this book. A keen student of South African history himself, Eugene argued persuasively that the time was right for a reappraisal of Louis Botha, a larger-than-life figure from our past, about whom little is known by a modern audience. Eugene and Jonathan Ball, publisher emeritus, were the first to scrutinise a draft of the manuscript and offer encouragement, for which I thank them.

I am indebted to many other people as well, most notably my friend Roger Crawford, another history buff, for his independent appraisal of the manuscript, and Emeritus Professor Fransjohan Pretorius, author of many works on the Anglo-Boer War, who vetted the manuscript with extreme care and saved me from egregious error. Dr Anne Samson, expert on the German South West African and East African campaigns of 1915–1916, Charles van Onselen and Graham Dominy were other historians to offer valuable insights and assistance. I thank them all.

Histories cannot be written without the aid of librarians and archivists, and I have been fortunate in having help close at hand at the Brenthurst Library and the South African National (now Ditsong) Museum of Military History in Johannesburg. At the Brenthurst, Jennifer Kimble, especially, Sally MacRoberts and Ffyona Meyer, and Ilse Cloete at Ditsong, were unfailingly helpful and at all times a pleasure to work with. I must also acknowledge the kind assistance, in Britain, of Lucy McCann of the Bodleian Library, Oxford, as well as the helpful staff of the British Library and the National Army Museum in Chelsea. While in Oxford, I enjoyed the hospitality of my old friend the historian and lecturer Christopher Danziger and his wife, Seonaid.

I am especially grateful to my editor, Alfred LeMaitre, for his expert guidance and meticulous attention to detail; to Kevin Shenton and his assistant, Danel van Jaarsveld, for their design, layout and map-drawing; to Tracey Hawthorne, for her careful proofreading; and to Tessa Botha, for the indexing. Errors in the text are my responsibility, and I'd be grateful if you would let my publisher know of any so that they may be corrected online and in print.

Richard Steyn
Johannesburg
July 2018

INDEX

Page numbers in *italics* indicate photographs.